MW01167055

SE Great Trips

Day Trips & Vacation Trips
In The Southeast

by
Linda L. Burton

Explore
Tennessee, North Carolina
Georgia & Alabama

Phase II: Publications
Chattanooga, Tennessee

Printed in the United States of America. First edition published in 1996.

Library of Congress Catalog Card Number 96-70440
          Burton, Linda L.
                    SE Great Trips
guidebook to trips in Tennessee, North Carolina, Georgia, Alabama
and the Chattanooga area; first edition.
          Includes index.
ISBN 0-9644760-1-0. $11.95.

Editing by Winston B. Brooks
Research assistance by Leah Gore
Special contributions by students in the Hospitality Management program at Chattanooga State Technical Community College, and instructor Randy Schulte
Maps by Carol Lycan and Dimitrius Mitsouras
Color separations by CompuColor: Tony Arp, Jim Gunn, Drew Queen and Jeremy Johnson
Cover preparation by Graphic Advertising: Linda Peppers and Lori Cleghon
Cover layout and photographs by Linda L. Burton

This is a personal guidebook, with evaluations based on numerous reports from traveling inspectors. Final judgments are made by the publisher. Our inspectors never identify themselves (except over the phone) and never take free meals or other favors during reviews. The publisher welcomes information conveyed by users of this book, as long as they have no financial connection with the establishment concerned.

Published by Phase II: Publications
5251-C Hwy 153, # 255
Chattanooga, Tennessee 37343
Office 423-875-4795 Fax 423-877-4089

Dedication

I dedicate this book to my working partner and buddy

Winston B. Brooks

I've worked a lot of years, but never with another person as smart and insightful and innovative and encouraging and hardworking and non-complaining and never-say-quit as Winston.   Did I mention fun, too?   Mixed with our hard work this past year we've had a lot of laughs, from talking about Elvis to talking about figs and followup.   But the fact of the matter is, without Winston's unfailing support in so many ways, this book wouldn't have happened.

Thanks Winston, for having the faith!

A Special Acknowledgement to Leah Gore, who verified every phone number and researched every fact in this book.   What perseverance!   What tenacity!   What a great job!   What a delightful person to work with!
Thanks Leah, for staying the course!

Special Thanks and Love for These Very Important People Too

Jim & Maude Burton and Andrew & Callie Sizemore were wonderful grandparents. Memories of things we shared still hang around in my mind, like sitting in the front porch swing, digging into a giant slice of coconut-topped Lane cake, and building frog houses in the dirt at the edge of the field.   But the best memory is how their eyes would light up at the sight of me. I knew I was special.

I consider it my job to make my grandchildren feel just that special. Andrew Burton Shumate is our newest family member, joining us on February 7, 1996 and carrying on some family names. Memory-making years are ahead with my Chattanooga G-Boys Jeffrey, Jason and Justin Shumate and my Seattle G-Boys Matthew and Andrew Shumate.   Guess How Much I Love You, guys!

Major thanks to the rest of the gang: Mom & Dad (Ivous & Craig), and Mike & Karen, and Rick & Tess, and Scott (picture on back cover), and Craig, and Hal for making me feel special and for being patient with me during another year's writing project.   I love you a bunch!

Lastly, I couldn't have finished the final version without the special feelings created by 23PO and my daily *quacks*.   :)

I hope you enjoy the book.   Be careful and have fun!

LindaLou

Contents

South East Area Map

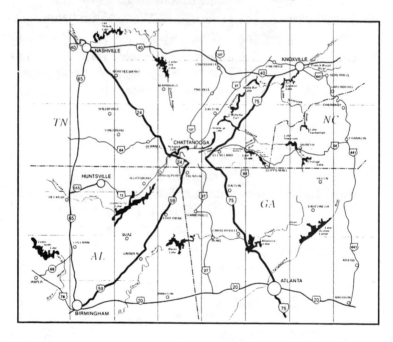

Welcome to Great Trips
by Linda L. Burton

I'm a great believer in traveling, and have been lucky enough to visit all 50 states. It's why I chose to be a travel writer -- what better thing in the world than doing what you love to do and then telling everyone you did it!

I'm guessing you love to travel too, or you wouldn't have this book in your hand right now. I hope it will help you find your way to your own adventures, and build memories that will last till you're too old to rock the rocking chair.

With 25 Great Trips, you can "hit the road" every other weekend for a year, and still have two weeks left to go to Europe, or Arizona, or your favorite condo on the beach. Some of the Trips offer so much to do you'll find yourself repeating the trip, but varying the focus each time you go.

You don't need to live in Chattanooga to take advantage of this book. Though the "loop" map shows Chattanooga as a starting point, if you live anywhere along the route, just hop in; many of the Trips can connect with others for an even Greater Trip.

The Trips are laid out in clockwise fashion, with the first one, to Crossville, at "noon" on the clock. They help you find your way through southeast Tennessee, the tip of North Carolina, north Georgia, northeast Alabama, and middle Tennessee.

Stop at the State Welcome Centers and get yourself a good road map that you fasten inside your car so it's always handy when you're on the road. The maps in this book will help to guide you, but you need a detailed map so you can add or change routes as suits your need.

Make use of the telephone numbers listed in the book to get call-ahead information. Visitor Bureaus will be happy to send you packets about their city. Many tours must be booked in advance, and some tours are irregularly scheduled. Call to be sure and avoid being disappointed.

Most of these Great Trips take advantage of Scenic Highways and Poke and Plum Places. No hurrying, now! As I once heard someone say, "The shortest distance between two points is no fun!" On the next pages are Ten Suggestions for Great Trips. Read, relax and have a Great Time!

Ten Suggestions for Great Trips

One

Make a Plan! Call the Chamber or Visitors Bureau; they will send you the maps and literature you request. Get it in advance, study it, be aware of distances, driving times, open hours; know what to expect. In busy seasons, reserve rooms ahead. Make a list of things you want to do. A family effort!

Two

Know Your History! If you don't, go on the tour or read the brochure! Don't drag kids around historic places and expect them to be anything but bored if they don't understand the significance of what they see. Have them play pretend games, as though they lived back then!

Three

Be Flexible! Road construction, traffic jams, sleepy eyelids -- all can throw your schedule out of whack. RELAX! Sometimes a thing you hadn't planned to stop for grabs your eye. STOP! LOOK! ENJOY! Vacation memories should be more than restroom pitstops!

Four

Take a Break! Don't be a drudgy driver. Make frequent stops. Get out and stretch. Drink some coffee, breathe fresh air. Reduce car-fighting (yours and the kids) with lots of chances to let off steam. State-line Welcome Centers generally have nice grounds; fast-food restaurants have playgrounds too.

Five

Dress for Comfort! Don't worry about how you look, but what you look at! You need to be warm (or cool) and dry. Avoid blisters and purse-snatchings with walking shoes and a lightweight pack. For parents with little hands to hold, for kids with games and snacks, for cameras, a pack's the best!

Ten Suggestions for Great Trips

Six
Have Options! For rain or shine have things in mind you'd like to do. Don't sit and motel-mope when things you can't control occur. Too stormy for boating? Go to the Aquarium instead. Too hot for the mid-day walking tour you scheduled? Take a nap, go later!

Seven
Do Your Thing! A Joined-at-the-Hip Trip can be boring. Need an early morning jog? Go and let the snoozer snooze in peace. Compromise makes for fun too: each person picks three things they want to do, you go with them, they go with you. Kids need to learn this compromise thing early in life!

Eight
Capture Memories! Make more pictures than you think you'll want! Get a good assortment -- some with people, some without. Twenty years from now they'll still bring smiles. Today's cameras are a snap to use, but remember, the quality of the memory is more important than the quality of the photo.

Nine
Be Impressed! Avoid comparisons with home. Or worse, too-high expectations of a place. Enjoy what is, find the good and interesting, don't complain or say "We've got this at home!" "Is that all there is?" "I thought it was going to be bigger than that!" It is what it is and you are there!

Ten
Be Nice to the Natives! When you travel, you are visiting someone else's home. Be a thoughtful guest! Give compliments to the local folks, ask them about their place. Show genuine interest and invite them to visit your part of the world! You'll spread goodwill and make new friends.

Chattanooga State and Closeups

My experience as a travel writer led to an invitation to speak to the Travel and Tourism class at Chattanooga State Technical Community College last year. CSTCC offers a program in Hospitality Management that leads to careers in hotel or restaurant management, or to various opportunities in tourism and convention planning. Randy Schulte heads the program, which is growing by leaps and bounds. The enthusiastic class became so interested in the *Great Trips* project that before I left, I had a passel of volunteers offering research assistance and writeups! Following is a record of some of the places they personally like to visit, and their suggestions for your enjoyment.

If you are interested in becoming part of the travel and tourism industry yourself, contact Chattanooga State Technical Community College, Business & Information Systems Division, at 423-697-4797.

And for Great Trips, compliments of the hardworking and knowledgeable students at CSTCC, please read on.

Closeup of Fall Creek Falls State Park
by Betty J. Solomon, CSTCC student

I grew up camping with my family. We camped in a lot of different places, but my favorite was and still is Fall Creek Falls State Park on the Cumberland Plateau in Tennessee. There is plenty to do there -- fishing, swimming, horseback riding, canoeing, bicycling, and my favorites, hiking and camping.

There are many waterfalls to enjoy and hike to, but the most spectacular of all is the one the park is named for -- Fall Creek Falls. It tumbles 256 feet into the Cane Creek Gorge, and hiking to the bottom of it should be at the top of anyone's list of things to do.

The best treat of all is camping at Fall Creek Falls. It is sheer heaven to be outdoors in the mountain air. I love to go to sleep or wake up to the smell of a campfire. To this day whenever I smell a campfire it brings up happy memories. What are you waiting for? See p. 206.

Closeup of Mentone
by Becky Price, CSTCC student

Mentone sits on the west brow of Lookout Mountain in Alabama. There is something for just about everyone here, such as interesting restaurants, antiques, crafts, and even a wedding chapel for those thinking about getting hitched!

My recommendation however, is that you mark your calendar for the four big weekends Mentone hosts every year, as every season looks different on the mountain. The third weekend in May, there's the Rhododendron Festival, featuring live music, contests, food, and more. The Mentone Crafts Festival, the first weekend after July 4, draws over 100 craftspeople and artists. Don't miss the Fall Colorfest the third weekend in October; it includes storytelling and a costume ball. Local businesses host open houses during Musical Mountain Christmas, the first weekend in December.

I made these notes during a delightful lunch at the Mentone Inn. When I come back in May, I'm staying overnight in one of the bed & breakfasts...let me check my list. See p. 128.

Closeup of Barnsley Gardens
by Marge Kinser, CSTCC student

Barnsley Gardens is a splendid, unique spot nestled in the North Georgia mountains near Adairsville. I enjoy it for its history as much as its continuing beauty. I can imagine the life of the family that lived here, and created this lovely place

It was built in the 1840's by Godfrey Barnsley to escape the oppressive Savannah heat. It played a part in the Civil War and is a source of numerous ghost stories. Today only the aged brick walls remain, and the gardens themselves. Elegant English boxwoods date back to the original owner, and there are over 700 varieties of roses, native and exotic rhododendrons, and daffodils.

Visit in spring or summer for full effect. The colorful flowers, the history, and the mystery create a setting that has a wonderful impact on the visitor. See p. 106.

Closeup of Falls Mill
by Peggy Weddington, CSTCC student

Falls Mill, an authentic antique grist mill near the New Salem
community of Belvidere, Tennessee, is the most beautiful place
I have ever found to fall back in time. Several large waterfalls
along with the gushing water coming off the huge water wheel
of the mill give the constant sounds of water flowing and creates
a relaxing atmosphere. I have spent many happy times here,
picnicking, and walking alongside the river admiring the
wildflowers and butterflies and birds.

My dream has always been to have a good book, a jug of lemonade,
an easy chair and the whole day free just to sit by the mill
stream. Leaving Falls Mill is the hard part, for I have to come
to my senses and realize life does travel at a faster pace. Still, I
had the joy of dropping out of the 20th century for just a little
while! See p. 170.

Closeup of The Anton Heiller Memorial Organ
by Christine Crawford-Hornbaker, CSTCC student

If you like organ music, or appreciate beautiful craftsmanship, you'll
want to see the Anton Heiller Memorial Organ on the Southern
College campus in Collegedale, Tennessee. If you stop by the
office first, someone will gladly open the doors for you.
Someone may be practicing, and invite you to come in and ask
questions. The organ is valued at $1.2 million, stands three
stories high, and is the largest North American tracker pipe
organ built in this century.

Anton Heiller was a Viennese organist, composer, and harpsichordist
who taught and influenced many of today's accomplished
organists, including Judy Glass, who is associate professor of
music at Southern. The College sponsors an organ festival in
June each year with instruction and concerts open to anyone
interested. I enjoy listening to the beautiful organ music
whenever I can, both when someone is practicing, and when I
attend the Organ and Orchestra Concerto every year. See p. 225.

Closeup of South Cumberland Recreation Center
by Randy Schulte, CSTCC Instructor

When the kids are climbing out of their seat belts, the perfect one-stop shop for history, recreation and nature on Monteagle Mountain in Tennessee is at the Visitors Center of the South Cumberland Recreation Center.

Our children love the mini-museum of Monteagle Mountain geology and history where they can peer into a pioneer cabin and even find fossils in the coal exhibit. A three-dimensional model of the mountain dramatically shows the topography and the location of trails to such scenic spots as the Fiery Gizzard and Buggytop Cave.

Just outside are tennis courts, a softball diamond, playgrounds and picnic tables. The kids love the self-guided Nature Trail where chipmunks scurry, hawks circle, and we all feel closer to the beauty of the mountain. See p. 204.

Closeup of Rainbow Lake Wilderness
by Winston Brooks, CSTCC Instructor

I like the out-of-doors, so I'm always looking for a good place to hike. Rainbow Lake Wilderness in Tennessee is one of my favorite spots. It was built as a recreation area for the Alexian Hotel in the early 1900's, and was once the center of Sunday activity on Signal Mountain. Choose a short or long hike; either gives you the chance to see the great scenery we're so famous for.

The short hike begins at the Rainbow Lake Trail Head; follow the path to Rainbow Creek. Head upstream until you see the dam, here you'll pick up the trail around Rainbow Lake. If you have more time and can handle a steep climb, follow the creek below the dam until you see the remains of a bridge (about .4 of a mile). Cross the creek near the remains. The trail picks up on the other side.

You will go through lush forest and dark hemlock groves, but best of all you'll wind up with spectacular views of the Tennessee River Gorge, known as the "Little Grand Canyon" of Tennessee. See p. 16.

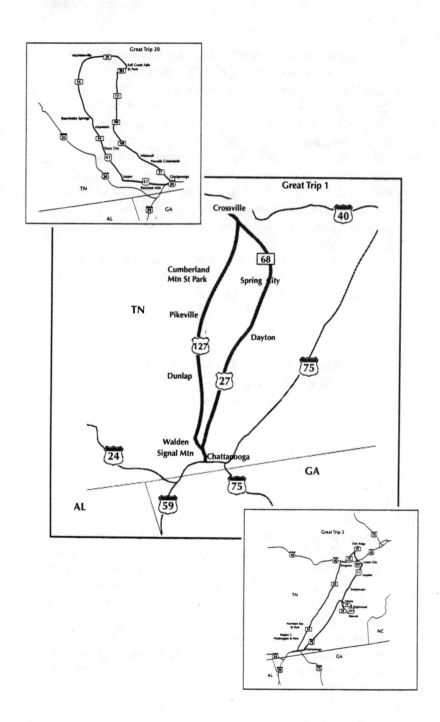

Great Trip 20

McMinnville
Fall Creek Falls
St Park
111

Beersheba Springs
Altamont
Tracy City
Whitwell
Powells Crossroads
41
Jasper
Raccoon Mtn
Chattanooga

TN

AL

GA

Great Trip 1

Crossville
40

68

Cumberland
Mtn St Park
Spring City

TN

Pikeville

Dayton

127

75

Dunlap

27

Walden
Signal Mtn
Chattanooga

24

GA

75

AL

59

Great Trip 2

Oak Ridge

40

Kingston
Lenoir City
40

Loudon

TN

Sweetwater

Athens
Englewood
Etowah

Harrison Bay
St Park
Booker T.
Washington St Park

Chattanooga
75

NC

GA

AL

Great Trip 1

Chattanooga to Crossville, TN
the ridge and valleys route
via Dayton, Spring City, Crossville, Cumberland Mountain State Park, Pikeville, Dunlap, Walden, Signal Mountain, returning to Chattanooga approximately 170 miles round-trip, 3.5 hours driving time

Why Go
Mountain Scenery & Cumberland County Playhouse &
Performing Arts Camp & Scopes Evolution Play &
Watts Bar Lake & Fishing & Laurel-Snow Pocket Wilderness &
Cumberland General Store & Antique-shopping &
Historic Coke Ovens & Pumpkin Patches & Mountain Opry &
Rainbow Lake & Nature Trails & Waterfalls &
100-foot Suspension Bridge & Resort Golf & Hunting

Suggested route with approximate mileages

Instruction	Road	Dir	Miles
Chattanooga to Dayton	U27	N	40
Dayton to Spring City	U27	N	16
Spring City to Crossville	S68 & U127	N	28
Crossville to Cumberland Mountain St Park	U127	S	5
Cumberland Mountain St Park to Pikeville	U127	S	27
Pikeville to Dunlap	U127	S	20
Dunlap to Walden	U127	S	18
Walden to Signal Mountain	U127	S	3
Signal Mountain to Chattanooga	U127	S	9
Total Mileage			166

This trip takes you over and back across **Walden Ridge** (not Walden's, as so often misspelled!), a plateau extending from the Tennessee River northeastward for about 90 miles, averaging 7 miles across its flat top and ranging in elevation from approximately 1,500 feet to the 3,048-foot Hinch Mountain at the northern end of the **Sequatchie Valley**. Half the Ridge sits in the Eastern Time Zone, and half in Central -- a fact to remember when you are considering "open hours" of places you want to visit.

Beginning on the new Corridor J in Chattanooga, travel north, crossing the waters of Soddy Creek and hugging the eastern side of the Ridge and the western side of the Tennessee River on a wonderful 4-lane cruise to **Dayton**. There the road narrows for the next 17 miles till you arrive at **Spring City**. Here clear signage directs you onto Scenic Hwy S68N, where you quickly ascend the Ridge, travel northwestwardly across its flat terrain, and meander down into Grassy Cove, surrounded by Black Mountain, Bear Den Mountain, and Brady Mountain. Then onto the next plateau and into **Crossville**.

Crossville sits squarely in the center of the plateau, resorts everywhere taking full advantage of the landscape. Golfing and hunting abound; so does water recreation in plateau-top lakes. The always popping **Cumberland County Playhouse** has three stages, one outdoors, with musicals, dramas, children's variety, and music. It's Tennessee's family theater, and even sponsors a performing arts camp for the kids!

The return route is Scenic Hwy U127, which winds its way past **Cumberland Mountain State Park**, worth a drive in the fall just for lunch in the restaurant overlooking Byrd Lake. Come off the Cumberland Plateau into the beautiful Sequatchie Valley, (pumpkin capital of the world, signs proclaim) and through **Pikeville** and **Dunlap** before climbing to the top of Walden Ridge once again. This part of the drive brings you through the towns of **Walden** and **Signal Mountain**, and then provides a dizzying descent "off the mountain" onto Signal Mountain Boulevard and a return to Chattanooga.

Dayton, TN
pop 5,671
Eastern Time
Chamber of Commerce 423-775-0361

To See and Do
Probably most famous as the site of the **Scopes Evolution Trial,** sometimes called the **"Monkey Trial,"** the courtroom in the **Rhea County Courthouse,** *423-775-7801, 1475 Market St;* has been restored and retains its 1925 authenticity. Pop in for a visit or call for information about the annual re-enactment in July of the trial which featured William Jennings Bryan and Clarence Darrow arguing the ?'s of evolution. The Courthouse is a National Historic Landmark. Nearby is **Bryan College,** *423-775-2041, 130 Mercer Dr;* a four-year Christian liberal arts college named for William Jennings Bryan.

Just 2.5 miles out of town, on Richland Creek Road, is the **Laurel-Snow Pocket Wilderness** area -- 710 acres with waterfalls and a hiking trail; ascents of about 900 feet.

Accommodations
Best Western, *800-437-9604, 7835 Rhea County Hwy.* Bed and Breakfasts include the **Magnolia House,** *423-775-9288; 656 Market St,* fireplaces, full breakfast, dinner with reservations; and the **Rose House,** *423-775-3311, 123 Idaho Ave;* Victorian cottage built in 1892, antique furnishings.

Spring City, TN
pop 2,199
Eastern Time
Chamber of Commerce 423-365-5210

To See and Do
Spring City sits beside the wide waters of **Watts Bar Lake,** and with so much water on one side, and Walden Ridge on the other, outdoor activities are prime. Go northwest on Shut-In Gap Road for trails and wilderness areas. Hike **Piney River Trail,**

423-336-7424, Shut-In Gap Rd, 1 mi NW of city; the ten-mile trail connects Piney River Picnic Area and Newby Branch Forest Camp and features numerous bridges, one of which is a 100-foot suspension bridge. **Twin Rocks Nature Trail,** *Shut-In Gap Rd, 1 mi NW of city;* is a fairly easy 2.5 mile trail from the Piney River picnic area to Twin Rocks, which overlooks the Tennessee Valley and the Soak Creek and Piney River gorges. **Stinging Fork Pocket Wilderness,** *Shut-In Gap Rd, 5 mi NW of city;* is a 104--acre Pocket Wilderness with a 3-mile loop leading from Shut-In Gap Road to Stinging Fork Falls on Stinging Fork Creek. All are open daily year round.

Watts Bar Dam, *Hwy S68,* has an overlook on the west side; the lock is 60 x 360. **Watts Bar Lake** has 72 miles of water and 783 miles of shoreline providing outstanding fishing and water recreation.

Accommodations

Cottages, cabins, boating resorts, and campgrounds are the ticket here. **Watts Bar Resort,** *800-365-9598, 6767 Watts Bar Hwy;* has 52 units and a restaurant, near dam.

Note time change from Eastern to Central as you cross Walden Ridge

---

Crossville, TN
pop 6,930
Central Time
Chamber of Commerce 615-484-8444

To See and Do

The play's the thing in Crossville, the **Cumberland County Playhouse,** *615-484-5000, Hwy 70W,* has been entertaining folks since 1965. Billed as **"Tennessee's Family Theater,"** it is the prime performing arts resource in rural Tennessee. There's always something going on with two indoor stages and one outdoors; **Mainstage** variety has included such diversity as *Singin' in the Rain, Godspell, The Tempest, Camelot,* and *Oliver; Captains Courageous* has played the **Adventure Theater** and

Smoke on the Mountain the **Theater-in-the-Woods.** The Southern Pops and Classic series has variety too, with past performances by the Jimmy Dorsey Orchestra, Grandpa Jones and Family, Mr. Jack Daniels Original Silver Cornet Band, and the Atlanta Symphony Brass Quintet; the Kids of All Ages series is geared to families, and features puppets, dance, and touring theaters. Call for schedules, season ticket prices and group rates; special prices for students, seniors. The **Summer Performing Arts Camp (SPARC)** is designed for children 3-18 and offers extensive training in tap, jazz, ballet, music, and speech, with workshops in acting and musical theater.

Downtown you'll find **Simonton's Cheese House,** *615-484-5193, 2010 N Main St;* where they've been serving up cheese since 1947 -- check out the 3-lb hoop cheddar. Nearby is **Great Upper Cumberland Trading Company,** *615-456-6270, 204 W First St;* where the work of many fine Tennessee artists and artisans is displayed for sale. On Main Street is the **Pioneer Hall Museum,** *615-277-3872,* where you can find exhibits of the local history; it's on the National Register of Historic Places.

Grapes grow well on the plateau, stop in at **Stonehaus Winery,** *615-484-WINE, I-40 Exit 320;* for a taste and a tour; picnic facilities here too. On the other side of town is the **Cumberland General Store,** *615-484-8481, Hwy U127 and S68.* Buy your old-time merchandise there or ask for the mail-order catalog. Just across the road is the **Homesteads Tower Museum,** *615-456-9663.* The Tower served as the Administrative Office when the Cumberland Homesteads Project was built during FDR's time; many photos, documents and artifacts of the 30's and 40's are there to see.

Accommodations

Lots of resorts on the Cumberland plateau -- **Fairfield Glade,** *615-484-7521, 101 Peavine Rd;* is one of the largest and most complete with over 12,000 acres and four golf courses; **Lake Tansi Village,** *615-788-6724, Hwy U127,* has water activities, tennis and golf. If your interest is hunting, contact **Caryonah Hunting Lodge,** *615-277-3113, Plateau Rd, off I-40;* the preserve covers several thousand acres and has an airport with 24-hr flight service. **Best Western,** *615-484-1551, Hwy*

U127N & I40; **Ramada,** 615-484-7581, Hwy U127N & I40. **Betty's Bed & Breakfast,** 615-484-8827, *Peavine Rd;* has five rooms and full breakfast, children welcome. **Talavera De La Reina,** 615-277-3749, *Jim Garrett Rd,* is a dinner-only, reservations-required restaurant filled with mementos and costumes of Hollywood stars from the owner's 40 years as a designer; for quick country eats stop in at the **Bean Pot,** 615-484-4633, *Peavine Rd;* **Halcyon Days,** 615-456-3663, *230 Woodmere Mall,* offers continental cuisine, dinner only.

Tennessee State Park
Central Time

The **Cumberland Mountain State Park,** 615-484-6138, *Hwy U127S,* is worth a visit for many reasons -- one of the best being a delightful lunch in the restaurant overlooking **Byrd Lake.** The restaurant serves two meals daily; open all year except during Christmas. For recreation, there's an Olympic-size pool; rowboats, paddleboats and canoes for rent to use on Byrd Lake; hiking and nature trails; a 10-mile overnight backpacking trail; playgrounds; and picnic areas. With 1,720 acres, there's room to roam. Most buildings are made of Crab Orchard sandstone; the Crab Orchard bridge is the park's best known landmark. The park has 37 cabins, 147 campsites and a group lodge.

Pikeville, TN
pop 1,771
Central Time
Chamber of Commerce 423-447-2791

To See and Do

The city is filled with many stately homes listed on the National Register of Historic Places. Be sure to visit in the fall -- when the pumpkins are at their peak! Check out **Everett Farms,** 423-447-6317, *off Hwy 30;* **Bucky Wooden Family Orchard,** 423-447-6277, *Hwy 30;* or **Oren Wooden's Farm,** 423-447-6376, *Hwy 443E;* for pumpkins, apples and cider.

Accommodations

Colonial Bed & Breakfast, *423-447-7183, 303 S Main;* has three rooms, offers full breakfast and southern hospitality, children welcome.

Dunlap, TN
pop 3,731
Central Time
Chamber of Commerce 423-949-3479

To See and Do

See the remains of early coal-mining and coke-producing at the **Coke Ovens Historic Site**, *423-949-2156, 114 Walnut St.* At the 62-acre site you'll find 268 beehive coke ovens and some mining apparatus. A sign in town proclaims the Valley as the Hang Gliding Capital of the East, watch for gliders coming off the bluff; and you can **Canoe the Sequatchie**, *423-949-4400, Hwy U127S,* in one of Scott & Ernestine Pilkington's canoes; you'll find their place on the river, naturally, just south of town.

**Note time change from Central to Eastern
as you cross Walden Ridge**

Walden, TN
pop 1,523
Eastern Time
Chamber of Commerce 423-886-4362

To See and Do

A regular attraction is the **Mountain Opry**, *423-886-5897, Fairmount Rd;* Friday night entertainment in the Walden Ridge Civic Center is old-time bluegrass; a fun family show; no charge but drop your contribution in the hat that is passed. **Mountain Java Coffeehouse**, *423-886-1129, 1832 Taft Hwy,* has live music weekends and some weeknights and, of course, coffee. Near the Civic Center is **Fairmount Orchard**, *423-886-1226, 2204 Fairmount Pike,* open September 1 to Christmas Eve

2204 Fairmount Pike, open September 1 to Christmas Eve daily; buy apples, jams and jellies, ciders and spices; and pumpkins at Halloween.

Accommodations

Stop at the place with the rocking chairs on the front porch; **Waycrazy's Bar-B-Que**, 423-886-3283, 3720 Taft Hwy, and relax with a fruit jar filled with iced tea; the place is known for its barbecue and homemade pies.

Signal Mountain, TN
pop 7,034
Eastern Time
Chamber of Commerce 423-886-2177

To See and Do

Signal Point Park, *Signal Point Rd*, at the tip end of the ridge; you're 1,000 feet up with a fabulous view overlooking the Tennessee River Gorge; this is part of Chattanooga-Chickamauga National Military Park. Start your hike at historic **Signal Point** and see some of the most scenic areas in the state; the Chattanooga section of the **Cumberland State Scenic Trail** begins in **Prentice Cooper State Forest**, and winds along escarpments and stream valleys 20 miles northward to the rim of the Sequatchie Valley. Primitive campsites on the trail. **Rainbow Lake Wilderness**, just past Alexian Village, is the site of Rainbow Lake and several nice hiking trails.

Looking for antiques? Clustered near the highway are **Church's Antiques & Accessories**, 423-886-9636, 1819 Taft Hwy; **Crabtree Booksellers**, 423-886-5944, 2905 Taft Hwy, for antiquarian and used books; **Log Cabin Herbs & Antiques**, 423-886-2663, 4111 Taft Hwy; **Victorian Cottage**, 423-886-2175, 1404 James Blvd; and **Woody's Goodies**, 423-886-4095, 4702 Taft Hwy.

Accommodations

The mountain's favorite spots to eat include **Just Delicious**, 423-886-7210, 1309 Taft Hwy; open breakfast through dinner and serving unique family recipes; **Pizza Place**, 423-886-3761,

1309 Taft Hwy; where the dough is hand-thrown and you can even get whole-wheat crust; **Vittles**, *423-886-3892, 1210 Taft Hwy;* great breakfasts, seafood, steaks, daily specials. Shop and eat at **Victorian Cottage Tea Room**, *423-886-2175, 1404 James Blvd;* the tables are set on antiques for sale, so the decor is always changing; try the chicken salad for lunch. Don't go home till you've stopped at the **Bread Basket**, *423-886-7771, 2116 Taft Hwy;* specialty breads, jumbo muffins, cakes, pies and gift baskets.

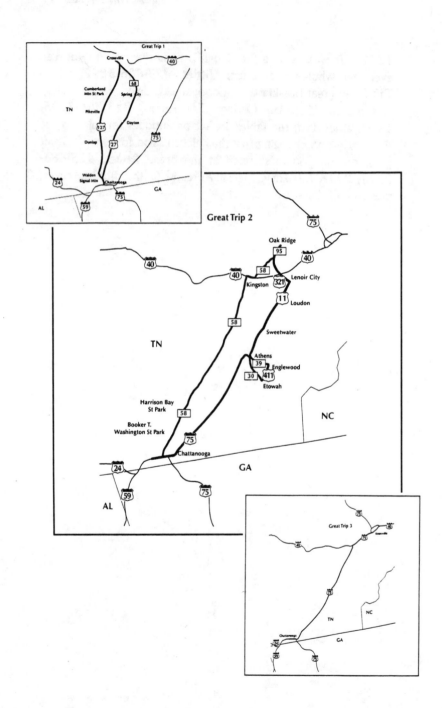

Great Trip 2

Chattanooga to Oak Ridge, TN
the water and wine route
via Booker T Washington State Park, Harrison Bay State Park, Kingston,
Oak Ridge, Lenoir City, Loudon, Sweetwater, Athens, Englewood,
Etowah, returning to Chattanooga
approximately 245 miles round-trip, 5 hours driving time

Why Go
Secret City Story ℘ American Museum of Science and Energy ℘
Wine Tastings ℘ Vineyards ℘ Living Heritage Museum ℘
Textile Museum ℘ Ice Cream ℘ Underground Lost Sea ℘
Boating ℘ Swimming ℘ Camping ℘ TVA Lakes ℘ State Parks

Suggested route with approximate mileages

Instruction	Road	Dir	Miles
Chattanooga to Booker T. Washington St Pk	S58	N	15
Booker T. Washington St Pk to Harrison Bay St Pk	S58	N	7
Harrison Bay State Park to Kingston	S580	N	60
Kingston to Oak Ridge	S58	N	25
Oak Ridge to Lenoir City	S95 ℘ I-40	S	17
Lenoir City to Loudon	U11	S	8
Loudon to Sweetwater	U11	S	14
Sweetwater to Athens	U11	S	15
Athens to Englewood	S39	E	10
Englewood to Etowah	U411	S	10
Etowah to Chattanooga	S30 ℘ I-75	W ℘ S	64
Total Mileage			245

This Trip takes you along picturesque and lightly-traveled State Highway 58, showing off Tennessee's farmlands and gently rolling hills to absolute best advantage. Don't go this way when you're in a hurry, make sure you start with a pleasant mood so you can delight in the white-board fences, red silos, and signs advertising everything from Horse Stables to Woodtick Bantams. What's more, you're never more than a few miles from recreational and scenic waters, passing over **Wolftever Creek**, the **Hiwassee**, and then the broad **Tennessee River** when you get to **Kingston**; the entire trip is near the shores of **Chickamauga Lake** and **Watts Bar Lake**.

Allow plenty of time in the interesting town of **Oak Ridge** -- this former Secret City, site of the WWII Manhattan Project, now tells the Energy Story. A mural of Einstein looms over the **American Museum of Science & Energy**; fascinating walk-through exhibits trace the construction of the city of 75,000 that was not on the map, and the weapon that forever changed warfare. The rest of the museum focuses on energy sources and peacetime uses, with displays that dazzle and hands-on buttons to push.

Return on Hwy U11 through Lenoir City, where many rivers come together; nearby **Melton Hill Dam** backs up the **Clinch River**, **Fort Loudoun Dam** the **Tennessee**, and **Tellico Dam** the **Little Tennessee**. In historic **Loudon** there are vineyards to visit. Most of the state's 15 wineries are clustered in the Tennessee Valley region; two are described on this Trip, seven on other Trips. The wineries invite you in to tour and taste; they'll explain grape growing, or viticulture, and how to select the wines that suit your taste. Even if you're not an oenophile, you'll enjoy walking and picnicking on the lovely grounds overlooking the river at **Loudoun Vineyards**, or the sweet smell of grapes at harvest time.

Down the road is the world-famous **Lost Sea** in **Sweetwater**, the college town of **Athens**, and historic **Etowah** and **Englewood**. Stay a while, keeping in mind that I-75 is handy to speed you home when traveling time is done.

Tennessee State Parks
Eastern Time

Booker T. Washington State Park, *423-894-4955, 5801 Champion Rd off Hwy S58,* is named for famous educator Booker Taliaferro Washington; in its 353 acres there are boating and fishing opportunities, boat launching ramp, swimming pool, picnic areas, play fields, and nature trails.

Harrison Bay State Park, *423-344-6214, 8411 Harrison Bay Rd off Hwy S58,* has camping available in its 1200 acres, some waterfront; the marina has one of the finest launching ramps in the area; 140 slips are available for boats up to 48 feet; boat rental, fishing, picnic shelter, pool, snack bar, showers, playground, tennis courts. Planned activities include arts and crafts and campfires. Parklands have historical significance, covering site of last Cherokee Campground, 3 villages were ruled by Chief Joe Vann, one of the great Cherokee chieftains.

Kingston, TN
pop 4,552
Eastern Time
Chamber of Commerce 423-376-5572

To See and Do
Lot of pretty water here, at a big bend in the Tennessee River. History too -- the **Roane County Museum of History**, *423-376-9211, 119 N. Kentucky St,* is located in one of only a few remaining antebellum courthouses in the state. For more history, visit **Fort Southwest Point**, *423-376-3641, Hwy S58,* a 1799 fort reconstructed on its original foundation; call for more details.

Accommodations
Comfort Inn, *800-221-2222, I-40, Exit 352;* **Days Inn**, *423-376-2069, I-40 Exit 356;* and a number of campgrounds, including **Watts Bar Lake Campground & Marina**, *423-376-8847, 511 DeArmond Rd.*

Oak Ridge, TN

pop 27,310
Eastern Time
Chamber of Commerce/Visitors Bureau 800-887-3429

To See and Do

Secret City invites one and all to visit now -- start at the **American Museum of Science & Energy**, 423-576-3200, 300 S Tulane Ave, and watch the slide show telling *The Oak Ridge Story*. You'll learn how these hidden hills became the secret site of part of the Manhattan Project during WWII, at one time housing over 75,000 people working on this wartime effort. The museum is fabulous, with live demonstrations and over 200 interactive exhibits. It's all about ENERGY -- Einstein's picture overlooks the area, where you'll learn about everything from Atoms to Quarks. A must for school groups, or any science-loving kids and adults who are fascinated by "what makes things work." They can tailor demonstrations and films for a specific age group -- call ahead to get just what you need arranged in advance. Open daily, free.

In connection with the Manhattan Project, you also are allowed to visit the **Historic Graphite Reactor**, 423-574-4160, Bethel Valley Rd. The world's oldest nuclear reactor, it was built during World War II and later used for peacetime applications. Active until 1963, it's a National Historic Landmark and is open daily. Down the road in tiny **New Bethel Church** you can see pictures and mementos of the Old Bethel community before Oak Ridge was built. Other "energy" attractions are the **Oak Ridge National Laboratory** from the Visitor's Overlook, the U. S. Department of Energy's largest energy laboratory; and TVA's coal-fired **Bull Run Steam Plant;** easy to find following the **Oak Ridge Self Guided Driving Tour**, 423-482-7821, Visitors Center, 302 S Tulane Ave.

Art, history and science are presented for children and adults at the **Children's Museum of Oak Ridge**, 423-482-1074, 461 W Outer Dr; major emphasis is on the Appalachian region. There's a permanent collection of contemporary international artists and changing exhibits of local and regional artists at the

Oak Ridge Art Center, 423-482-1441, 201 Badger Ave, home of the Gomez collection of 60 works by contemporary artists, open daily, free. And you can enjoy nature's artistry at the **UT Arboretum,** 423-483-3571, 901 Kerr Hollow Rd, where trails wind through 250 acres in this forestry experiment station and arboretum. Displays and other information at on-site Visitor's Center. Trails open 8 AM-sunset daily and it's free. Don't miss **Jackson Square Historic Park,** Tennessee Ave, which is the original townsite of Oak Ridge. It's now a retail area, with craft shops, a playhouse, and several nice restaurants; kiosks display photographs of early city scenes and tell the story of John Hendrix, turn-of-the-century visionary who prophesied the beginnings of Oak Ridge. As you head south, you'll go by **Melton Hill Dam & Lake,** Hwy 95, 1-mi north of I-40, exit 364, on the Clinch River; campground, picnic area, swimming and boat ramp; observatory visitors center; free but charge for camping, daily all year.

Accommodations
Comfort Inn, 800-553-7830, 433 S Rutgers Ave; **Days Inn,** 423-483-5615, 206 S Illinois Ave; **Garden Plaza,** 800-3-GARDEN, 215 S Illinois Ave; **Hampton Inn,** 800-426-7866, 208 S Illinois Ave; **Super 8,** 800-800-8000, 1590 Oak Ridge Turnpike. Local restaurants include **The Daily Grind, A Coffee Emporium,** 423-483-9200, **Simply D'Vine Wine & Cheese Bistro,** 423-482-0077, offering live music along with your food, and the **Soup Kitchen,** 423-482-3525, all in historic Jackson Square.

Lenoir City, TN
pop 6,147
Eastern Time
Chamber of Commerce/Visitors Bureau 423-458-2067/423-986-6822

To See and Do
From one overlook you can see three TVA lakes! Listed are the following recreation areas:

Watts Bar Lake (Tennessee River): Watts Bar Dam Reservation, Rhea Springs Recreation Area, Froshee Pass Recreation Area,

Hornsby Hollow Recreation Area, Riley Creek Recreation Area.
Tellico Lake (Little Tennessee River): Tellico Dam Reservation
Fort Loudoun Lake (Tennessee River): Ft Loudoun Dam Reservation, Yarberry Peninsula Recreation Area, and Poland Creek Recreation Area.
All are beautiful facilities offering an abundance of recreational opportunities -- get TVA's recreational map "Great Lakes of the South" for a complete listing of boat docks, resorts, state parks, US Forest Service camp areas, and county and municipal parks along TVA's shores by writing *TVA, Communications & Public Relations, 400 W Summit Hill Dr, Knoxville, TN 37902.*
Fort Loudoun Dam, *Hwy U321*, is on the main channel of the Tennessee River; free tours of the hydro-power dam available with prior arrangements; groups welcome; picnic, swimming, fishing, boat ramp.

Accommodations
Econo Lodge, *800-553-2666, 1211 Hwy U321N;* and **Ramada Limited**, *800-2-RAMADA, 400 Interchange Park Dr;* many campgrounds on all that water.

Loudon, TN
pop 4,026
Eastern Time
Chamber of Commerce/Visitors Bureau 423-458-206/423-7986-6822

To See and Do
Historic Loudon is within easy reach of the water, yet this pretty spot entices those who like to visit interesting buildings and homes too -- many here are on the National Register. Follow the **Downtown Loudon Walking Tour**, *423-458-9020, 501 Poplar St*, a self-guided tour of the downtown area; blue street banners proclaim the Loudon limits; see pre and post Civil War architecture; stop in at the **Carmichael Inn Museum**, *423-458-1442, 501 Poplar St, Courthouse Square*, an 1810 log cabin used as a stage coach inn during the heyday of river and train transportation, now a museum with memorabilia of the county.
Two wineries in the area offer pleasant visits: the **Tennessee Valley**

Winery, 423-986-5147, 15606 Hotchkiss Valley Rd, annually produces 14,000 gallons of muscadine wines and French hybrids and is open all year; the **Loudon Valley Vineyards & Winery**, 423-986-8736, 555 Huff Ferry Rd N, has 51 acres on the Tennessee River; tours, hikes and tastings, all year, free. Drop by at the end of August for the **Smoky Mountain Fiddlers Convention and Antiques Festival**, 423-458-4352, Grove St near courthouse; prize money for bands and individual fiddle, banjo, guitar and dancing; play area for the kids.

Accommodations

Holiday Inn Express, 800-HOLIDAY, 12452 Hwy S72N; **Knights Inn**, 800-843-5644, 15100 Hwy S72N; **Mason Place Bed & Breakfast**, 423-458-3921, 600 Commerce St, family-owned 130-year old plantation home on National Register; antiques and feather beds, pool and garden.

Sweetwater, TN
pop 5,066
Eastern Time
Chamber of Commerce/Visitors Bureau 423-442-9147

To See and Do

Go underground in Sweetwater and find the **Lost Sea**, 423-337-6616, 140 Lost Sea Rd. The cavern is a US Registered Natural Landmark, and holds the Guinness World Record as the World's Largest Underground Lake. You can ride in a glass-bottom boat on the 4.5 acre lake and see anthodites, rare cave flowers found only in a few caves throughout the world. A great place to visit on a hot summer day -- it's always cool here!

At the **Orr Mountain Winery**, 423-442-5340, 1 mi off Hwy 68 between Sweetwater and Madisonville, enjoy the Grape Experience from Vine to Wine; award-winning wines; picnic facilities; daily summer; call for other hours and group tour information, free.

Accommodations

Comfort Inn, 800-228-5150, 803 S Main St; **Days Inn**, 800-325-2525, 229 Hwy S68; **Hillside Heaven Bed & Breakfast**, 423-

337-2714, 2920 Hwy 68, historic log cabin, wraparound porches, swing, rockers; full breakfast; **Sweetwater Valley KOA Campground**, 800-KOA-9224, 269 Murray's Chapel Rd.

Athens, TN
pop 12,054
Eastern Time
Chamber of Commerce/Visitors Bureau 423-745-0334

To See and Do
The **McMinn County Living Heritage Museum**, 423-745-0329, *522 W Madison Ave*, is worthy of a long visit -- there are 26 permanent exhibit areas. They cover the Cherokee heritage, Tennessee's pioneer years and secession from the Union, and the Civil War and its economic transformation. One of the South's largest quilt shows is held here every year. Get the scoop at **Mayfield Dairy**, 423-745-2151, *4 Mayfield Lane;* at the Visitor's Center you are treated to a film and then a tour of the plant; there are some steps to climb; wear slip-resistant shoes; stop in the ice cream parlor for treats when you're done. **Tennessee Wesleyan College**, 423-745-9522, *204 E College St,* has a beautiful campus gracing the downtown area; co-ed four-year institution supported by United Methodist Church.

Accommodations
Days Inn, *800-329-7466, I-75 & Hwy S30;* **Holiday Inn Express**, *800-HOLIDAY, I-75 & Mt Verd Rd;* **Quality Inn Motel**, *423-337-3541, I-75 & Hwy S68;* **Sweetwater Hotel & Convention Center**, *423-337-3511, 180 Hwy S68;* **Woodlawn Bed & Breakfast**, *800-745-8213, 110 Keith Lane,* gourmet breakfast in National Historic Register home built in 1858; original smokehouse still stands; downtown location; **Athens KOA Campground**, *423-745-9199, 2509 Decatur Pike.*

Englewood, TN
pop 1,611
Eastern Time
Chamber of Commerce 423-745-0334

Englewood Textile Museum, *423-887-5455, 109 Niota Rd in downtown Englewood;* museum shows the history of the textile industry and focuses on the role of women in "public work;" textile manufacturing was the one Appalachian industry that employed large numbers of women; free but donations appreciated.

Etowah, TN
pop 3,815
Eastern Time
Chamber of Commerce 423-263-2228

To See and Do
Get visitor information and tour the **L&N Depot/Railroad Museum,** *423-263-7840, Tennessee Ave in downtown Etowah;* this restored Victorian railroad passenger station has a museum on 1st floor; art gallery on 2nd. Groups call for tour arrangements, free. Another historic spot is the **Gem Theatre,** *423-263-2202, Tennessee Ave;* opened in 1928, it's considered the largest privately owned theatre in E Tennessee, now shows both film and live. For outdoor recreation, the **Hiwassee Ranger Station, *423-263-5486, Hwy 310,*** provides trail maps and information on the **Cherokee National Forest.**

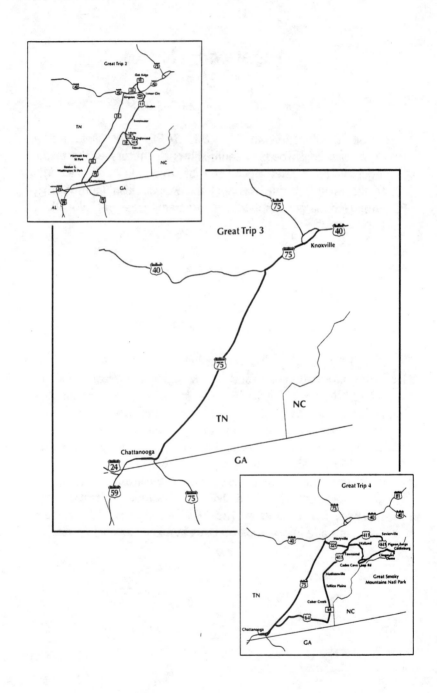

Great Trip 3

Chattanooga to Knoxville, TN
the dogwoods and history route
via I-75
approximately 245 miles round-trip, 4.5 hours driving time

Why Go
Dogwood Trails & Big Orange Football &
Largest Campus Stadium in US & World's Fair Sunsphere &
Cheetah Savanna & African Plains & Gorilla Valley &
Historic Old City & Archives & Genealogy & Planetarium &
IJAMS Nature Center & Memorial Gardens &
Birthplace of Tennessee & Civil War Relics &
Pioneer Houses & Victorian Cemetery &
Owl Prowls & Sightseeing Cruises &
Farmer's Market & Chocolate Factory

Suggested route with approximate mileages

Instruction	Road	Dir	Miles
Chattanooga to Knoxville	I-24 & I-75	N	122
Knoxville to Chattanooga	I-75 & I-24	S	122
Total Mileage			244

Dogwoods in the spring and football in the fall -- two real draws to any nature-and-sports lovers heart. And in Knoxville, these things are big time. Every year, the mid-part of April gives over to the **Dogwood Arts Festival**. Pink and white dogwood trees bust their buds on the hillsides, in the residential neighborhoods, and clustered among the office buildings downtown. You can drive the **"Dogwood Trails"** -- sixty miles of gorgeously manicured lawns filled with glorious flowers and trees, in six of Knoxville's most prestigious neighborhoods. Or hop a free bus at Market Square and relax during the drive around the city. There also are over 100 public and private gardens that are open during the festival and enough events to please everybody. Are you interested in quilts? photography? architecture? tennis? dancing? cars? storytelling? arts, crafts, and activities for the kids? It's all there, during April in Knoxville.

The Knoxville campus of the **University of Tennessee** is the site of **Neyland Stadium**, the largest on-campus stadium in the U. S, and it's river side, so you can come in your boat! See SEC football on glorious autumn days and cheer the Big Orange, or the other team if you dare; remember you're in Orange territory.

Visit an incredible number of restored homes filled with period furnishings -- including historic **Blount Mansion**, which served as territorial capital and was the birthplace of Tennessee Statehood. You can research to your heart's content in the **East Tennessee Historical Center**, perusing more than 35,000 volumes of history and genealogy. Eat and shop in Knoxville's **Old City** district, and check out **World's Fair Park**, site of the 1982 World's Fair and now housing interesting galleries and more; go to the huge **Regional Farmer's Market** too.

And of course, another great reason to go to Knoxville is its marvelous **zoo** -- where you'll find more than 850 creatures housed in natural habitats. You'll enjoy **Gorilla Valley**, with rocks and cliffs and special viewing windows; the zoo is well known for its **Big Cats** too -- the collection includes cheetahs, leopards, lions, pumas, and even a white tiger.

Knoxville, TN
pop 165,121; metro pop 604,816
Eastern Time
Convention & Visitors Bureau 423-523-2316

To See and Do

Free and Historical

East Tennessee Historical Center, *423-544-5744, 314 W Clinch Ave.* More than 35,000 volumes of history and genealogy covering Tennessee and the southeastern U. S. are located here; the building was formerly the U. S. Custom House and Post Office; built in 1874, it's an outstanding example of 19th century architecture and is on the National Register of Historic Places; it houses both the Calvin M. McClung Historical Collection and the Knox County Archives through the Knox County Public Library System. You'll find documents, maps, newspapers, photographs and paintings here too; open daily, call for hours.

Beck Cultural Exchange Center, *423-524-8461, 1927 Dandridge Ave;* this museum displays the achievements of Knoxville's black citizens from the early 1800's with books, photographs, newspapers, recordings, biographies and works of art; open Tuesday-Saturday.

Old City Historic District, *423-523-2316, Jackson Ave & Central St;* restored 19th-century brick warehouses are now filled with restaurants, nightclubs, shops, and galleries; go antiquing by day and enjoy live entertainment in the evenings.

Museums and Galleries Unique to the Area

East Tennessee Discovery Center. Museum/Science Discovery, *423-594-1494, 516 N Beaman St,* has exhibits on life, energy, transportation, fossils; lots of hands-on things to do with holograms, electricity, and lasers; includes aquarium and the famous AKIMA Planetarium; open Monday-Saturday. **KAMA Health Discovery,** *423-594-1294, 1060 World's Fair Park Dr,* is famous for its age-appropriate multimedia programs such as Lifetime Fitness, Family Life, and Drug Awareness; taught by health education specialists; open to public by appointment.

Knoxville Museum of Art, 423-525-6101, *1050 World's Fair Park Dr;* the permanent collection focuses on contemporary American art; there are four galleries, lovely gardens, an ARTcade computer-interactive learning gallery, and the Junior League of Knoxville Exploratory Gallery. Lectures, workshops and traveling exhibits from all over the country.

Museum of East Tennessee History, 423-544-4318, *600 Market St;* managed by the East Tennessee Historical Society, this museum has exhibits covering 200 years of life in the river valley. Located in the former U. S. Custom House and Post Office, it is next to Krutch Park and only a few blocks from the historic Old City.

Ewing Gallery of Art & Architecture, 423-974-3200, *1715 Volunteer Blvd on the UT campus,* carries the work of avant-garde artists and architects of international and local stature; also on the UT campus are the **Frank H. McClung Museum,** *423-974-2144, 1327 Circle Park Dr,* with collections in anthropology, archaeology, and local and natural history; traces 12,000 years of Tennessee Indian history and the geology and fossil history of Tennessee; and the **Gallery Concourse,** *423-974-5455, 1502 W Cumberland Ave,* with two permanent collections and twenty-one different shows annually.

Historic Homes and Gardens in Knoxville

Armstrong-Lockett House and W. P. Toms Memorial Gardens, Crescent Bend, 423-637-3163, *2728 Kingston Pike;* the house was built in 1834 and restored in 1977; houses 18th Century English and American furniture and outstanding collection of English silver; the gardens are on seven terraces going down to the rivers edge.

Blount Mansion, 423-525-2375, *200 W Hill Ave;* built between 1792 and 1830; oldest section was home of William Blount, Governor of the SW Territory; the site also was the territorial capitol and birthplace of Tennessee Statehood; it's a National Historic Landmark restored to period of late 1700's; The **Blount Mansion Interpretive Center,** *Gay St and Hill Ave,* serves as orientation facility and museum shop.

Confederate Memorial Hall, 423-522-2371, *3148 Kingston Pike SW;* this Antebellum mansion was headquarters of Confederate

Gen. James Longstreet during siege of Knoxville; its brick walls are still pitted with bullet holes and an inside wall is embedded with a cannon ball; home contains collection of southern and Civil War relics, library of southern literature.

James White's Fort, *423-525-6514, 205 E Hill Ave*, is an original pioneer house built in 1786 by the founder and first settler of Knoxville. On site are guest house, museum, smoke house, blacksmith shop and loom house; you'll see tools and artifacts of the period. Call for hours; also available for weddings and special events.

John Sevier Historic Site, Marble Springs, *423-573-5508, 6 mi S via Hwy U441, S 33, E on S168.* Restored farmhouse of John Sevier, state's first governor between 1796-1809; on 36 acres; seven original and reconstructed log buildings give a glimpse of pioneer life; trading post, pavilion and outdoor stage.

Mabry/Hazen House, *423-522-8661, 1711 Dandridge Ave*, constructed in 1858 and occupied by Union forces in 1863, the house then remained in the same family for three generations; many original family furnishings.

Ramsey House, Swan Pond, *423-546-0745, 6 mi NE on Thorngrove Pike*; first stone house in Knox County; built in 1797; social, religious, political center of early Tennessee; restored gabled house, period furnishings; on National Register of Historic Places.

Old Gray Cemetery, *423-522-1424, 543 N Broadway*; stroll past many examples of Victorian art and architecture in this 13-acre spot; established in 1850 as part of the rural cemetery movement, it was named for English poet Thomas Gray, author of *Elegy Written in a Country Churchyard*.

Parks and Entertainment

Knoxville Zoological Gardens, *423-637-5331, E via I-40, Rutledge Pike exit*; over 850 animals representing 225 species wander in a park-like setting; you're invited to walk on the wild side as animals roam in Gorilla Valley, the Cheetah Savanna, and the African Plains where you'll see lowland gorillas, African elephants, white rhinoceros, cheetahs, red pandas, Bengal tigers and tall giraffes; also a world-class reptile collection; the wooded hillsides feature over 125 varieties of trees and shrubs;

don't miss the summer Bird Show in the amphitheater and the Seal and Sea Lion demonstrations.

IJAMS Nature Center, 423-577-4717, 2915 Island Home Ave; an 80-acre park with 20 acres of trails through woods, meadows, and bluffs overlooking the Tennessee River; lectures and programs also; some of the most popular are the "Owl Prowl" and the canoe trips.

Star of Knoxville, 423-525-7827, 300 Neyland Drive; 325-passenger sternwheeler riverboat offers dinner and lunch cruises; sightseeing cruises show off historic sites and the Knoxville and UT skyline.

Knoxville Chamber Orchestra and Knoxville Symphony Orchestra, 423-523-1178; and the **Knoxville Opera**, 423-523-8712, for tickets. The **UT Musical Arts Series and Opera Theater**, 423-974-5678, has Sunday afternoon concerts and student/faculty recitals.

UT football, 423-974-2491, is played at **Neyland Stadium**, which seats 102,544 in the largest on-campus stadium in the U.S.; **UT basketball**, 423-974-2491, is played at the **Thompson-Boling Arena**, which seats 25,000.

The **Sunsphere** looms over **World's Fair Park**, 423-523-2316, Clinch Ave; built for the 1982 event; the **Victorian Houses** and the **Candy Factory**, 423-546-5707, 1060 World's Fair Park Dr, are filled with galleries and even a working chocolate factory; you'll find jewelry, crafts, pottery, toys, dolls and works by national and regional artists; some of the studios are open for visitors so you can watch artists at work; you can watch the chocolatiers too! More foods and finds at **Knox County Regional Farmer's Market**, 423-524-FARM, 4700 New Harvest Lane; stop in for fresh produce or crafts; within their 79 acres and 27,000 square-foot pavilion they stage special events and demonstrations throughout the year. And, don't forget the already mentioned **Dogwood Arts Festival**, 423-637-4561; 150 events, public and private gardens on display, 60 miles of marked dogwood trails for auto or bus tours; mid-late April.

Accommodations

No shortage of fine accommodations here, but book way ahead during football and events weekends. Downtown you'll find a

Hyatt Regency, 423-637-1234, 500 Hill Ave SE; Radisson Summit Hill, 423-522-2600, 401 Summit Hill Dr; Hilton, 423-523-2300, 501 W Church Ave; and Holiday Inn, 423-522-2800, 525 Henley; most chains can be found on each side of town; call About Tennessee Bed & Breakfast, 800-458-2421 for reservations in area B & B's; or try the Maple Grove Inn, 423-690-9565, 8800 Westland Dr; old-world style in a 1799 Georgian-style home on 15 acres; tennis court, pool, sunroom, private porches. Park and walk the Old City to find such interesting restaurants as Sullivan's, 423-522-4511, 1375 Central St, offering seafood, beef, and southwestern; Lucille's, 423-546-3742, 106 Central Ave N, featuring jazz and blues; The Big Easy, 423-523-7711, 125 E Jackson Ave, strictly cajun; near the World's Fair site is the Butcher Shop, 423-637-0204, 801 W Jackson Ave; anywhere in town you'll be able to find everything from barbecue to Chinese to family style, and plenty of college-student fare.

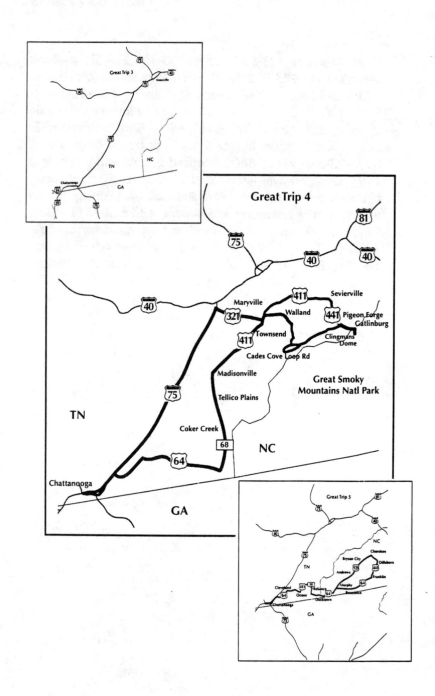

Great Trip 4

Chattanooga to Clingmans Dome, TN
the mountain magic route
via Maryville, Sevierville, Pigeon Forge, Gatlinburg, Clingmans Dome,
Townsend, Walland, Madisonville, Tellico Plains, Coker Creek,
returning to Chattanooga
approximately 370 miles round-trip, 7.5 hours driving time

Why Go
Clingmans Dome, 6,643 ft, Highest Point in Tennessee
Great Smokies & Crafts & Dollywood & Hiking & Horseback Riding &
Autumn Foliage & Spring Rhodies & Spruce-Fir Trail & Cades Cove Deer

Suggested route with approximate mileages

Instruction	Road	Dir	Miles
Chattanooga to Lenoir City	I-75 & U321	NE	90
Lenoir City to Maryville	U321 & U411	NE	22
Maryville to Sevierville	U411	E	27
Sevierville to Pigeon Forge	U441	S	9
Pigeon Forge to Gatlinburg	U441	S	5
Gatlinburg to Newfound Gap	U441	S	11
Newfound Gap to Clingmans Dome	Park Road	S	7
Clingmans Dome to Newfound Gap	Park Road	N	7
Newfound Gap to Pigeon Forge	U441	W	15
Pigeon Forge to Townsend	U321	W	19
Townsend to Walland	U321	W	8
Walland to Maryville	U321	W	9
Maryville to Madisonville	U411	S	28
Madisonville to Tellico Plains	S68	S	14
Tellico Plains to Coker Creek	S68	S	11
Coker Creek to Ducktown	S68	S	22
Ducktown to Chattanooga	U64 & I-75	W & S	67
Total Mileage			371

Let's face it folks -- there's far more to do on this Trip than any moderately energetic person can do in a week's time! After all, you're in serious mountain territory here -- **Gatlinburg** is the Gateway to the **Great Smoky Mountains National Park**, much of the route goes through the **Cherokee National Forest**, and more than half your drive is on **Scenic Highways**.

You'll be treated to everything from take-your-breath-away mountain-top views to quiet little crafts galleries tucked among the hills, such as **Coker Creek Crafts Gallery**, where you'll find white oak baskets so fine they are in permanent museum collections as far away as Paris and Tokyo.

Tightly confined mountain streams create rushing waters that make you want to fly fish, even if you don't know how. You might wind up wading in the coolness on a hot summer's day, or snapping pictures when surrounded by blazing foliage in the fall. Count among the mountain wildlife black bear, deer, mountain lions and red wolves; rhododendron and laurel are everywhere, combined with ferns, trillium and a multitude of wildflowers. Every season of the year offers different delights.

If you're a hiker, gather a supply of trail maps and go for the elevation climbs on **Alum Cave Bluff Trail** or **Gregory Bald Trail**. If you're not, get yourself in good enough shape to walk the paved pathway to the observation tower at **Clingmans Dome**. You'll be standing at 6,643 feet, the highest point in Tennessee. Prefer horseback? Outfitters are everywhere, offering trips and trails for experienced or beginning riders.

Add extra mileage to your Trip by taking the Park Road to **Cades Cove** (get a map at Sugarlands Visitor Center) for a one-way scenic drive back in time. Go late in the afternoon and you'll see more deer than you can count, peacefully enjoying their evening meal in the broad pastures of the Cove.

And, if it's NOT peace and quiet you're after, you'll find all the hoopla your heart desires in fast-paced **Pigeon Forge**, packed corner-to-corner with water slides, miniature golf, car racing, **Dollywood**, and an unusual five-course meal sans silverware at the rip-roaring-rodeo called the **Dixie Stampede**.

Maryville, TN
pop 19,208
Eastern Time
Chamber of Commerce/Visitors Bureau 800-525-6834

To See and Do
If you like the out-of-doors, you're probably interested in Scouting too; visit the **Peregrine Scout Museum**, 423-856-0244, 6588 Hwy U411S, where you can see the international history of scouting in a fun setting; open daily. Other interesting history at the replica of the **Sam Houston Schoolhouse**, 423-983-1550, 3650 Old Sam Houston School Rd, built in 1794, two years before Tennessee became a state. Sam Houston was only 18 years old when he taught here.

Accommodations
Shannondale Boarding Stables & Bed & Breakfast, 423-983-7197, 2543 Tuckaleechee Pk; country French stone home, pool, view of mountains; horses boarded; 25-stall barn.

Sevierville, TN
pop 7,178
Eastern Time
Chamber of Commerce 800-255-6411

To See and Do
See the sights on horseback from here; stables in the area are **Cedar Ridge Riding Stables**, 423-428-5802, Hwy U441; **Douglas Lake View Horse Riding**, 423-428-3587, 1650 Providence Rd; **Walden's Creek Horseback Riding Stables**, 423-429-0411, 2709 Walden Creek Rd; and **Willowbridge Farm**, 423-453-2257, 2920 Jones Cove Rd; or take to the air at **Scenic Helicopters**, 423-453-6342, 2791 Pkwy; or **Wind Works Hot Air Balloon Co**, 423-453-5277, 240 Riverwalk Dr; MUST have reservations. Go underground at **Forbidden Caverns**, 423-453-5972, 455 Blowing Cave Rd, where you'll see sparkling formations and natural chimneys; enjoy wandering

out-of-doors at **Smoky Mountain Deer Farm & Petting Zoo,** *423-428-3337, 478 Happy Hollow Lane,* among the deer, zebra, miniature horses, and exotic cattle; also pony rides for the little ones. Before you leave for Pigeon Forge and Dollywood, check out the tribute to hometowner **Dolly Parton** on the **Sevier County Courthouse** lawn. Other recognizable names: **Lee Greenwood Theater,** *800-769-1125, 870 Winfield Dunn Pkwy,* a 1,776-seat showplace where Lee performs over 200 shows a year; **Arnold Palmer's Eagle's Landing Golf Club,** *423-429-4223, 1556 Old Knoxville Hwy.*

Accommodations

Best Western, *800-528-1234, 3426 Winfield Dunn Pkwy;* three **Comfort Inns,** *800-233-3443, 1850 Parkway* and *800-228-5150, 155 W Dumplin Valley Rd* and *800-441-0311, 860 Winfield Dunn Pkwy;* **Days Inn,** *800-590-4861, 1841 Parkway;* **Fairfield Inn,** *800-228-2800, 1650 Parkway;* **Hampton Inn,** *800-HAMPTON, 681 Winfield Dunn Pkwy;* **Ramada Limited,** *800-939-9448, 2863 Winfield Dunn Pkwy.* Plenty of cabins, campgrounds, chalets, condos and bed & breakfasts in the area; call the Chamber for a complete listing. Pay a visit to the **Apple Barn & Cider Mill,** *423-453-9319, 230 Apple Valley Rd;* eat in the **Applewood Farm House Grill;** purchase apples, cider, apple butter and fried apple pies too; get ribs and onion loaf at **Damon's,** *423-428-6200, 1640 Parkway.*

Pigeon Forge, TN
pop 3,027
Eastern Time
Chamber of Commerce/Visitors Bureau 800-251-9100

To See and Do

Pigeon Forge is mile-after-mile of water slides, mini-golf, skydiving, bungee jumping, speedway, arcade-ish entertainment; with music shows and Elvis museums interspersed. If you love theme parks, you'll surely love **Dollywood,** *800-DOLLYWOOD, 1020 Dollywood Lane.* Great rides and music shows of course, the park highlights the folklore of the Smokies too.

Fantastic is the word for the **Dixie Stampede**, *800-356-1676, 3049 Parkway;* billed as the Most Fun Place to Eat in the Smokies, it's a feast at a rodeo show; you're seated facing the ring, watching the dazzling horses-in-action while being served soup and salad and chicken and just about everything else a person can eat with no silverware! It ends in a rousing flare of patriotism and applause, after you've wiped your fingers.

Racing and car lovers will find speedways, and museums such as the **Smoky Mountain Car Museum**, *2970 Parkway*, with gas, electric and steam autos, and famous personality cars.

When you're done playing, try your hand at shopping in the **Tanger Factory Outlet**, *423-428-7001, 175 Davis Rd*, where you'll find discounts up to 70% off. The **Old Mill**, *423-453-4628, 2944 Middle Creek Rd*, was built in 1830, and has been in operation ever since; the water-powered mill grinds corn, wheat, rye and buckwheat into 28 kinds of flour, meal, grits and pancake mixes; take some home.

Accommodations

Best Western, *800-422-3232, 3810 Parkway;* **Days Inn**, *800-645-3079, 2760 N Parkway;* **Hampton Inn & Suites**, *800-388-1727, 2492 Parkway;* **Holiday Inn**, *800-HOLIDAY, 3230 Parkway;* **Microtel**, *800-431-ROOM, 202 Emert St;* **Ramada Limited**, *800-269-1222, 2193 N Parkway;* **Ramada Inn**, *800-345-6799, 4025 Parkway;* many more choices include cabins, campgrounds, chalets, condos, and bed & breakfasts. Eat at the **Dixie Stampede**, *800-356-1676, 3049 Parkway*, or other dinner shows; along the Parkway are restaurants of every type.

Gatlinburg, TN
pop 3,417
Eastern Time
Visitors Bureau 800-822-1998 or 800-343-1475

To See and Do

Any visit to town should begin at the **Gatlinburg Welcome Center**, *423-436-0519, Hwy U441S*. Gatlinburg is the ultimate big-little town; with hawkers on every corner peddling T-shirts picturing the incredible natural beauty that surrounds you. You can stand atop a "space needle" in the heart of downtown and gaze at the full moon rising over 6,593-ft Mt LeConte. Down below, you can get married in a wedding chapel or play gooney golf by floodlight. Or, eat fudge you've just watched them make. Many folks are content to sit in a rocking chair on a porch hanging over the Pigeon River; sometimes they make extra effort and dangle a fishing pole down below. People-watching and shopping top the list of things to do.

Serious crafts-people visit the **Arrowmont School of Arts & Crafts**, 423-436-5860, 556 Parkway; this arts complex provides year-round changing programs and exhibits. Ride the **Arts & Crafts Trolley** for an 8-mile loop tour of the **Great Smoky Arts & Crafts Community**, 423-671-3600, Ext 3504, Hwy U321 N/Glades Rd/Buckhorn Rd, taking you to the shops and studios of more than 80 artists and craftspeople; watch and visit them while they work.

Shows you may want to catch: the **Gatlinburg Passion Play**, 423-430-3777, 322 Airport Rd, a musical drama depicting the life of Christ with choir, soloists, and special effects; **Smoky Mountain Travelers**, 423-436-4194, 715 Parkway, live bluegrass and mountain music; **Sweet Fanny Adams Theatre**, 423-436-4039, 461 Parkway, two musical comedies presented on alternate nights. Reservations advised.

A quick ride to the mountain tops on the **Gatlinburg Sky Lift**, 423-436-4307, 765 Parkway, #7 Traffic light, go up Crockett Mountain for a panoramic view of the Great Smokies; or **Gatlinburg Aerial Tramway**, 423-436-5423, 1001 Parkway, which takes you to **Ober Gatlinburg Ski Resort and Amusement Park**. If you're looking for a slower ride, try **McCarter's Stables, Inc**, 423-436-5354, Hwy U441S, horseback guided one to four-hour mountain trail rides inside Great Smoky Mountains National Park, daily, spring to fall.

Accommodations

Best Western Crossroads, 800-225-2295, 440 Parkway; **Best Western Twin Islands**, 800-223-9299, 539 Parkway; **Clarion Inn**, 800-CLARION, 1100 Parkway; **Comfort Inn**, 800-933-8679, 200 E Parkway; **Days Inn**; 800-362-9522, 504 Airport

Rd; **Holiday Inn,** *800-435-9201, 520 Airport Rd;* **Quality Inn,** *800-933-8674, 938 Parkway;* **Ramada,** *800-933-8678, 756 Parkway;* many non-chains such as downtown's **Edgewater,** *423-436-4151, 402 River Rd;* **Greystone Lodge,** *800-451-9202, 559 Parkway;* and **River Terrace,** *800-251-2040, 240 River Rd.* The Chamber can give you a listing of cabins, campgrounds, chalets, condos and bed & breakfasts; also call **About Tennessee Bed & Breakfast Reservation Service,** *800-458-2421* to make reservations at B & B's all over the state; they have over 200 listings. Walk down any street to find your **restaurant** of choice; lots of sidewalk or over-the-river dining; during peak seasons you may wind up waiting in line if you don't start early.

U. S. National Park
Eastern Time
Start your visit to the **Great Smoky Mountains National Park** and your drive to Tennessee's highest point at **Sugarlands Visitor Center,** *423-436-1200, 107 Park Headquarters Rd.* Exhibits to view here, and rangers to assist you with trip-planning advice. The park is open year round, although Clingmans Dome Road is closed in winter and Newfound Gap Road may close during winter storms. The park encompasses 520,000 acres and is well-loved, logging over 9 million visits a year. Half the park lies in Tennessee and half in North Carolina, and the Appalachian Trail winds through, nearly following the state line. There are more than 800 miles of trails throughout the Park.
It is 35 miles through the Park on Hwy U441 from Gatlinburg to Cherokee, NC. When you've driven about 11 miles to **Newfound Gap,** you are at an elevation of 5,048 feet. The air is much cooler here, so bring a jacket even though it may be a sweltering August day when you leave home. You can hike a portion of the Appalachian Trail from here, or stand with one foot in Tennessee and one in North Carolina and enjoy the view from the overlook.
Drive seven miles more on **Clingmans Dome Road;** park and hike the uphill path to the 6,643-foot peak. You'll be standing at the

highest point in the state of Tennessee, go even higher on the observation ramp; if the weather is clear you'll have a 360-degree view of the Smokies. Follow the **Spruce-Fir Trail,** round-trip of .75 miles, for a close look at the forest.

If you want to connect with Great Trip 5 and continue to Cherokee, you may do so on returning to Newfound Gap. Otherwise, head back towards Gatlinburg on Hwy U441. For hiking, the **Alum Cave Bluff Trail** takes off from Newfound Gap Road and climbs 2,500 feet, passing unusual geology such as **Arch Rock, Alum Cave Bluff,** and steep cliffs.

Driving on, to stay in the Park, head west at Sugarlands; follow the signs to Cades Cove, and ultimately, Townsend. **Cades Cove** gives a glimpse of the past; in the 6-mile-long valley nestle cabins and churches; there are 19 tour stops on the 11-mile one-way road. If you are there late in the day, you'll see deer grazing in the fields. A great biking spot; and more good hikes from here too -- **Abrams Falls Trail** is level and treats you to a beautiful plunge pool; **Gregory Bald Trail** takes you through changing landscapes on a 3,000-foot climb; go for the June azaleas. It's one-way into Townsend from Cades Cove.

Townsend, TN
pop 4,749
Eastern Time
Visitors Center 423-448-6134

To See and Do

Want to ride? **Cades Cove Riding Stables,** *423-448-6286, 4035 E Lamar Alexander Pkwy,* offers guided horseback rides and carriage rides through the foothills; hayrides around Cades Cove; reserve in advance. **Davy Crockett Riding Stables,** *423-448-6411, 505 Old Cades Cove Rd,* has guided trail rides by the hour outside the Park; horses can be boarded too. **Double M Ranch,** *423-995-9421, 4033 Miser Station Rd,* has horseback riding, plus hiking trails, a paved bike trail, and streams for trout fishing.

Inside, visit the **Little River Railroad & Lumber Company Museum,**

423-448-2211, 7747 Hwy U321; see memorabilia from the railroad and lumber company operations of this old company town; or go underground at **Tuckaleechee Caverns**, 423-448-2274, 825 Caverns Rd, and see the Big Room, gorgeous onyx formations, and high waterfalls; 58 degree temperature.
For performing arts see **Christy, the Musical**, 423-448-0215, 329 Bethel Church Rd, in a beautiful outdoor setting; the drama is based on Catherine Marshall's novel about East Tennessee's Appalachian heritage; May-October Monday-Saturday. Visual arts at **K Collection of Catherine Girard**, 423-448-6141, 7720 Chestnut Hill Rd, and **Lee Roberson Gallery**, 800-423-7341, 758 Wears Valley Rd; both feature wildlife and scenery.

Accommodations
Best Western Valley View Lodge & Convention Center, 800-292-4844, 7726 E Lamar Alexander Pkwy; **Hampton Inn**, 800-257-1932, 7824 E Lamar Alexander Pkwy; **Family Inns of America**, 800-332-8282, 7239 E Lamar Alexander Pkwy; numerous non-chain motels, cabins, campgrounds and chalets; **Richmont Inn Bed & Breakfast**, 423-448-6751, 220 Winterberry Ln; Appalachian barn furnished with English antiques and French paintings; breathtaking views; candlelight dessert; luxurious. **Tuckaleechee Inn**, 423-448-6442, 160 Bear Lodge Dr; 10 rooms, full breakfast, rocking chair front porch, beautiful views.

Walland, TN
pop 525
Eastern Time
Visitors Center 423-448-6134

Accommodations
Walland is known for the fabulous **Inn at Blackberry Farm**, 800-862-7610, 1471 W Millers Cove Rd; elegance and pampering here, in a 29-room country house/hotel/estate on 1,100 acres in the foothills of the Smokies. Gourmet meals, beverages, and use of recreational equipment included in daily rates; member of Relais & Chateaux; 4 Diamond Award winner.

Madisonville, TN
pop 3,033
Eastern Time
Chamber of Commerce 423-442-9147

To See and Do
An interesting stop here is the **Lucky Pine Herb Farm**, 423-442-1221, 155 Big Creek Cemetery Rd, where you'll find 227 varieties of herbs, gardens, greenhouses and classes in cooking, harvesting, and local crafts.

Tellico Plains, TN
pop 657
Eastern Time
Chamber of Commerce 423-442-9147

To See and Do
Tellico Plains is a gateway to the **Cherokee National Forest**, and offers abundant trout fishing, canoeing, camping, horseback riding and hiking. Many waterfalls in the area; on the road to **Coker Creek Falls** you'll find **Bentwood Farm Llamas**, 423-261-2500, 243 Ironsburg Rd. **Arrowhead Land Company**, 423-253-7670, Hwy S165E, was once the location of the Cherokee Indian village Telequa; area also was site of first gold strike in America in the 1820's and was a lumberjack town in the 1900's.

Coker Creek, TN
Eastern Time
Chamber of Commerce 423-442-9147

To See and Do
Coker Creek Village, 800-448-9580, Hwy 68, is a 250-acre mountain ranch in the historic gold district. You can still pan for gold here; also horseback trail rides in the Cherokee National Forest, and whitewater rafting. Plan to spend time at

Coker Creek Crafts Gallery, *423-261-2157, 206 Hot Water Rd;* more than 30 artists and craftspeople represented; owners Kathleen and Ken Dalton are internationally known white oak basket makers; Kathleen also is a watercolorist and Ken does folk art sculptures.

Accommodations
Mountain Garden Inn Bed & Breakfast, *423-261-2689, Hwy S68,* new 3-story log home with 3-state mountain view; rockers on the porch, full breakfast; cabins in the area too.

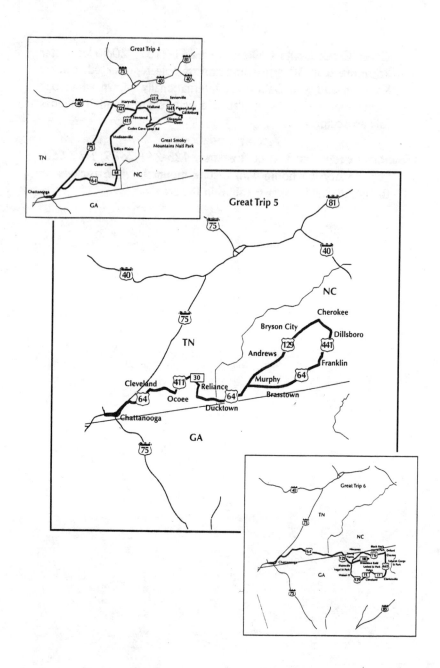

Great Trip 4

Great Trip 5

Great Trip 6

Great Trip 5

Chattanooga to Cherokee, NC
the heritage and whitewater route
via TN - Cleveland, Ocoee, Benton, Reliance, Ducktown
NC - Murphy, Andrews, Bryson City, Cherokee, Dillsboro, Franklin,
Brasstown, and returning to Chattanooga
approximately 350 miles round-trip, 7 hours driving time

Why Go
Cherokee Heritage & Hiwassee Float Trips & Ocoee River & Nantahala
Gorge & Whitewater Rafting & Slickrock Wilderness & Qualla Boundary &
Unto These Hills & Ruby Mining & Great Smoky Mountain Train &
Folk School & Mountain Lodges & Mingus Mill & Cowee Valley

Suggested route with approximate mileages

Instruction	Road	Dir	Miles
Chattanooga to Cleveland	I-75 & S64	NE	31
Cleveland to Ocoee	S64	E	8
Ocoee to Benton	U411	N	8
Benton to Reliance	U411 & S30	NE	20
Reliance to Murphy	S30 & U64	SE	45
Murphy to Andrews	U129	N	12
Andrews to Bryson City	U129	N	30
Bryson City to Cherokee	U129	N	20
Cherokee to Dillsboro	U441	S	12
Dillsboro to Franklin	U441	S	18
Franklin to Brasstown	U64	S	48
Brasstown to Murphy	U64	W	8
Murphy to Ducktown	U64	W	23
Ducktown to Chattanooga	U64 & I-75	W & S	67
Total Mileage			350

If it's whitewater you crave, whether to test your own daring or to marvel at someone else's, this is your route! This takes you to Tennessee's world-famous **Ocoee River**, site of the 1996 Whitewater Slalom and Canoe Olympic competition, and to North Carolina's fabulous **Nantahala Gorge**.

In North Carolina's southwest tip a town's elevation often surpasses its population. Many mountains are higher than 5,000 feet, creating the rushing streams that, in turn, make for the exciting whitewater you'll see. The **Cherokee and Nantahala National Forests** are lush; within the forest boundaries are the **Slickrock Wilderness** area and the **Joyce Kilmer Memorial Forest**, dedicated to the author of the poem, *Trees*.

The **Cherokee Indian Reservation** spreads over 56,000 acres known as the **Qualla Boundary** at the eastern edge of the **Great Smoky Mountains National Park**. This is the North Carolina entry into the Park; well-loved and often crowded. In downtown **Cherokee** you'll find today's commercialism mixed with the most ancient of traditions and unspeakable natural beauty. See the play, *Unto These Hills*, running for over 40 years in a beautiful outdoor amphitheater, and learn even more about Cherokee history in the **Cherokee Museum**.

Head south for **gem country**; rubies and sapphires are in the hills around Franklin; the mines invite you to dig for your own. Roll up your sleeves with a guaranteed ruby bucket, or go for pink and purple sapphires at a flume beside a tree-lined stream.

By all means ride the **Great Smoky Mountains Train**; a raft and rail trip takes you up the Nantahala Gorge by train and back down on the white water. They offer numerous excursions, including twilight gourmet dinner rides, and special events trips. But this can't be a last-minute whim, the train is often booked in advance, so call ahead and get your schedule in mind.

Speaking of schedules, tune into events at the **John C. Campbell Folk School** in Brasstown. In addition to the classes on this 365-acre campus, there are concerts, dances, and special crafts festivals and auctions. They claim one of the best dance floors in the country in the Community Room; come early for supper before the free Friday-night folk music and storytelling time.

Cleveland, TN
pop 30,354
Eastern Time
Visitors Bureau 800-472-6588

To See and Do

Much Cherokee heritage here; start with a look at the **Cherokee Chieftain** in downtown Johnston Park -- it's the state's only Peter Toth sculpture. While you're there you'll want to do the downtown historic walking tour; then take the **Cherokee Heritage Wildlife Tour**; get a brochure at the **Visitors Bureau,** *423-472-6587, 2145 Keith St;* or take the **Cherokee Scenic Loop Tour,** which leads you south of town to **Red Clay State Historic Park,** *423-478-0339, 1140 Red Clay Rd SW.* This was the site of the last Cherokee Councils before the Trail of Tears began; you'll see an interpretive center and replicas of Cherokee structures of the 1830's.

Stop at the **Primitive Settlement,** *423-476-5096, 693 Kinser Rd SE,* and visit an interesting collection of log cabins which have been restored and furnished with household and farm items once used by early Americans.

Headquarters for the **Cherokee National Forest,** *423-476-9700, 2800 N Ocoee St,* are located in Cleveland. The Forest covers 625,000 acres in ten Tennessee counties and offers 540 miles of hiking, horseback or mountain biking trails. Waterways in the Forest include the **State Scenic Hiwassee River** and the **Ocoee River.**

Accommodations

Comfort Inn, *800-221-2222, 153 James Asbury Dr;* **Days Inn,** *800-DAYS INN, 2550 Georgetown Rd;* **Econo Lodge,** *800-55-ECONO, 2650 Westside Dr;* **Hampton Inn,** *800-HAMPTON, 185 James Asbury Dr;* **Holiday Inn,** *800-HOLIDAY, I75 & S60;* **Quality Inn,** *800-221-2222, 2595 Georgetown Rd;* many campgrounds in area.

Benton/Ocoee, TN
pop 992
Eastern Time
Polk County Chamber of Commerce 423-338-5040

To See and Do
Nancy Ward Grave, 423-745-3573, Hwy U411 near Benton. Nancy Ward was the "Wild Rose of Cherokee" and was a beloved woman. Friend to pioneers, she helped to prevent war between the Indians and settlers. **Old Fort Marr Blockhouse,** 423-745-3573, Hwy U411, is oldest original block house in USA; it was used to confine the Cherokee during the months prior to their removal. Donated to Polk County schools in 1922; moved from original site.

Ocoee River. TVA manages the three dams here; there is a five-mile stretch of Class III-IV rapids to challenge you with such names as Grumpy and Hell Hole. Be aware of the following restrictions for rafting.

- *Guided raft trips are available between March and November; call ahead for information and reservations.*
- *You must be at least 12 to raft the Ocoee River; it's a Tennessee law.*
- *When it's warm, wear your swimsuit or t-shirt and shorts; cooler weather bring wool sweaters, socks and windbreakers; bring a change of clothes.*
- *Leave non-waterproof watches and cameras behind; anchor your glasses.*
- *Use of alcohol or drugs is strictly prohibited.*

There are more than two dozen Ocoee River outfitters, here are a few of them: **Adventures Unlimited,** 800-662-0667; 12-acre base camp has hot showers, a campground, picnic areas, and volleyball and basketball courts. **High Country,** 800-233-8594; 27 acres of meadow and forest, spacious changing area, hot tub, store, picnic pavilion, and group camping area. **Ocoee Inn Services,** 800-272-7238; family-style restaurant, rustic motel rooms, cabins on the water, boat dock, pontoon boats, fishing boats, canoes, photo services, rafting; hiking trails,

swimming holes, picnic areas and campgrounds. **Ocoee Outdoors**, *800-533-7767*; changing area and showers, store and picnic area, private campground. **Outdoor Adventures Rafting (OAR)**, *800-627-7636;* bathhouse and bunkhouses on 10-acre riverside outpost, photos and videos of trip.
In addition to the whitewater, you can also book mild-mannered float trips below Dam #1.

Accommodations

In the area are many rustic cabins and campgrounds; check **Lake Ocoee Inn & Marina**, *423-338-2064, Hwy U64*, for an on-the-water stay, with restaurant; **Horn's Creek Cabins & Lodge**, *800-864-2856, off Hwy U64*, rustic cabins with kitchens, lofts; for bed & breakfast there's **Southern Memories Country Inn**, *423-338-4351, Hwy U411*, a plantation house on 25 acres; and **Chestnut Inn B & B**, *800-993-7873*, a 1940's country house.

Reliance, TN
Eastern Time
Chamber of Commerce Polk County 423-338-5040

To See and Do

The **Hiwassee River** is a designated State Scenic River, Class I and II, and safe for beginners. **Hiwassee Outfitters**, *800-338-8133*, and **Webb Brothers Float Service**, *423-338-2373, Hwy S30*, will get you floating in a funyak, raft or tube. Before you depart, step back in time in the **Webb Brothers Store**, *423-338-2373, Hiwassee River St*; open since 1936.

Accommodations

Spring Creek Retreat, *800-488-7218, Hwy 315*, two houses on 22 acres of woodland on Spring Creek; sleep 12 and 8; kitchens, porches, fireplaces; near Webb's Store.

Note state change from Tennessee to North Carolina

Murphy, NC
pop 1,575
Eastern Time
Cherokee County Chamber of Commerce 704-837-2242

To See and Do
Murphy is positioned halfway between Tennessee's Ocoee River and the Nantahala Gorge, a great spot for river rafters who want to take advantage of both.

Some sights to see in the area are the **Cherokee County Historical Museum**, *704-837-6792, 205 Peachtree St,* which reflects the life of the Cherokee Indian during the time of the Cherokee nation and removal along the Trail of Tears to Oklahoma; housed in old Carnegie Library Building; and **Fields of the Wood**, *704-494-7855, Hwy S294, 18 miles west of Murphy,* a Biblical Theme Park owned and maintained by Church of God of Prophecy; the 10 Commandments are spread in stone across the mountainside; an All-Nation's Cross is at the top; gift and book shop; snack bar; daily, free.

Accommodations
Best Western, *704-837-3060, Andrews Rd.* **Huntington Hall Bed & Breakfast**, *704-837-9567, 500 Valley River Ave,* located in downtown area; five rooms, private baths, full breakfast. **Stone Manor Inn Bed & Breakfast**, *704-837-8676, 505 Peachtree St,* has **Mama Sue's Kountry Kitchen**, breakfast and lunch Monday-Saturday, full dinner menu Friday and Saturday; **Oak Barrel Restaurant**, *704-837-7803, Hwy U19,* has fine country dining, steaks, seafood, reservations suggested.

Andrews, NC
pop 2,551
Eastern Time
Chamber of Commerce, 704-321-3584

To See and Do
Nantahala means Land of the Noonday Sun; the **Nantahala Gorge** is so deep and narrow that the sun reaches the bottom only at

noonday. Beginning here are scenic drives through the Southern Appalachians **Nantahala Forest** and opportunities for hiking, swimming, fishing for bass and trout, and hunting for deer, wild boar, turkey, and ruffed grouse. Several of the **Great Smoky Mountains Railway Excursions,** *800-872-4681*, depart from here; Red Marble Gap goes through the Nantahala Gorge; Three-In-One combines the Tuckasegee, Nantahala and Red Marble Gap with a one-hour layover at the gorge; box lunch included.

Accommodations

Hawkesdene House, *800-447-9549, Phillips Creek Rd*, bed and breakfast on 20 acres adjoining Nantahala National Forest; deck, fireplace.

Robbinsville is a side trip off the suggested route. Take Hwy U129 between Andrews and Bryson City to get to Robbinsville.

Robbinsville, NC
pop 709
Eastern Time
Chamber of Commerce 704-479-3790

To See and Do

The Ranger District office is located here, where you can get information about the **Joyce Kilmer-Slickrock Wilderness**, a 17,013-acre area within the Nantahala Forest; the **Joyce Kilmer Memorial Forest** is a 3,840-acre stand of virgin timber dedicated to the author of the poem *Trees*.

Fontana Dam, in the southwest corner of Great Smoky Mountains National Park, is a 480-ft dam crossed by the **Appalachian Trail; Fontana Lake** is 30 miles long. These mountains have served as the backdrop for a number of Hollywood movies; namely *The Fugitive*, with Harrison Ford; and *Nell*, with Jodie Foster. Nell's "cabin" is in a remote cove along the shores of Fontana Lake; the Joyce Kilmer Restaurant, Blue Beacon Pool Hall, and county courthouse were other locations used in the movie.

Accommodations

Snowbird Mountain Lodge *704-479-3433, 275 Santeetlah Rd, 12 mi NW off Hwy U129, open* mid-April to early November; dining room, hiking trails, lawn games, rec room, stone lodge with great room. **Fontana Village Resort,** *800-849-2258, Hwy S28,* has 94 rooms in the inn, and 225 kitchen cottages; open June-October; pool, sauna, playground, supervised childrens activities; dining room, cafeteria, picnics, cookouts; grocery, laundry, trout pond, square dancing, movies, game room, rec room; some fireplaces, balconies.

Bryson City, NC
pop 1,145
Eastern Time
Chamber of Commerce/Visitors Bureau 704-488-3681

To See and Do

The **Nantahala Outdoor Center,** *704-488-2175, 13077 Hwy U19 W,* has lodging, mountain bike rentals, an outfitters store, and three restaurants in this large complex. Hang out at the many overlooks just to watch the rafters on the river, or join in. Call for a calendar of events; there are festivals and races from mountain biking to whitewater paddling; even the oldest triathlon in the country. NOC offers canoeing and kayaking classes and rafting trips on five whitewater rivers in the Appalachian mountains. Rafting available also with **Wildwater,** *800-451-9972;* guided rafting trips with minimum weight of 60 pounds; if you're already a skilled rafter you can rent everything you need to do it yourself. You might enjoy a **Raft & Rail Trip,** *800-872-4681;* for a 2-hour ride up the Nantahala Gorge on the **Great Smoky Mountains Railway** and a 7-mile assisted raft trip down; picnic lunch included. **Nantahala Village Riding Stable,** *704-488-9649, 9 mi W on Hwy U19 at Nantahala Village,* offers guided half-day, all day and overnight horseback trips, reservations must be made in advance.

Accommodations

Nantahala Village Resort, *704-488-2826, 9400 Hwy U19W, 9 mi*

W on Hwy U19/74; 14 rms in native stone mountain lodge with chestnut paneling and huge stone fireplaces; 40 kitchen cottages; free supervised childrens activities; dining room; tennis; lawn games; rec room; observation tower; fireplaces; on 200 acres. **Nantahala Village Restaurant,** *704-488-2826, in the lodge,* homemade soups, breads and desserts, mountain trout, old-time traditional favorites; open daily from mid-March through December; limited menu other times. **Fryemont Inn,** *800-845-4879, 1 Fryemont Rd off Spring St;* overlooking Great Smoky Mountains National Park, enormous stone fireplaces and hardwood floors, breakfast and dinner included; listed in National Register of Historic Places.

Cherokee, NC
pop 8,519
Eastern Time
Cherokee Visitors Center 800-438-1601

To See and Do
The **Cherokee Indian Reservation** covers 56,000 acres in an area east of the Great Smoky Mountains National Park known as the Qualla Boundary. Most of the 10,000 members of the Eastern Band of the Cherokee Tribe live within the Boundary in the communities of Yellowhill, Birdtown, Painttown, Snowbird, Big Cove, and Wolftown.

The **Visitors Center,** *704-497-9195, downtown,* is a good place to start gathering information on the museums and attractions in town. Souvenir shops and trading posts abound, but two things you don't want to miss are the **Museum of the Cherokee Indian,** *704-497-3481, Hwy U441 at Drama Rd,* where artifacts and displays show the history of the Cherokee People; and the spectacular outdoor drama, **Unto These Hills,** *704-497-2111, Mountainside Theater.* Get tickets in advance at the box-office on Hwy U441, many hotels offer shuttle service for the performance. This play has been in production over 45 years, and features more than 100 actors telling the story of the Cherokee. Near the theater is **Oconaluftee Indian Village,**

704-497-2111, Drama Rd, a replica of an Indian village of more than 200 years ago; there is a seven-sided council house, and demonstrations of craftwork such as flint chipping, fingerweaving, beads, and dugout canoes. Next door to the Museum is **Qualla Arts & Crafts,** *704-497-3103, Hwy U441,* an Indian-owned arts and crafts cooperative.

Cherokee Fish and Game Management, *704-497-5201,* stocks the 30 miles of streams on the Reservation; get your permit and go for the rainbow, brook and brown trout, daily limit of 10.

You can enter the **Great Smoky Mountains National Park** on Hwy U441, stop first at **Oconaluftee Visitors Center,** *704-497-9146, 2 miles from Cherokee,* to plan your drive through the Park; visit the **Oconaluftee** living history area and a 19th-century farm; see farm-life chores being done at the John Davis house; cornmeal made at **Mingus Mill.**

Accommodations

Best Western, *800-528-1234, Hwy U441N at Acquoni Rd;* **Days Inn,** *800-325-2525, Hwy U19N;* **Holiday Inn,** *800-HOLIDAY, Hwy U19N;* **Hampton Inn,** *800-HAMPTON, Hwy U19;* **Quality Inn,** *800-4-CHOICE, Hwy U441S.*   The **Tee Pee Restaurant,** *704-497-5141, Hwy U441N,* serves rainbow trout with a river view; **Hungry Bear Restaurant,** *704-497-2073, Hwy U441S,* specializes in hickory-smoked ribs and Carolina country ham. The **Country Boy Restaurant,** *704-497-2307, Hwys U441 & U19, behind the Visitor Center,* is open for breakfast; **Ponderosa Steak House,** *704-497-9559, Hwy U441N, across from the Ceremonial Grounds,* features a buffet.

Dillsboro, NC
pop 940
Eastern Time
Jackson County Chamber of Commerce 704-586-2155

To See and Do

The train's the thing here, visit the **Historic Railway Museum,** *next to the depot in the heart of downtown,* and see over 3,000 articles of railroad memorabilia, model trains, and a video booth. Then board the **Great Smoky Mountains Railway**, *800-872-4681 for reservations;* daytime round-trip excursions along the Tuckasegee River or a seated buffet gourmet dinner at twilight. Special excursions include the Cottontail Express and an Easter egg hunt, a Halloween Ghost Train with trick or treating, a Santa Express and a New Year's Gala. The streets of Dillsboro are made for strolling; get a walking tour map and stop in at the many interesting shops for a pleasant day.

Accommodations

The Jarrett House, *800-972-5623, 100 Haywood St,* is one of the oldest inns in western North Carolina, offering lodging and food since 1884; designated a National Historic Place. The **Jarrett House Restaurant**, *800-972-5623, in the hotel,* serves breakfast, lunch and dinner on seasonal schedules; reservations needed for large groups.

Franklin, NC
pop 2,873
Eastern Time
Chamber of Commerce, 704-524-3161

To See and Do

Since Franklin is famous for its ruby mines, stop first at the **Franklin Gem and Mineral Museum**, *704-369-7831, 2 W Main St in the Old Jail;* and get gem fever as you look at the displays. Then roll up your sleeves and go dig for your own; try **Gem City Mine**, *704-524-3967, Hwy U441 1 mi north of Franklin,* where they have guaranteed ruby buckets; **Mason Mountain Mine**, *704-524-4570, 895 Bryson City Rd,* with assistance for beginners; **Rocky Face Gem Mine**, *704-524-3148, 260 Sanderstown Rd,* covered flume beside a tree-lined creek; **Rose Creek Mine**, *704-524-3225, 115 Terrace Ridge Dr,* home of the Star Garnet; **Sheffield Mine**, *704-369-8383, off Leatherman Gap Rd,* rubies, pink and purple sapphires.

Another interesting museum is the **Scottish Tartans Museum and Heritage Center**, *704-524-7472, 33 E Main St,* showing tartan and Highland dress from 1700 to the present; the evolution of the kilt and weaving of the tartan. A pretty spot and free is **Perry's Water Garden**, *704-524-3264, 1183 Leatherman Gap Rd*, a water park with a 4-1/2-acre sunken garden, waterfall, hundreds of water lilies and other flowers, trails, and picnicking.

The **Cowee Valley**, in the heart of the Nantahala National Forest, is filled with waterfalls, mountain lakes, and streams, and offers excellent fishing for trout and bass, as well as boating, tubing, and swimming. The **Appalachian Trail** bisects the western part of the county through **Standing Indian Wildlife Management** area and over **Wayah Bald Mountain**.

Accommodations

Heritage Inn Bed & Breakfast, *704-524-4150, 101 Heritage Hollow;* private entrances and porches, full breakfast and evening dessert; **Snow Hill Inn**, *704-369-2100, 531 Snow Hill Rd;* nine rooms with private baths, spectacular mountain views, breakfast buffet; **Wayah Creek Cottages**, *704-524-2034, 610 Wayah Rd;* seven rustic mountain cottages by mountain stream in Nantahala valley; fireplaces, kitchens; call Chamber for complete listing of cabins, cottages, chalets. **Mountain Vittles Restaurant**, *704-524-9980, 103 Highland Rd*, cooks up everything from scratch; **Buglino's Sausage Factory Deli**, *704-369-6081, 59 Palmer St Circle*, offers pizzas, Italian entrees, imported food specialties, and homemade baked goods.

Brasstown, NC
Eastern Time
Clay County Chamber of Commerce 704-389-3704

To See and Do

The **John C. Campbell Folk School**, *800-FOLK-SCH, off Hwy U64*, was founded in 1925 and is patterned after the "folkehojskole" of Denmark. Today's 365-acre campus has 42 buildings, which include a saw mill; craft studios, a craft shop, meeting rooms, rustic lodgings, a covered dance pavilion, and the Community Room, with one of the best dance floors in the country. Instruction at the Folk School is non-competitive, emphasizing discussion and conversation rather than reading and writing. Students must be 18 to attend; many courses also are available through Elderhostel. Subjects range from Basketry to Woodworking, including Blacksmithing, Calligraphy, Dance, Drawing, Knitting, Music, Painting, Photography, Quilting, Weaving and more.

Free concerts are held most Fridays; folk music and stories in an informal setting; if you want to come early for supper, make reservations ahead for your meal, *704-837-9571*. Contra and square dances are held every other Saturday, no experience necessary. Special events are festivals and auctions that feature crafts from the school and music and dance; call for schedule; also summer program for youngsters.

Note state change from North Carolina to Tennessee

Ducktown, TN
pop 421
Eastern Time
Chamber of Commerce Copper Basin 423-496-9000

To See and Do
If you are wondering about the barren hillsides all around, stop in at **Ducktown Basin Museum**, *423-496-5778, Burra Burra Hill*, at the Burra Burra Mine site. Listed on the National Register, it traces the history of copper mining in the Basin. Slide program and tour of buildings. Monday-Saturday year round; admission fee.

Accommodations
Best Western Copper Inn, *800-528-1234, Hwy U64*; bed and breakfasts include **The Company House**, *800-343-2909, 125 Main St*, a restored 1870 home with a rocking chair porch; and **The White House Bed & Breakfast**, *800-775-4166, 104 Main St*, which is listed on the National Register; full breakfast, view of Blue Ridge Mountains.

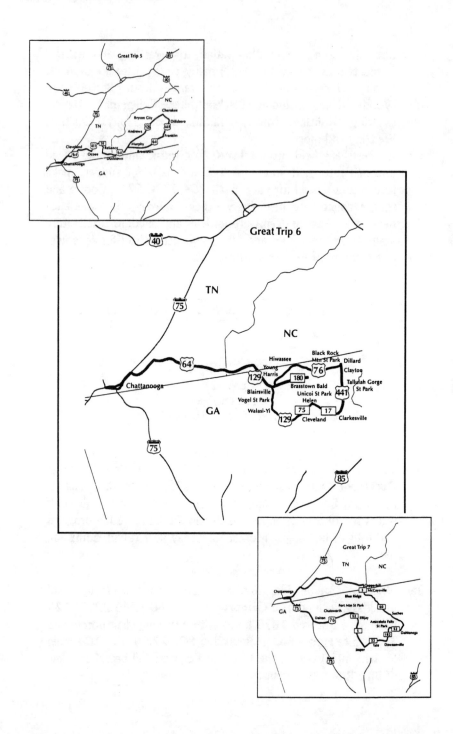

Great Trip 6

Chattanooga to Brasstown Bald, GA
the high country route
*via Young Harris, Hiwassee, Clayton, Mountain City, Black Rock Mtn St Pk,
Dillard, Tallulah Gorge St Pk, Clarkesville, Helen, Unicoi St Pk, Cleveland,
Walasi-Yi, Vogel St Pk, Brasstown Bald, Blairsville, and returning to
Chattanooga
approximately 350 miles round-trip, 7.5 hours driving time*

Why Go
Brasstown Bald, 4,784 ft, Highest Point in Georgia
Mountain Fair & Oktoberfest & Reach of Song & Cabbage Patch Babies &
Eastern Continental Divide & Warwoman Wildlife Refuge & Ancient
Petroglyphs & Oldest Gorge in US & Resort Lodges & Foxfire Museum

Suggested route with approximate mileages

Instruction	Road	Dir	Miles
Chattanooga to Blairsville	I-75 & U64 & U129	N	102
Blairsville to Young Harris	U76	E	9
Young Harris to Hiwassee	U76	E	11
Hiwassee to Clayton	U76	E	20
Clayton to Mountain City	U441	N	2
Mountain City to Dillard	U441	N	4
Dillard to Tallulah Gorge	U441	S	19
Tallulah Gorge to Clarkesville	U441	SW	12
Clarkesville to Helen	S17	NW	13
Helen to Cleveland	S75	S	13
Cleveland to Brasstown Bald	U129 & S180	N	31
Brasstown Bald to Blairsville	S180 & U129	W & N	11
Blairsville to Chattanooga	U129 & U64 & I-75	NW	102
Total Mileage			349

The **Blue Ridge Mountains** of northeast Georgia sit like a crown at the top of the state; **Lakes Nottley, Chatuge, Burton, Rabun and Yonah** are the sparkling jewels. The highest point in the state is lofty **Brasstown Bald**, rising to a glorious 4,784 feet; the lowest is **Tallulah Gorge**, carved to a depth of 1,100 feet by time and the ancient workings of the river.

The lifestyle of the mountain people is revered and celebrated at every turn; at Young Harris College **"The Reach of Song,"** Georgia's Official Historic Drama, brightens summer months, as does the **Georgia Mountain Fair** in Hiwassee, where quilt making and board splitting are demonstrated while the sounds of bluegrass fill the air. The **Foxfire Museum** in Mountain City displays **Appalachian artifacts** in a mountain cabin; the Foxfire series of books tells about the people of Appalachia and their crafts.

Good eats, such as you find at the **Dillard House**, comfortable resorts and fine state parks make you want to settle in and stay a while, or come back again and again. Come for the rhododendron-covered mountainsides in the spring; swimming, boating and fishing all summer long, and the festivals of autumn. The **Official State Fiddler's Convention** on the shores of Lake Chatuge marks October; tiny Helen celebrates what is billed as the nation's largest **Oktoberfest**, complete with oompah bands.

There are enough hiking trails, waterfalls, and wilderness areas here to occupy a year's worth of weekends; the **Appalachian Trail** passes under a covered archway at **Neels Gap at Walasi-Yi**, the only place between here and Maine that can make such a claim! Hikers stop here to shower and check their blisters; the **Mountain Crossing** store is a good place to buy supplies, books, and trail maps too.

Another unusual claim to fame for this part of the state is **Babyland General Hospital**, birthing place of world-famous **Cabbage Patch Dolls**. If you're present when a birth occurs, you get to name the baby!

Young Harris, GA
pop 604
Eastern Time
Chamber of Commerce 706-896-4966

To See and Do
In the summertime see **"The Reach of Song"** **Appalachian Drama,** *800-262-7664, on the campus of Young Harris College,* a musical celebration of the Appalachian mountains and Georgia's **Official Historic Drama.** The 700-seat theater is in the Clegg Fine Arts Building. **Dinner-on-the-Grounds** is a fun event; live mountain music and chicken salad while you sit on straw bales; reservations strongly recommended. Arts and Craft Show and other plays during the season in the 130-seat Dobbs Theater; call for schedule.

Accommodations
Brasstown Valley Resort, *800-227-6963, 6231 Hwy U76;* lodge, cottages, fireplaces, mountain views; golf, tennis, meeting facilities. **Brasstown Valley Resort Dining Room,** *706-379-9900,* serves breakfast, lunch, dinner; mountain views and spacious veranda; **Fireplace Lounge** is adjacent; **McDivots,** on clubhouse level, serves lighter fare.

Hiwassee, GA
pop 547
Eastern Time
Chamber of Commerce 706-896-4966

To See and Do
The **Georgia Mountain Fairgrounds,** *706-896-4191, Hwy U76 on the shores of Lake Chatuge,* are the site of the fabulous **Georgia Mountain Fair** held in early August. Over 100,000 attend this annual event, which has no commercial exhibits, but features the products and talent of the mountain folks. Daily demonstrations of mountain arts such as soap making, board splitting, hominy making, cider squeezing and quiltmaking; and the best of bluegrass, gospel and clogging. A **Fall Celebration** in

October is the scene of Georgia's **Official State Fiddler's Convention**, with prizes for guitar, banjo, mandolin, dulcimer and buck dancing too. The summer-long **Schedule of Stars** brings in such guests as Waylon Jennings, Barbara Mandrell, and Sawyer Brown; call for season tickets. At Georgia's "country music capital," you'll find a campground, ole-timey pioneer village, exhibits, farm museum, and, of course, a music hall! Also on the Fairgrounds is **Fred Hamilton Rhododendron Garden**, 706-896-4966, with over 2,000 rhododendron and azaleas; season is mid-April to June.

Lake Chatuge is a 7,000-acre TVA lake, and the **Lake Chatuge Recreation Area**, 706-745-6928, Hwy S288, offers camping, boating, fishing and hiking; call for a Recreation Guide; rent pontoon boats and fishing boats at **Boundary Waters Marina**, 706-896-2530, 528 Sunnyside Rd, off Hwy S288.

Accommodations

Fieldstone Inn Resort & Conference Center, 800-545-3408, Hwy U76, on the shores of Lake Chatuge; lakefront restaurant, marina. **Lake Chatuge Lodge**, 706-896-LAKE, Hwy U76, also has marina and restaurant; **Mountain Memories Inn**, 800-335-VIEW, 385 Chancey Dr, has suites, jacuzzis, full breakfast and evening desserts; **Swallows Creek Country Cabins**, 706-896-4707, 3461 Jordan Rd, kitchens, fireplaces, on 17 acres.

Clayton, GA
pop 1,613
Eastern Time
Chamber of Commerce 706-782-4812

To See and Do

Stop in at the well-stocked **Welcome Center** on Hwy U441 and get maps and info that will guide you to the incredible variety of designated **Wildlife and Scenic Areas**, high mountain lakes, hiking trails, waterfalls, and rafting opportunities; just out from the city are **Lakes Burton and Rabun**, the **Chattahoochee National Forest**, and the wild and scenic **Chattooga River** (yes, that's where they filmed the movie *Deliverance*!).

Accommodations
Downtown is the **Old Clayton Inn**, *706-782-7722*, a historic mountain lodge; newest in town is **Stonebrook Inn**, *706-782-2214, Hwy U441S*. The excellent **Stockton House Restaurant**, *706-782-6175, Warwoman Road*, overlooks a beautiful valley and across at Screamer Mountain; it's open daily and year-round.

Mountain City, GA
pop 784
Eastern Time
Chamber of Commerce 706-782-4812

To See and Do
Stop in at the **Foxfire Museum**, *706-746-5828, Hwy U441*, for a self-guided tour of Appalachian artifacts housed in a mountain cabin; buy the entire Foxfire series of books on Appalachian handicrafts in the gift shop.
Accommodations
York House Bed & Breakfast Inn, *800-231-YORK*, Yorkhouse Rd; a B & B with a country flair, since 1896.

Georgia State Park
Eastern Time
Black Rock Mountain State Park, *706-746-2141, Hwy U441*, has steep rhododendron-covered banks along the winding road to the top of **Black Rock Mountain**, elevation 3,640; cross the Eastern Continental Divide along the way, stop at the overlooks for great valley-gazing.
The 1,830-acre park is named for its sheer cliffs of dark colored biotite-gneiss; it encompasses some of the most outstanding mountain country in the southern Blue Ridge with six mountains over 3,000 feet. Picnicking, fishing and hiking are available; there are 10 cottages for rent and 48 campsites with water, others for hike-in.

Dillard, GA
Eastern Time
Chamber of Commerce 706-782-4812

To See and Do
The **Dillard House**, 706-746-5348, off Hwy U441, is certainly the biggest draw in Dillard, with 1,200 people a day partaking of the bountiful country-style breakfasts, lunches and dinners in the spacious dining room overlooking a beautiful valley. **Dillard House Stables**, 706-746-2038, offer guided horseback rides along the Little Tennessee River, or into the backwoods of the **Warwoman Wildlife Refuge**. Stop at the **Dillard Antique Mall** and browse for a while; then drive on to **Sky Valley**, Georgia's only spot for skiing. **Rabun Bald** is just beyond, elevation 4,696 feet.

Accommodations
Best Western, 706-746-5321, Hwy U441; **The Dillard House**, 800-541-0671, rooms in original Dillard House, also separate cottages, fully equipped houses; restaurant, pool, riding stables; **Sky Valley Resort**, 800-262-8259, 39 Sky Valley Resort, Georgia's only skiing; championship golf, tennis.

Georgia State Park
Eastern Time
Tallulah Gorge State Park and Terrora Park; stop at the **Terrora Visitors Center**, 706-754-3276, Hwy U441. Time to be impressed: this is the oldest gorge in the United States, and at 1,100 feet, it is second in depth only to the Grand Canyon! Cross the road and hike along the **North Rim Trail** to get a top-side view. The state park offers camping, picnicking, and fishing; 50 campsites, 63-acre lake. Also in the area you'll find **Tallulah Falls**, **Tugalo** and **Yonah Lakes**, and **Panther Creek Trail**. See the work of local and regional artists at **Tallulah Gallery**, 706-754-6020, on old Hwy U441 Bypass.

Clarkesville, GA
pop 1,151
Eastern Time
Hospitality Center 706-754-5259

To See and Do
Stop 10 miles before you get to town at **Mark of the Potter**, *706-947-3440, Hwy S197.* Grandpa Watts' Grist Mill, built beside the picturesque Soque River in 1931, now houses pottery and handmade crafts from more than 40 artists and craftspeople; watch potter Jay Bucek at work, or relax on the big porch that extends over the river. Then, walk or drive **Clarkesville,** *706-778-4654,* to see the refurbished downtown square and enjoy the galleries and crafts shops.

Accommodations
Glen-Ella Springs Inn & Conference Center, *706-754-7295, 1789 Bear Gap Rd,* a historic country inn on 17 acres, gardens, gourmet dining; **Happy Valley Cabins,** *706-754-3377,* Col. Hough Rd, housekeeping cabins with jacuzzis, fireplaces; **Adams Rib Restaurant,** *706-754-4568, Hwy 441S,* barbecue ribs, prime rib, oyster bar.

Helen, GA
Eastern Time
Welcome Center 706-878-2181

To See and Do
Alpine Helen is one of the most popular destinations in the high country of Northeast Georgia. A declining logging community in the 60's, local businessmen came up with the idea of embellishing local buildings with Alpine designs; now you can wander among shops and restaurants in a thriving tourist town.

Helen's **Oktoberfest** claims to be the nation's largest, with events every weekend in September and every day but Sunday in October. You'll find oom-pah bands from Europe and cloggers from everywhere. The Chattahoochee River flows through town, rent a tube and float past the shops and restaurants.

In the **Museum of the Hills**, 706-878-3140, *Main Street*, there's the "Story of Helen" and a fantasy kingdom for the kiddies. **Nora Mill Granary**, 706-878-2375, uses Chattahoochee River water to power its original 1876 grindstones; watch them in action; buy grits, flours and even jams and pies here. Want to look for gold? **Historic Gold Mines of Helen**, 706-878-3052, shows you the mines and tells about the "gold rush" years; pan for your own.

Accommodations

Comfort Inn, 800-443-6488, *101 Edelweiss Strasse;* **Helendorf River Inn**, 800-445-2271, *33 Munichstrasse*, downtown, riverfront balconies; **Innsbruck Resort & Golf Club**, 800-20 HELEN, golf, tennis, one-bedroom suites to four-bedroom homes. **Heidelberg Restaurant & Lounge**, 706-878-2986, serves lunch/dinner; oom-pah band, 2 dance floors; **Hofbrauhaus Inn Restaurant & Lounge**, 706-878-2248, overlooks Chattahoochee River, German & American cuisine.

Georgia State Park
Eastern Time

Unicoi State Park, 706-878-2201, *Hwy S35;* two miles from Helen, the park's 1,081 acres have 84 campsites, 30 cottages, and a 100-room lodge and conference center; Friday/Saturday programs offered year round; swim, fish or boat in the 53-acre lake. **Unicoi Lodge Restaurant** is buffet style, features mountain trout at night; fireside dining or mountain views.

Cleveland, GA
pop 1,653
Eastern Time
Chamber of Commerce 706-865-5536

To See and Do

Top attraction here is a hospital! **BabyLand General**, 706-865-2171, *19 Underwood St*, is home to the world-famous

Cabbage Patch dolls; you can tour the "clinic" and be present at a birth -- when the crystals under the giant tree begin flickering, you know a delivery is imminent, gather round as the cabbage unfolds to reveal the newest "kid," and participate in its name-giving. Hundreds of dolls in all shapes and sizes are displayed in "what-kids-do" settings from nurseries to playgrounds to schools; you can adopt one for your very own. The soft-faced dolls carry collector-item prices; the molded kind are in the toy-price range.

Walasi-Yi, GA
Eastern Time
706-745-6095

To See and Do
Walasi-Yi has a Blairsville address, but its historical significance and uniqueness make it worthy of its own listing. A must-see stop! It's the only place on the entire **Appalachian Trail** that is covered -- the trail passes under a stone archway that's part of a 1937 CCC construction; hikers can shower, do their laundry, doctor their blisters, pick up their mail, and get complete supplies, equipment, maps and books in the well-stocked store, **Mountain Crossing at Walasi-Yi,** *706-745-6095, Hwy U129.* This is **Neel Gap,** on Blood Mountain; nearby is the **Blood Mountain Archaeological Area,** site of a Cherokee and Creek Indian battle, and it's accessible via the Appalachian Trail.

Georgia State Park
Eastern Time
Vogel State Park, *706-745-2628, Hwy U129,* 280-acre Blue Ridge Mountain refuge; 36 cabins, 100 campsites; hiking trails, picnicking, paddle boats for rent; weekend programs

Brasstown Bald, GA
Eastern Time
Visitor Center 706-896-2556

To See and Do
Brasstown Bald, *off Hwy S180,* is the highest mountain in the state of Georgia, with an elevation of 4,784 feet. Park and ride the shuttle to the fabulous **observation deck** with a 360-degree view. While you're there, check out all the exhibits and watch the video program. There are picnic facilities and hiking trails; stay a while. A craft shop too. Call for the Recreation Guide.

Blairsville, GA
pop 564
Eastern Time
Chamber of Commerce 706-745-5789

To See and Do
Pop into the **Blairsville/Union County Chamber of Commerce** for information on the numerous scenic trails, lakes and streams in the area. It's **Chattahoochee National Forest** country, and Blairsville sits on **Lake Nottley,** with 106 miles of shoreline. Make sure you track down **Track Rock Archaeological Area,** *706-745-6928, Track Rock Gap Rd,* a 52-acre area with ancient petroglyphs of Indian origin; they resemble bird and animal tracks, and even human footprints. On the square is the **Union County Historical Society Museum,** *706-745-5493,* with exhibits on county history.

Accommodations
God's Country Farm, *706-745-1560, Hwy S325,* fully-equipped log cabins on 50 acres, stocked fishing pond, pontoon boat on Lake Nottley; **7 Creeks Cabins,** *706-745-4753,* fully-equipped cabins, 70-acres, private lake, fishing, swimming; **Trackrock Campground & Cabins,** *706-745-2420, 4887 Track Rock Gap Rd,* secluded, cabins and campsites, horseback riding, hayrides, playground.

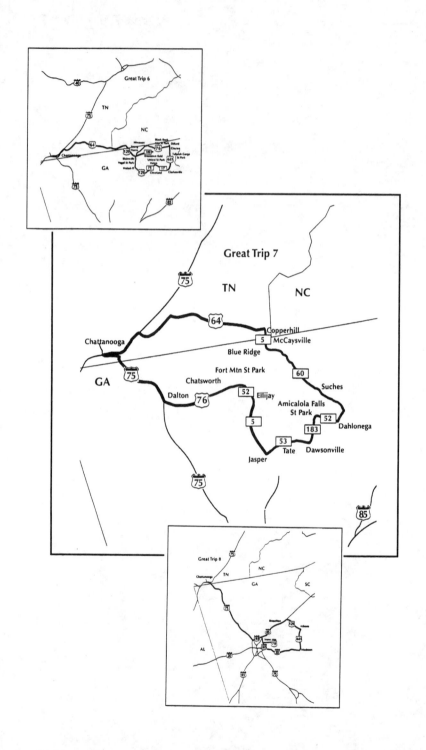

Great Trip 7

Chattanooga to Dahlonega, GA
the gold'n apple route
*via TN- Copperhill; GA - McCaysville, Blue Ridge, Suches, Dahlonega,
Amicalola Falls St Pk; Dawsonville, Tate, Jasper, Ellijay, Ft Mountain St Pk;
Chatsworth, Dalton, returning to Chattanooga
approximately 275 miles round-trip, 5.5 hours driving time*

Why Go
Golden Delicious & Cohutta Wilderness & Toccoa River &
Gold Panning & Ancient Ruins & Sugar Creek & Praters Mill &
Highest Waterfall & Deepest Lake & Largest Marble Quarry &
Family-style Dining Wonder & NASCAR Museum & Peacock Alley

Suggested route with approximate mileages

Instruction	Road	Dir	Miles
Chattanooga to Copperhill/McCaysville	I75 & U64 & S68	N & S	71
McCaysville to Blue Ridge	S5	S	11
Blue Ridge to Suches	U76 & S60	E & S	32
Suches to Dahlonega	S60	S	16
Dahlonega to Amicalola Falls St Park	S52	W	18
Amicalola Falls St Park to Dawsonville	S183 & S53	S	14
Dawsonville to Tate	S53	W	19
Tate to Jasper	S53	N	5
Jasper to Ellijay	S5	N	20
Ellijay to Fort Mountain St Park	S52	W	17
Fort Mountain St Park to Chatsworth	S52	W	8
Chatsworth to Dalton	U76	W	12
Dalton to Chattanooga	I-75	N	31
Total Mileage			274

The **Apple Capital** of the state, the **Carpet Capital** of the world, the largest open-pit marble quarry anywhere, site of the country's first gold rush -- is that reason enough to visit the north-central part of Georgia? Add to that the beginning of the Appalachian Trail, one of the most-loved hiking trails in the country; state parks with waterfalls cascading almost into your lap, or ancient, mysterious stone ruins; and wilderness areas so remote there is no access except on foot. You can even learn the history of NASCAR racing! Highest waterfall and deepest lake bragging rights "east of the Mississippi" go to **Amicalola Falls** and **Carter Lake**.

From Ducktown head south to **Copperhill** and **McCaysville**, two towns that share a river; stand on the bridge where the sign marks the **Toccoa** changing to the **Ocoee**. Beyond McCaysville the hills become dotted with apple trees; to the west is the **Cohutta Wilderness** area. If it's outdoor adventure you crave, stop at the Ranger Station in **Blue Ridge** to get the scoop. Or take the slow road on to Dahlonega and enjoy the mountain views.

Allow enough time in **Dahlonega** to sit on the square, partake of at least one meal at **The Smith House**, go through the **Gold Museum**, and delight in what was, and is. Did you know that gold mined in this area gilds the dome of the capitol in Atlanta? Do a little mining yourself at **Consolidated Gold Mines**; they'll take you on a tour of what was once the largest operation east of the Mississippi.

From Dahlonega, drive to **Amicalola Falls State Park**, where even those who don't want to walk a step can drive right to the bottom of the 729-ft falls and enjoy their beauty without getting out of the car! A variety of things from this point on, such as the history of NASCAR racing in **Dawsonville** at **Awesome Bill Elliott's Museum**, and marble mining in **Jasper**, where once a year the world's largest open pit marble quarry is open for public tours. Then into **Ellijay** and a drive through Gilmer County's **apple orchards**. Go in apple season, of course; that way you can enjoy the fall foliage as you drive the mountain on to **Ft. Mountain State Park**.

By the time you reach **Dalton**, you are back to fast-moving freeway traffic. Don't let that put you in a hurrying mood, however; stick around and explore this interesting town, which dominates the world's carpet industry. Then hit the outlet mall. It won't take you long to get back home from here.

Copperhill, TN/McCaysville, GA
pop 362/ pop 1,065
Eastern Time
Chamber of Commerce Copper Basin 423-496-3221

To See and Do
Copperhill has its connections with Ducktown -- the offices of the mines are in Copperhill and the Museum about mining is in Ducktown (see p. 61); the Basin's hills, showing years of copper mining, surround the drive between the two. But Copperhill and McCaysville are even more connected, as they sit facing each other across a river and a state line. Called the Toccoa in Georgia, the river name changes to Ocoee as it crosses the Tennessee state line; a sign on the bridge marks the spot. These are good walking towns.

Accommodations
Bed and Breakfasts, by advance reservation, **Maloof's**, 800-475-2016, 80 Ocoee St; and **The Terry House**, 423-496-1100, Hwy U64.

Blue Ridge, GA
pop 1,336
Eastern Time
Chamber of Commerce 706-632-5680, 800-899-MTNS

To See and Do
Wilderness adventurers will be in their element here; the **Chattahoochee National Forest Ranger Station**, 706-632-3031, 990 E Main St, can help with recreation maps and information on hiking trails, scenic rivers, and camping areas. The **Cohutta Wilderness Area** makes up 31,400 acres of the National Forest land; here access is by footpath only. Forest roads can take you to a Wilderness Boundary; don't enter unless properly prepared; and, of course, leave the area like you found it to preserve it for the next visitor. The **Benton MacKaye Trail** is accessible from roads beginning in Copperhill and Blue Ridge.

In the fall, the smell of apples will get your attention as you travel Highway 5 from McCaysville to Blue Ridge; stop at **Mercier Orchards**, 706-632-2364, Hwy S5, for some Golden Delicious,

Rome, Winesap or Jonagolds; fresh cider too.

Also on the north side of town is **Sugar Creek Music Park**, *706-632-2560, Hwy S5, 8 mi south of McCaysville, 3 mi north of Blue Ridge;* camping is available at the park; weekends feature storytelling, clogging, and mountain music with dulcimers, banjos, fiddles, guitars and mandolins; gospel music and shape note singing too; plus a Buckskinners Encampment; pre-1840 America, Buckskinners in period dress with Native Americans; arts, crafts, cooking; call *706-492-3819* for schedule of events.

The **Historic Railroad Depot** in the center of downtown is the site of a **Labor Day Bar-B-Q Weekend**, *706-492-3819*, with family entertainment.

Accommodations

Days Inn, *800-325-2525, Appalachian Hwy;* call for listing of cabins and campgrounds in the area. **Toccoa Riverside Restaurant and General Store**, *706-632-7891, Aska Rd*, offers a smoked trout appetizer, steaks, specialty dishes, has a large outdoor deck overlooking the Toccoa River; tube rental here too; **Becky's Country Kitchen**, *706-632-2197, Hwy U76*, serves breakfast, lunch, and homemade desserts.

Suches, GA
Eastern Time
Union County Chamber of Commerce
706-745-5789

To See and Do

You cross over the **Benton MacKaye Trail** twice on the way south to Suches, and the **Appalachian Trail** once, near **Woody Gap**. Between McCaysville and Dahlonega, cross over or go around these **Mountains: Tipton, Wilscot, Rocky, High Top, Pilot and Three Sisters**, ranging in elevation from 3,000+ to 1,500 feet.

Dahlonega, GA

pop 3,086
Eastern Time
Chamber of Commerce/Visitors Bureau 706-864-3711

To See and Do

The town square has benches for resting in between shopping and eating in authentic 19th Century buildings, such as the **Dahlonega General Store**, *706-864-2005*, where you can get 5-cent coffee and old-fashioned candies. Cars are routed in and around the center attraction, the **Dahlonega Gold Museum**, *706-864-2257*, located in a former courthouse; built in 1836 and restored to house the history of the area. The word "Dahlonega" has Cherokee origins, a term for "yellow;" named for the color of the gold found here. In the Museum you can learn about the first major gold rush in the United States, which began in 1828.

The large **Welcome Center** faces the square, and the friendly folks there will direct you to the many attractions and scenic spots in the area; just up the street is **Kinsland's Hometown Book Store**, *706-864-7225*, where you can find new and used books, topographic maps, and more information about what's happening in the Lumpkin County area; good historical information here too.

After you've checked out the Gold Museum, visit a gold mine and pan for some of your own: **Consolidated Gold Mines**, *706-864-8473, Hwy U19/60 Bypass*, takes you inside what was once the largest gold mining operation east of the Mississippi; although it closed in 1900, there's still enough there to give you a good day's panning, and their expert gold panners will teach you how. **Crisson Gold Mine**, *706-864-6363, Hwy U19 Connector*, lets you pan for gold and gemstones, with indoor panning during the colder months.

For over 70 years people have come from everywhere to have a meal at the "family-style dining wonder," the world-famous **Smith House**, *706-867-7000, 202 S Chestatee St*, where you can get fried chicken, sweet baked ham, a dozen vegetables, and angel biscuits; as many as 2,000 meals get served at Sunday dinner. **North Georgia College** is located here; free Friday shows at the **George E. Coleman Planetarium**, *706-864-1511*, when school is in session. Don't miss the town's annual **Bluegrass Festival**, *706-864-7203*.

Accommodations

Day's Inn, 706-864-2338; Econo Lodge, 800-55-ECONO; and Ho-Jo, 706-864-4343. B&B's and Inns include Smith House Inn, 800-852-9577; Royal Guard B&B Inn, 706-864-1713; Stanton Storehouse B&B Inn, 706-864-6114; Cavender Castle Winery and B&B, 706-864-4759; and Mountain Top Lodge, 706-864-5257. Forest Hills Mountain Hideaway, 800-654-6313, has hottub cabins, banquet facilities, and group accommodations. Plenty of campgrounds in the area too. In addition to the famous Smith House mentioned above, you'll find good food at Nature's Cellar Cafe, 706-864-6829; Caruso's Italian, 706-864-4664; Park Place Family Restaurant, 706-864-4625; Robyn's Nest Cafe, 706-864-9169; and Wagon Wheel Restaurant, 706-864-6677; they're either on the square or close to town.

Georgia State Park
Eastern Time

Amicalola Falls State Park, 706-265-8888, Hwy S52. "Tumbling waters" in Cherokee translates to Amicalola, and this park's falls tumble down seven cascades for a total of 729 feet. This is the highest waterfall east of the Mississippi River, and it's easy to see; there's a porch swing beside a beautiful pool at the bottom of the falls; simply park and swing while you drink in the view. Or drive up the mountain and take a short walk to the wooden bridge at the top of the falls. There is trout fishing in this beautiful 1,020-acre park, and picnic facilities. But its greater claim to fame is hiking; the Approach Trail to the 2,160-mile Appalachian Trail begins here -- hike 8.5 miles to Springer Mountain to access the trail, and don't stop till you get to Mt. Katahdin in Maine!

Accommodations

Amicalola Falls Lodge, 706-265-8888, from the parking lot you can see the mountains through all the glass in the lobby; the lodge has 57 rooms and a restaurant with a view. The Park also has 14 cottages with mountain view or creekside; and 17 campsites. Trailers are limited to 17 feet due to the steep incline.

Dawsonville, GA
pop 9,429
Eastern Time
Chamber of Commerce/Welcome Center 706-265-6278

To See and Do

The **Dawson County Courthouse** sit squarely in the square; built in 1859, it's the only working courthouse of its era in the state. You'll find the C of C and **Welcome Center** there, so stop in and stock up on area information. Then step across the street to the **Dawsonville Pool Room**, *706-265-2792,* where you'll learn about Dawsonville's Most Famous Citizen, "Awesome Bill from Dawsonville." Bill Elliott's #9 NASCAR memorabilia fills the Pool Room, sometimes you can catch Bill there too. **Elliott Museum,** *706-265-2718, Hwy S183,* is 5 miles outside of town; this is the home of Elliott's auto racing operation. It was moonshine-running that led to NASCAR racing; get tuned into the history here via video and displays.

Tate/Jasper, GA
pop 1,000/pop 1,772
Eastern Time
Pickens County Chamber of Commerce 706-692-5600

To See and Do

The **Tate House,** *770-735-3122, Hwy S53,* was built in 1926 of rare Etowah pink marble which was quarried in the area; it's now listed on the National Register of Historic Places. You can tour the house, or enjoy a Sunday brunch; come in October during the **Georgia Marble Festival,** *706-692-5600, Jasper;* the **Georgia Marble Company** opens the world's largest open-pit marble quarry to the public for tours during the festival; also enjoy marble sculpture contest, air exhibit, golf tournament, and parade, along with arts, crafts, music, and of course, food.

Accommodations

The **Woodbridge Inn Restaurant & Lodge,** *706-692-6293, 44 Chambers St, Jasper,* offers continental American cuisine; dinner nightly; **The Tate House Bed & Breakfast,** *770-735-3122, Hwy S53, Tate,* has suites, private cabins, fireplaces, gardens.

Ellijay, GA
pop 1,178
Eastern Time
Gilmer County Chamber of Commerce 706-635-7400

To See and Do
The word "Ellijay" has Cherokee origins, meaning "green earth." And out of that green earth comes red apples, and golden apples, for Ellijay is the **Apple Capital of Georgia.** The apple houses open in late summer and you can stop and shop through December. **Carter's Lake,** *706-635-7400,* is just outside of town; the deepest lake east of the Mississippi River, it offers fabulous swimming and fishing. The **Rich Mountain Wildlife Area** provides 9,000 acres of wilderness for hikers, campers, and hunters. Visit the **Perry House,** *706-635-5605, 10 Broad St;* a historic home that now houses the Gilmer Arts and Heritage Association and has changing exhibits throughout the year.

Accommodations
An interesting B&B is the **Home of Gardener Fatness,** *706-276-7473, 59 River St,* a historic home on the river with theme rooms.

Georgia State Park
Eastern Time
Fort Mountain State Park, *706-695-2621, Hwy S52;* at the point of the mountain stand the ruins of an ancient fortification for which the mountain was named; a 1.3 mile loop trail takes you there. The Park has many hiking trails and a 14-acre lake for fishing, swimming and boating.

Accommodations
Fort Mountain State Park, *800-864-7275 for reservations,* has 15 two and three bedroom cabins and 70 tent and trailer sites; in the area is **Cohutta Lodge and Restaurant,** *706-695-9601,* open year-round for mountain-top dining and lodging; 60 rooms; restaurant open daily; spectacular views; indoor pool, tennis.

Chatsworth, GA

pop 2,865
Eastern Time
Chamber of Commerce/Welcome Center 706-695-6060

To See and Do

The **Welcome Center** can direct you to the many scenic attractions and recreation areas surrounding the town; nearby **Lake Conasauga,** 706-695-6736, is the highest lake in Georgia. Visit the **Vann House Historic Site,** 706-695-2598, 82 Hwy S225N, a beautiful two-story classic brick mansion built for Chief James Vann in 1804. It served as a meeting place for Cherokee Tribes before they were forced to move to Oklahoma. This site is on the Chieftains Trail.

Dalton, GA

pop 21,761
Eastern Time
Visitors Bureau/NW Georgia Trade & Convention 706-272-7676

To See and Do

Dalton is unquestionably the **Carpet Capital of the World,** with over 150 carpet mills and more than 100 carpet outlet stores. Start with **Crown Gardens and Archives,** 706-278-0217, 715 Chattanooga Ave, where you'll learn about local history and how bedspread tufting led to the carpet industry; hear the story of a young girl named Catherine Evans who admired a handtufted bedspread and copied it as a gift; this turn-of-the-century act was the beginning of the bedspread industry, which eventually led to the tufted carpet industry. Over the years, tufters hung their spreads on the clothesline to dry in the breeze; tourists driving by on Highway 41 would see the colorful displays and stop to buy. One of the favorite designs was two colorful peacocks with their tails spread, and the road became known as "Peacock Alley." The creation of a machine that could tuft carpet in 1945 began to shift the focus from bedspreads to carpet and today Dalton's carpet mills produce over 1 billion square yards of carpet annually.

If you are interested in shopping or browsing outlet malls, **Dalton's Factory Stores**, *706-278-0399, I-75 Exit 136*, has a huge West Point Pepperell Store plus Corning, Revere and Farberware; many options for clothing too.

Prater's Mill Country Fair, *706-275-MILL, Hwy S2, 10 mi NE of Dalton;* the 1855 mill is on the National Historic Register; every May and October it's the backdrop for an old-fashioned country shindig that brings in fiddling and food, hundreds of crafts, and demonstrations including a Civil War encampment and a "Peacock Alley" display.

Accommodations

Comfort Suites, *706-217-6200, 417 Holiday Dr;* **Days Inn**, *706-278-0850, 1518 W Walnut Ave;* **Hampton Inn**, *706-226-4333, 1000 Market St;* **Holiday Inn**, *706-278-0500, 515 Holiday Dr.*

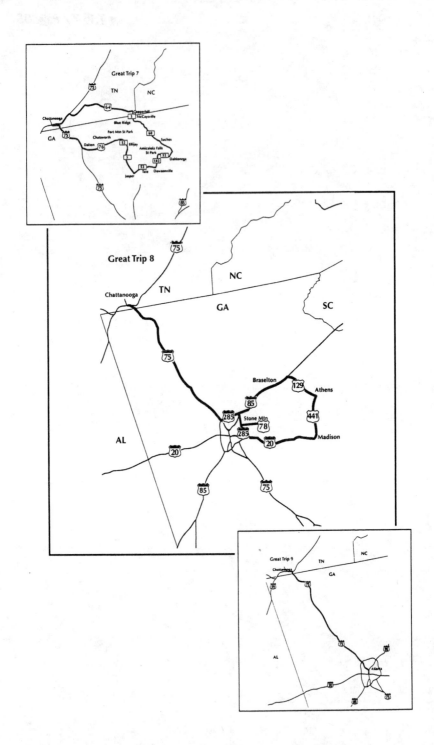

Great Trip 7

TN

NC

73

I-64

Chattanooga

Copperhill

McCaysville

Blue Ridge

GA

75

Fort Mtn St Park

40

Suches

Chatsworth

Dalton

76

5

Ellijay

Amicalola Falls
St Park

103

52

Dahlonega

Jasper

Tate

Dawsonville

75

85

Great Trip 8

75

NC

TN

Chattanooga

GA

SC

75

Braselton

129

Athens

85

285

Stone Mtn

78

441

285

Madison

AL

20

20

85

75

Great Trip 9

TN

NC

Chattanooga

GA

75

75

Atlanta

AL

20

85

75

Great Trip 8

Chattanooga to Athens, GA
the classics route

via Braselton, Athens, Madison, Stone Mountain,
returning to Chattanooga
approximately 400 miles round-trip, 8 hours driving time

Why Go

French Chateau & European Spa & Classic College Town &
Double Barreled Cannon & Botanical Gardens & Bulldogs Football &
100 Antebellum Homes & Piedmont History &
Boiled Peanuts & Fresh Peaches & Giant Stone Monolith &
Confederate Sculpture & Skylift & Mountain Laser Show &
Southern Plantation & Riverboat

Suggested Route with approximate mileages

Instruction	Road	Dir	Miles
Chattanooga to Braselton	I-75 & I-285 & I-85	S & E	153
Braselton to Athens	I-85 & U129	E & S	32
Athens to Madison	U441	S	29
Madison to Stone Mountain	U441 & I-20 & I-285 & U78	S & W & N	61
Stone Mtn to Chattanooga	U78 & I-285 & I-75	W & N	128
Total Mileage			403

This Trip is one of the longest, mileage-wise, so there are not as many cities and towns included for stopping. The "classics" Trip, it takes you from look-alike 16th century castles in Braselton to a center of classic learning in Athens, the University of Georgia. See authentic antebellum homes in Madison, where Sherman was persuaded to leave the scene untouched; and a cluster of restored 18th and 19th century buildings that have been moved to Stone Mountain Park from around the state.

If you want a faster pace, tune into the football season for the Georgia Bulldogs in Athens -- see red! Much good music comes from that part of the state too. And there is plenty of entertainment at Stone Mountain Park -- you can ride a skylift up the mountain or a train around it. Buy peaches or boiled peanuts from stands beside the road in the rolling farmland between Athens and Madison; select from a variety of wines at Chateau Elan.

The trip takes you south on I-75 until you reach the I-285 Bypass; stay on the Bypass to I-85 and Braselton, where you'll find delightful Chateau Elan. Relax with a wonderful meal, or a winery tour, or a game of golf. Then, to Athens, where you should park the car! Walk through the campus and enjoy the lovely gardens and many fine examples of Greek revival architecture. This is the oldest state-chartered university in the United States, created in 1785. Cross Broad Street for outdoor seating in numerous eateries, or a stroll through town.

From Athens to Madison, the town that's famous for something that didn't happen. As General Sherman marched through on his way to a Union victory in 1864, a delegation led by Senator Joshua Hill asked him to spare the torch. Hill had not voted for secession; Sherman honored his request. As a result, Madison is blessed with many antebellum homes and historic churches; go for a Historic Homes Tour, held during the summer and at Christmas time. Any time of year, stop at the Madison-Morgan Cultural Center and get a walking-tour guide; there are 45 points of interest you'll see as you stroll through the community.

West on I-20 to the I-285 Bypass again, and follow the signs to Stone Mountain Park. You'll want to be there after dark to take advantage of the mountain-side laser show.

Braselton, GA
Eastern Time

To See and Do
Two wineries here, one as part of a world-class resort. Start at the **Chestnut Mountain Winery**, *770-867-6914, Exit 48 off I-85*. This pretty spot is set in 30 wooded acres, and after enjoying a tour and tasting, you can wander through the vineyards and make use of the picnic areas. On the opposite side of I-85 is **Chateau Elan Winery and Resort**, *800-233-9463*, a 16th-century style French chateau on 2,400 acres, with 200 acres of vineyards. Winery tours here, plus an equestrian center, and within the resort, golf, tennis, and a European Health spa.

Accommodations
Chateau Elan Winery and Resort, *770-932-0900, 100 Rue Charlemagne*, six restaurants on property; inn and conference center, spa. **Cafe Elan** restaurant is next to the winery's extensive gift shop, and offers casual fare; **Le Clos** will serve you a 6-course meal matched with their finest wines.

Athens, GA
Athens is a Georgia Main Street City
pop 45,734
Eastern Time
Athens Welcome Center 706-353-1820
Convention & Visitors Bureau 706-546-1805

To See and Do
Start at the **Welcome Center**, *280 E Dougherty St*, an 1820's restored house; get information on attractions in the area. The town is filled with lovely antebellum homes; scenic tour signs guide you through the historic districts and residential areas.

This charming, easy-to-manage-size college town is home to the **University of Georgia**, the nation's oldest state chartered university. For a guided tour of the campus, stop at the **University Visitor Center, College Station Road**, or call *706-542-0842*. Spend time walking the campus grounds; the architecture and landscaping will soothe and delight. The **Georgia Museum of Art**, 706-542-4662, has a permanent collection of over 5,000 works of art valued at over $12 million. If football is your game, call the **Ticket Office**, 706-542-1231, to see the **Georgia Dawgs.**

From the campus, step across Broad Street and stroll the historic, compact downtown shopping, dining and entertainment district. Three square blocks of historic buildings are generously sprinkled with outdoor dining and tree-shaded sitting spots.

The State's **Botanical Garden of Georgia**, 706-542-1244, 2450 S Milledge Ave, has an **International Garden** and a **Conservatory.** You may want to check out two interesting historic churches: **Athens First Presbyterian**, 185 E Hancock St, was built in 1855, restored in 1902, and retained its Italinate marble pulpit and pine and walnut pews; **Emmanuel Episcopal**, Pope & Prince Sts, is an 1899 Victorian Gothic structure constructed of Georgia granite.

Athens brags of two unusual attractions you won't find anywhere else: **The Tree That Owns Itself** and a **Double Barreled Cannon!!** The Tree can be found at the corner of Dearing and Finley Sts; Professor W. H. Jackson deeded the tree to itself in the late 1800's; he simply enjoyed its shade! The Cannon, at College and Hancock Sts, was designed locally; the intent was to protect Athens from Sherman's Army (1863); the result was less than successful!

Lots of great musicians have come out of Athens, such as R.E.M. and Kenny Rogers; a variety of music can be found in and around town on any day.

Accommodations

Best Western, 706-546-7311, 170 N Milledge Ave; **Courtyard by Marriott**, 800-321-2211, 166 Finley St; **Hampton Inn**, 706-548-9600, 2220 W Broad St; **Holiday Inn**, 800-TO-ATHENS, 197 E Broad St; **Howard Johnson**, 706-548-1111, 2465 W Broad St; **Ramada**, 800-448-4245, 513 W Broad St; and several other chains. B&B Inns include **Magnolia Terrace**, 800-891-1912, 277 Hill St, a 1912 guest house in the Cobbham historic district; **The Nicholson House**, 706-353-2200, 6295 Jefferson Rd, on six wooded acres, history dates to 1779; **Oakwood Bed & Breakfast**, 800-546-7886, 4959 Barnett Shoals Rd, 130-year-old Victorian-style house on 5 acres; renovated barn with exercise facilities.

Madison, GA
Madison is a Georgia Main Street City
pop 3,483
Eastern Time
Madison-Morgan Chamber of Commerce 706-342-4454

To See and Do
Madison is the town that's famous for something that didn't happen. In 1864, as General Sherman marched through on his way to a Union victory, a delegation led by native son Senator Joshua Hill asked him to spare the torch. Sherman and Hill's brother had been friends at West Point, and Hill had not voted for secession; Sherman honored the request and left the town untouched.

As a result, Madison is blessed with a number of lovely antebellum homes and historic churches along its tree-lined streets. Start at the **Madison-Morgan Cultural Center**, *706-342-4743, 434 S Main St*, where you can see Senator Hill's uniform and other Civil War memorabilia. This 1895 former schoolhouse now houses art galleries, and a **Piedmont History Museum**, showing the area's development prior to 1900. Get a walking-tour guide here; there are 45 points of interest you'll see as you stroll through the **National Historic District**. Down the street is **Heritage Hall**, *706-342-4454*; you can tour this house museum; it was built in 1833, with furnishings of the period. The **Morgan County African-American Museum**, *706-342-9197, 156 Academy St*, is in the downtown district. Other homes may be toured during the May and December **Tour of Homes**, *706-342-4454*.

On the antebellum trail, this town was on the stage route from Charleston to New Orleans. Some of the south's earliest colleges were located here, and one of the first female colleges. Many movies have been filmed here to take advantage of its 19th century atmosphere. Spring flower displays are worth a trip to see in this picturesque town.

Accommodations
The Brady Inn, *706-342-4400, 250 N Second St*, Victorian cottages with period antiques; **Burnett Place**, *706-342-4034, 317 Old Post Rd*, 1830-s Federal-style house; also a **Days Inn**, *706-342-1839, 2001 Eatonton Hwy*.

Stone Mountain, GA
pop 6,494
Eastern Time
DeKalb County Chamber of Commerce 404-378-8000

To See and Do
You see **Stone Mountain** long before you get there; the giant granite monolith rises 825 feet above the plain; on its north face is the huge **Confederate Memorial,** a 90x190-foot high-relief sculpture of Jefferson Davis, Robert E. Lee, and Stonewall Jackson that took 50 years to carve.

Stone Mountain Park, *770-498-5702, Highway U78,* is a 3,200-acre park surrounding the mountain, with enough to keep you coming back again and again. A **skylift** takes you past the carving to the summit, the **Stone Mountain Railroad** takes you five miles around the base of the mountain, past granite quarries and natural forests.

Nineteen buildings have been moved from their original Georgia sites and restored to create a **Southern plantation** of the 1800's. There's a paddle wheel **Riverboat,** for lake cruising; and over 20 acres of woodlands with wildlife trails. Evenings in the summer, catch the 50-minute laser show, spotlighting the north side of the mountain. For more to do, there are golf courses, tennis courts, swimming and fishing.

At **Villages of Stone Mountain,** *770-879-4971,* browse a quaint 19th Century town with more than 70 shops and restaurants.

Accommodations
Stone Mountain Inn, *800-277-0007,* colonial atmosphere; **Evergreen,** *800-722-1000,* conference center and resort; **Family Campground,** *770-498-5710,* 400 tentsites, full or partial hookups.

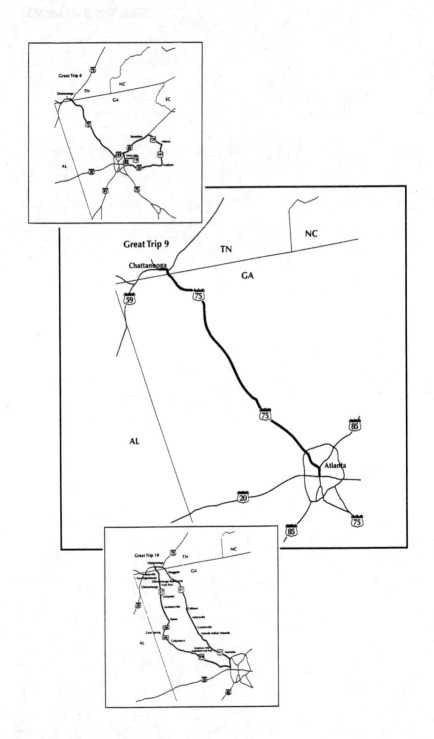

Great Trip 9

Chattanooga to Atlanta, GA
the skyscrapers and sports route
via I-75
approximately 235 miles round-trip, 4.5 hours driving time

Why Go
Underground Atlanta & State Capitol & Jimmy Carter Library &
Martin Luther King Jr. National Historic Site & Fernbank Planetarium &
Georgia Archives & High Museum of Art & SciTrek Science Museum
& Piedmont Park & Cyclorama & Tullie Smith Farm & Wren's Nest &
Atlanta Braves & CNN Studios & Fabulous Fox & Coca-Cola &
African Rain Forest & Six Flags & Georgia Dome & Motor Speedway
& Tallest Hotel & Pittypats Porch & Gone With the Wind

Suggested route with approximate mileages

Instruction	Road	Dir	Miles
Chattanooga to Atlanta	I-75	S	116
Atlanta to Chattanooga	I-75	N	116
Total Mileage			232

Georgia's capital city may have been leveled during the Civil War, but it's the place to go now if you want to see skyscrapers, luxury shops, and major league sports. Its 29 colleges include **Georgia Tech**, **Georgia State**, and **Emory**. It's a big city filled with cultural activities, incredible museums, great restaurants, and entertainment for every age.

The city had small beginnings as **Terminus**, in 1837 a mere stake marking the end of the Western and Atlantic Railroad line. Renamed Atlanta, it grew due to the rail trade, and Mile Post Zero became the commercial center of town. In those days, the railroad tracks converged on the spot where **Underground Atlanta** now stands. With no major body of water near, it was railroads that started this city and linked the Southeast with other regions, and railroads that made it a key supply center during the Civil War.

Federal headquarters for reconstruction after the Civil War, the city offered facilities for state government if it could be chosen capital. It was, in 1868. Another boom after WWII led to the modern scene you see today. Though Georgia was one of the original 13 colonies and the 4th state to ratify the U. S. Constitution, Atlanta is a "new" city.

It's a modern-day boom town, home of **Coca-Cola** and **CNN**. **Hartsfield International Airport** is among the busiest in the U. S. In 1996, the city hosted the summer **Olympics**. A former President keeps offices here; the **Jimmy Carter Library** and Museum has exhibits of life in the White House. A Nobel Peace Prize winner was born here and preached at Ebenezer Baptist Church; **Martin Luther King Jr** is buried at a site near his birth home, which is open for public tours.

It's home of the pennant-winning **Braves** and their famous tomahawk chop, and **Falcons** football, **Hawks** basketball and **Knights** hockey. The **Woodruff Arts Center** on Peachtree is the largest arts complex in the Southeast. **SciTrek Science and Technology Museum** is ranked one of the top ten science centers in the country.

The city's restaurants serve, every type of food, from good ole Georgia bar-b-q pork to the most exotic continental cuisine. There's always someplace interesting to go in the big city. So, go dancing, go shopping, go gallivanting; just go. They don't call it **Hot-lanta** for nothing!

Atlanta, GA
pop 394,017
metro pop 2,833,511
Eastern Time
Visitors Bureau 404-222-6688
Welcome Centers at Underground Atlanta, Peachtree Center Mall,
Lenox Square Mall

To See and Do

Any visit to a capital city should include a visit to the **State Capitol**, *404-656-2844, Capitol Hill at Washington St*. The gilding on the dome is Georgia gold, mined in Dahlonega, 70 miles north, where the first gold rush in America happened in 1828. When the Capitol Building was renovated in the 1950's, the Dahlonega folks not only donated gold to cover the dome, they hauled it to Atlanta wagon-train-style to present it to the governor! Georgia materials make up most of the building: the wood and iron, and the marble on the walls and floors. People are proud to tell that the building was dedicated on schedule, July 4, 1889, with $118.43 remaining in the building fund!

It is open weekdays only but go; see the **Hall of Flags**, and the **Hall of Fame**, which honors outstanding Georgians. The **Georgia State Museum of Science & Industry** is located in the capitol and has exhibits of wildlife, fish, minerals and dioramas of Georgia. You can tour the **Governor's Mansion**, *404-261-1776, 391 West Paces Ferry Rd NW*, a Greek Revival style home with a fine collection of Federal Period furnishings Tuesday through Thursday mornings only.

Near the capitol is **Underground Atlanta**, *404-523-2311, bounded by Wall, Washington, S. Peachtree and Martin Luther King Jr Dr*; the birthplace of Atlanta, these six blocks are filled with promenades, fountains, shops, and restaurants where olden days blend with today in a well-preserved array of underground buildings; take time for an Underground lunch, indulge in a platter of fried green tomatoes and sweet tea.

Art and Museums

Federal Reserve Bank Monetary Museum, *404-521-8747, 104 Marietta St NW*; gold coins minted in Dahlonega, GA; rare coins, and a collection of various forms of money used from earliest times; history of the banking system too.

Fernbank, 404-378-0127, 767 Clifton Rd NE; this 150-acre environmental/educational complex includes a Museum of Natural History, Science Center, Planetarium and Observatory, and the Fernbank Forest. In the **Fernbank Museum of Natural History,** 404-370-0960, A Walk Through Time explores the chronological development of life on earth; gallery has exhibits dealing with light and sound; IMAX theater. **Fernbank Science Center,** 404-378-4311, 156 Heaton Park Dr NE, is home to one of the nation's largest planetariums; observatory is open to the public. The **Fernbank Forest** has nature trails.

Georgia Department of Archives and History, 404-656-2350, 330 Capitol Ave SE; this 17-story marble building has no windows; it is literally a "box" containing state records from 1733; also maps, and official papers. Open Monday-Saturday, free.

Hammonds House Galleries, 404-752-8730, 503 Peeples St; housed in a restored Victorian house in the Historic West End, this fine art museum is dedicated to African-American art; collection includes Romare Bearden, Haitian art.

High Museum of Art, 404-733-4400, 1280 Peachtree St NE; European art from early Renaissance to present; photography, graphics, and "Spectacles" gallery. **High Museum of Art Folk Art & Photography Galleries,** 404-577-6940, 30 John Wesley Dobbs Ave; major works in the heart of downtown from the uptown permanent collection; rotating traveling exhibits.

Jimmy Carter Library and Museum, 404-331-0296, One Copenhill Ave; exhibits of life in the White House, full-scale replica of Oval Office; films and videos portraying President Carter's life as well as the office of the presidency; open daily.

Michael C. Carlos Museum, 404-727-4282, 571 S Kilgo St, Emory University; ancient cultures of Mediterranean and the Americas are emphasized here; Egyptian mummy, pre-Columbian pottery, Greek statues.

SciTrek Science and Technology Museum, 404-522-5500, 395 Piedmont Ave; more than 100 interactive hands-on exhibits; traveling exhibits, live demonstrations, workshops, lectures and films; this museum is ranked as one of the top ten science centers in the country; bring the little Einsteins to Kidspace or explore the Hall of Light and Perception.

Woodruff Arts Center, 404-733-4200, 1280 Peachtree St NE; the largest arts complex in the SE houses the Atlanta Symphony Orchestra, Alliance Theatre, and the Studio Theatre; also Atlanta Children's Theatre, Atlanta College of Art, and High Museum of Art.

Historical Buildings, Homes, and Gardens

Atlanta Botanical Garden, 404-876-5859, 1345 Piedmont Rd; a real oasis within the big city, the Garden borders **Piedmont Park**. Go into the Fuqua Conservatory to see tropical plants, desert plants, and plants on the endangered list.

Atlanta Cyclorama, 404-658-7625, Georgia and Cherokee Ave SE, Grant Park; this three-dimensional, 358-foot painting-in-the-round depicts the 1864 Civil War Battle of Atlanta, complete with sound effects and narration to highlight each facet of the battle.

At the **Atlanta History Center/Buckhead**, 404-814-4000, 130 West Paces Ferry Rd, there are four structures and 32 acres of gardens and trails; includes: **McElreath Hall** which contains the biggest exhibits in the state on the Civil War; **Swan House**, a classic example of early 20th century architecture with fountains and gardens; and **Tullie Smith Farm**, an 1840 farmhouse where you can see craft demonstrations.

Martin Luther King Jr. National Historic Site, 404-524-1956, 449 Auburn Ave NE; two-block area in memory of famed leader of civil rights movement and winner of Nobel Peace Prize; Dr. King's grave is at the King Center site, and tours of his birth home depart from here. Ebnezer Baptist Church, where he preached, is in the area.

Wren's Nest, 404-753-7735, 1050 Ralph D. Abernathy Blvd SW. Victorian house of Joel Chandler Harris, transcriber of "Uncle Remus" stories; guided tours, special story-telling sessions; shop with Br'er Rabbit memorabilia.

Entertainment and Tours

World Series Winning Atlanta Braves, 404-249-6400 for tickets, Atlanta Fulton County Stadium; professional baseball. **Atlanta Falcons**, 404-223-9200 for tickets, The Georgia Dome, professional football. **Atlanta Hawks**, 404-249-6400 for tickets, Omni Sports Arena, professional basketball. **Atlanta Knights**, 404-525-8900, Omni Sports Arena, professional hockey. **Ticketmaster** 404-249-6400.

Atlanta Motor Speedway, *770-946-4211, I-75S Exit 77, 18 miles S on Hwy U19/41;* ARCA stock car races, NASCAR Winston Cup events, Busch Grand National.

CNN Studio Tours, *404-827-2300, One CNN Center, Techwood Dr & Marietta St;* call ahead to select the type of tour you want; these often fill up quickly. Tours give you an inside look at **Turner Broadcasting System's World Headquarters;** you'll see the studios of CNN, Headline News, and CNN International, three 24-hour news networks. Turner Store and Atlanta Braves Clubhouse here too; also restaurants and CNN Cinema 6. CNN Center is adjacent to the Omni Coliseum, the Georgia Dome, and the Georgia World Congress Center.

Fox Theatre, *404-881-2100, 660 Peachtree St NE;* the building is on the National Register of Historic Places, a 1920's theater in Egyptian/Art Deco design; tours are available year-round; wide range of performances and a summer movie series which includes the annual showing of *Gone With The Wind.*

Georgia Dome, *404-223-TOUR, One Georgia Dome Dr NW;* site of 1994 Super Bowl and 1996 Olympics gymnastics and basketball events, and where the Atlanta Falcons play, is the world's largest cable-supported dome; open for tours.

Six Flags Over Georgia, *770-948-9290, 12 mi W via I-20, exit Six Flags parkway;* a 337-acre family theme park with over 100 rides, coasters, live shows; for kids of all ages; all-inclusive ticket.

World of Coca-Cola, *404-676-5151, 55 Martin Luther King Jr Dr;* learn about Coca-Cola through interactive displays and exhibits; over 1,000 artifacts trace the history of Coca-Cola; visit the Soda Fountain of the Future.

Zoo Atlanta, *404-624-5600, Grant Park, 800 Cherokee Ave SE;* naturalistic habitats encourage natural behavior in the animals; some highlights are the **African Rain Forest** for the gorilla families and **Masai Mara,** resembling the plains of Kenya, where you'll see antelope, giraffes, and zebras on open land; rhinos, lions and elephants are nearby. **Ketambe** features high-climbing orangutans and in the lush **Sumatran Forest,** tigers are on the prowl.

Accommodations

Downtown you will find one of the tallest hotels in the world, the 73-story **Westin Peachtree Plaza,** *404-659-1400, Peachtree at*

International Blvd; also **Hyatt Regency Atlanta,** *404-577-1234, 265 Peachtree St NE;* **Marriott Marquis,** *404-521-0000, 265 Peachtree Center Ave;* **Omni Hotel at CNN Center,** *404-659-0000, 100 CNN Center;* and the **Ritz-Carlton,** *404-659-0400, 181 Peachtree St NE;* accommodations plentiful in all price ranges in all sections of town. **Atlanta International Bed & Breakfast,** *800-473-9449* and **Bed & Breakfast Atlanta,** *800-967-3224,* are reservation service organizations. Food spots that are Atlanta landmarks include **Pittypats Porch,** *404-525-8228, 25 International Blvd,* with a Southern menu and rocking chairs in the lounge; and **The Varsity,** *404-881-1706, 61 North Ave,* on the edge of the Georgia Tech campus; hot dogs and fried peach pie.

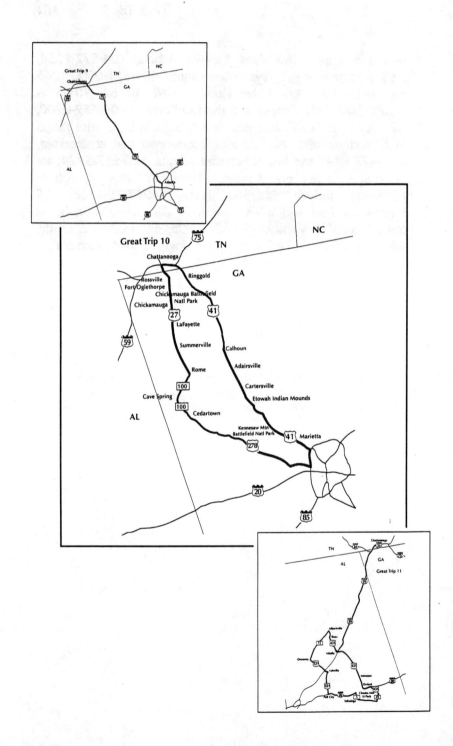

Great Trip 10

Chattanooga to Marietta, GA
the battlefields and backroads route
*via Ringgold, Calhoun, Adairsville, Cartersville, Etowah Indian Mounds St
Historic Site, Red Top Mountain St Pk, Marietta, Kennesaw Mtn Natl
Battlefield, Cedartown, Cave Spring, Rome, Summerville, LaFayette,
Chickamauga, Chickamauga Natl Battlefield, Fort Oglethorpe, Rossville,
returning to Chattanooga
approximately 245 miles round-trip, 5 hours driving time*

Why Go
Chieftains Trail & Cannonball Trail & Indian Mounds & Civil War
Battlefields & Great Locomotive & Barnsley Gardens & Paradise Gardens
& Rock Swaps & World's Deepest Caves & Main Street Cities

Suggested route with approximate mileages

Instruction	Road	Dir	Miles
Chattanooga to Ringgold	I-24 & I-75 & U76	S	17
Ringgold to Calhoun	U41	S	33
Calhoun to Adairsville	U41	S	10
Adairsville to Cartersville	U41	S	19
Cartersville to Marietta	U41	S	25
Marietta to Cedartown	S120 & U278	W	44
Cedartown to Cave Spring	S100	N	10
Cave Spring to Rome	U411 & U27	N	16
Rome to Summerville	U27	N	26
Summerville to LaFayette	U27	N	18
LaFayette to Chickamauga	U27	N	15
Chickamauga to Fort Oglethorpe	U27	N	8
Fort Oglethorpe to Rossville	U27	N	1
Rossville to Chattanooga	U27	N	1
Total Mileage			243

Go directly south without getting on I-75? Yes, please do, and explore the delightful and historic backroads of Northwest Georgia. Two famous trails criss-cross this area; the **Chieftains Trail** is 150 miles long and explores the history of the Native Americans in Northwest Georgia; the **Blue and Gray Trail** covers some of the Civil War's most dramatic events. Welcome Centers in towns along the route have mapped out walking and driving tours for you; start in Ringgold with a **Battlefields and Backroads Photo Tour** map; in Marietta they will supply detailed maps and history for the **Cannonball Trail Tour.**

Evidence of Native American presence is preserved throughout. **New Echota** was the **Cherokee Nation Capital,** the **Etowah Indian Mounds** near Cartersville date back to 1000 AD, the **Chieftains Museum** in Rome is located in the home of one of the signers of the New Echota treaty, and contains evidence of cultures as far back as 700 AD. **John Ross** was the **Cherokee Nation Chief,** and founder of Ross's Landing, which was renamed Chattanooga. His 1797 log cabin is in Rossville.

Two **National Battlefield Parks,** Kennesaw Mountain and Chickamauga, are the end pieces for Civil War battle history. The **Depot in Ringgold** was a significant location for transporting Confederate soldiers, near here **The General** was abandoned by Andrews Raiders during the **Great Locomotive Chase** in 1862. Battle reenactments are held each year on the dates of the events; the **Battles of Resaca, Kennesaw Mountain, and Chickamauga** are replayed in full costume with authentic weaponry. Confederate cemeteries are scattered through the area; **Cassville Cemetery** near Cartersville has over 300 graves.

This is an area of small-town charm too. **Cave Spring** bills itself as the "small town of your dreams;" imagine a place where all the citizenry are bilingual; they learn sign language to communicate with students at the Georgia School for the Deaf, which is located there. The towns on this tour have town squares for gathering, and benches for sitting. Notice how many are Georgia **"Main Street"** cities working towards adaptive preservation; their efforts are to preserve the past, but revitalize for the future. Drive slowly and enjoy.

Ringgold, GA

pop 1,675
Eastern Time
Catoosa County Chamber of Commerce 706-965-5201

To See and Do

Start with the **Chamber of Commerce**, 306 E Nashville St, for a copy of the **Battlefields and Backroads Self-Guided Photo Tour** of historic sites; don't miss the **Ringgold Depot**, one of the few remaining antebellum depots in the state. It was the backdrop of the Great Locomotive Chase in 1862 (see p. 108, where the locomotive now can be seen), and was significant in transporting Confederate soldiers. The **Whitman-Anderson House** served as Grant's headquarters during the Civil War. The **Old Stone Baptist Church**, which is 2 miles east of the city, was built in 1849 and still has its original altar and pews.

Accommodations

Best Western, 423-894-1860, 6650 Ringgold Rd; **South Lookout Mountain KOA**, 706-937-4166, off I-75, exit 141; 165 sites, social events.

Calhoun, GA

A Georgia Main Street City
pop 7,135
Eastern Time
Gordon County Chamber of Commerce 706-625-3200
Calhoun Local Welcome Center 800-887-3811

To See and Do

At the **Local Welcome Center**, 300 S Wall St, get a map of the **Blue & Gray Trail**; at nearby **Resaca** visit the **Confederate Cemetery** where the Battle of Resaca was fought; there's a reenactment the third weekend each May. Get directions too for the **Chieftains Trail**; **New Echota State Historic Site**, 706-629-8151, 1211 Chatsworth Hwy NE, was the Cherokee nation capital between 1825-1838. The **Gordon County Historical Society** is housed at **Oakleigh**, 706-629-1515, 335 S Wall St.

Enjoy the outdoors at **Salacoa Creek Park**, *706-629-3490, 10 miles east of Calhoun,* where there's boating, camping and swimming; and **Hidden Creek**, in the **Chattahoochee National Forest**, *10 miles southeast of town,* for camping, hiking and picnicking.

Want to shop? The **Calhoun Outlet Center**, *706-602-1300, 455 Belwood Rd,* offers designer outlet shopping with big discounts.

Accommodations

Budget Host Shepherd Motel, *706-629-8644;* Hwy S53 & I-75, **The Jameson Inn**, *800-541-3268, 189 Jameson St;* **Stoneleigh Bed & Breakfast**, *706-629-2093, 316 Fain St.* Eat at **B. J.'s**, *706-629-3461, next door to Shepherd Motel;* lunch and dinner in a pleasant setting.

Adairsville, GA
pop 2,131
Eastern Time
Bartow County Visitors Bureau 800-733-2280

To See and Do

In historic Adairsville visit the 1902 Stock Exchange, *770-773-1902, 124 Public Square,* a shopping emporium housing antiques, books, a cafe, and the **Public Square Opera House**, a living history dinner theater.

Then drive on to **Barnsley Gardens**, *770-733-7480, 597 Barnsley Gardens Rd,* a country estate with swans on the pond and wildflowers along the paths. The original home has been left in ruins, the brick walls and formal gardens providing a perfect backdrop for weddings, or just fantasizing about the past. Several buildings have been restored that are in use as a restaurant, a gift shop, and a bed and breakfast. There is an amphitheatre on the property; and the Barnsley Gardens Plant Shop, in an 1830's log cabin, sells cuttings right off the estate.

Accommodations

Barnsley Gardens Restaurant, *770-773-7480, 597 Barnsley Gardens Rd,* located in restored house, vintage 1854, the restaurant serves Southern cuisine prepared with herbs and salad greens grown right outside the kitchen door.

Cartersville, GA
A Georgia Main Street City
pop 12,035
Eastern Time
Cartersville-Bartow County Tourism Council 770-387-1357

To See and Do
At the **Visitor Services Center**, 16 W Main St, get directions for the self-guided tours; also events information. Downtown takes you by two courthouses, the depot, and the first outdoor Coca-Cola advertisement; on the wall of **Young Brothers Pharmacy**, it was painted in 1894. Lots of antiquing opportunities here too.

Stop in at the **Kingston Confederate Memorial Museum**, 770-336-5269, 13 E Main St, to learn about the town's history; and **Bartow History Center**, 770-382-3818, 319 E Cherokee Ave, to see the workshops, farmsteads, and mercantile of North Georgia pioneers between the 1840's-1940's. **Roselawn**, 770-387-5162, 224 W Cherokee Ave, was the home of Sam Jones, a Victorian evangelist.

Just outside of town is **Cooper's Iron Works**, 770-387-1357, River Rd, the only remnant of Mark Cooper's Iron Plantation at Etowah, which was an antebellum industrial center obliterated because of its contributions to the Confederacy. **Cassville Confederate Cemetery**, 770-387-1357, Cass-White Rd, is the burial site of 300 Confederate soldiers.

Other points of interest include the **William Weinman Mineral Museum**, 770-386-0576, US 411, which features a Rock Swap annually, and geology classes; **Air Acres Museum**, 770-382-7030, Cartersville-Bartow Airport, an all-flying military aircraft museum; **Noble Hill**, 770-382-3392, 2361 Joe Frank Harris Pkwy, a Black History Museum and Cultural Center; and **Euharlee Covered Bridge**, 770-387-1357, Euharlee Rd, which is Georgia's oldest covered bridge, built in 1886.

Accommodations
Holiday Inn, 770-386-0830; Hwy U411; **Red Top Mountain State Park Lodge**, 770-975-0055, see below.

Georgia State Park
Eastern Time

Etowah Indian Mounds State Historic Site, *770-387-3747, 813 Indian Mounds Rd SW*, a Mississippian Indian site dating from 1000 AD to 1500 AD, is a stop on the Chieftains Trail. The mounds served as a platform for the Priest-Chief, as temples, and as mortuary houses. Nobility were buried in elaborate costumes. The largest mound is 63 feet tall and covers three acres.

Red Top Mountain State Park, *770-975-0055, 653 Red Top Mountain Rd SE;* this park is located on beautiful **Lake Allatoona,** and offers 1,950 acres of rolling hills, forests, trails, beaches and boating on the 11,860-acre lake; a marina, two ramps, and five docks. Red Top Mountain was an important iron mining area; named for the red earth color caused by the iron in the soil; look for remains of old mines.

Accommodations
Red Top Mountain Lodge, *770-975-0055, 653 Red Top Mountain Rd SE,* 33-room lodge, 18 cottages and 125 campsites. **Mountain Cove Restaurant** in the lodge.

Marietta, GA
pop 44,129
Eastern Time
Marietta Welcome Center 770-429-1115

To See and Do
Stop at the Welcome Center in an 1898 railroad depot on Marietta Square. Get brochures about the four **National Historic Districts** containing 52 points of interest; The **Historic Marietta Walking/Driving** Tour and the Cannonball Trail Driving Tour will take you through this charming town.

Also around the square you'll find more than 20 antique shops, **Glover Park** for concerts and festivals, and **Theatre in The Square,** *770-422-8369,* for professional live theatre.

Big Shanty Museum, *770-427-2117, 2829 Cherokee St, in nearby Kennesaw;* houses **The General;** it's the locomotive, as

Chattanoogans know, that was hijacked twice!
Modern-day fun and foolishness, especially when it's hot and humid, can get you smiling at **White Water** and **American Adventures,** *770-424-9283, 250 N Cobb Parkway;* splashing in the wet or roller-coasting high and dry, for kids of all ages.

Accommodations

Best Western, *800-528-1234, 859 Cobb Pkwy SE;* **Courtyard by Marriott,** *800-321-2211, 2455 Delk Rd;* **Hampton Inn,** *770-425-9977, 455 Franklin Rd.* **Sixty Polk Street Bed & Breakfast,** *800-497-2075, 60 Polk St,* within walking distance of Marietta Square; 1872 French Regency Victorian house furnished with antiques; **The Whitlock Inn,** *770-428-1495, 57 Whitlock Ave;* Victorian Mansion, large ballroom and gardens.

National Battlefield Park
Eastern Time

Kennesaw Mountain National Battlefield Park, *770-427-4686, 900 Kennesaw Mountain Rd.* Two Civil War battles were fought here prior to the siege on Atlanta. Check out the slide show first, for a better understanding of the battle strategies; on the grounds you'll be able to follow the historic markers. Roads and trails lead to Kennesaw Mountain summit, with a panoramic view to downtown and Stone Mountain on a clear day. Recreational fields, 16 miles of hiking trails, and picnicking areas, but no overnight facilities.

Cedartown, GA
A Georgia Main Street City
pop 7,978
Eastern Time
Polk County Chamber of Commerce 770-748-3473

To See and Do

The folks at the **Polk County Chamber of Commerce** in the Courthouse, *100 Prior St, Room 207,* will furnish the information you need to enjoy the town; there is a **Historic**

Driving Tour. First walk the **Historic Downtown District;** preservation efforts have turned Main Street into a delightful spot to stroll and shop. The **West Cinema,** a fine example of Art Deco architecture, won the Georgia Trust Award for Historic Preservation.

The Big Spring, *just off Hwy 27 on Wissahickon Ave,* is where the Cherokee met for councils and ceremonies; now a park with picnic facilities.

Accommodations

As you walk Main Street, stop at **Moore's Pharmacy,** *770-748-2200, 402 Main St,* for an old-fashioned lemon sour at the soda fountain; **Red Onion Cafe and Main Street Gallery,** *770-748-4606, 308 Main St,* is a gathering spot "where the elite meet" for food, fun and trivia.

Cave Spring, GA
pop 950
Eastern Time
City of Cave Spring 706-777-3382

To See and Do

Called the **"small town of your dreams,"** this town of 950 has 90 structures and sites on the National Register of Historic Places. Beautifully maintained homes of Gothic, Victorian and Plantation styles, an 1880 train depot, and 19th century hotels and boarding houses are reminders of the past.

Georgia School for the Deaf, a state-operated elementary and secondary school, has been here since 1846. Cave Spring is a bilingual town, as almost everyone communicates by sign language with the students.

Located in **Rolater Park,** just off the town square, are the natural limestone cave and spring for which the town is named. The spring produces 3 to 4 million gallons a day of pure water; people come from miles around for a taste. The water goes on to fill the park's 1.5 acre swimming pool with its invigorating mineral water. **Arts and crafts** thrive in this community; an art bronze foundry and a working pottery studio downtown; lively

antique trade here too; many shops located in historic homes. The **Cave Spring Arts Festival** is held annually in early June.

Accommodations

Cedar Creek Lodge & Chalets, *706-232-3239, by Little Cedar Creek;* lodge for group gatherings, 8 chalets; **Creekside Inn,** *706-777-3124, 1 Georgia Ave,* across the road from Rolater Park; **Tumblin House Bed & Breakfast,** *706-777-0066, 38 Alabama St;* breakfast served; lunch/dinner available in **Tearoom** upon request. On the square is **Shumate's Diner,** *706-777-3766,* serving homecooked meals; **Dee's Place,** *706-777-9053, 118 Gadsden Rd,* specializes in steaks.

Rome, GA

A Georgia Main Street City
pop 30,326
Eastern Time
Rome Welcome Center, 800-444-1834

To See and Do

When in Rome stop first at the **Welcome Center,** *402 Civic Center Dr;* it's located in a restored 1901 depot and on the grounds are an 1847 machine shop lathe and an 1850 log cabin. Get info there and drive into the **Historic Downtown** area for a **Walking Tour;** see the **Capitoline Wolf Statue,** Romulus and Remus; the city's seven hills were factors in the naming of Rome. The **City Clock Tower Museum** is downtown too, where there are many examples of adaptive restoration. The downtown area is "between the rivers" -- the **Etowah** and **Oostanaula Rivers** join in the heart of Rome to form the **Coosa,** which flows to the Gulf of Mexico. The Riverways Development Plan calls for the development of Riverwalks and Nature Areas to take advantage of the water scenes.

The **Chieftains Museum,** *706-291-9494, 501 Riverside Parkway,* was the 1794 home of Major Ridge, who signed the New Echota Treaty. Experience the three cultures of the Coosa Valley here; the Mississippian Culture (700 to 1600), the Cherokee Indians (1700-1838), and the Agrarian South

(1834-1935). The house museum is on the **Chieftains Trail.**
North of Rome on Hwy 27 stop in at **Oak Hill** and the **Martha Berry Museum,** *706-291-1883, 189 Mount Berry Station;* the museum has an art gallery; see the 1847 plantation home and formal gardens. Drive the beautiful campus at **Berry College,** *706-236-2226, 227 Mount Berry Blvd;* 37 major building on 26,000 acres; one of the largest overshot waterwheels in the world; an operational dairy; and Possum Trot Church; built in 1850, it was Martha Berry's first school.
In mid-October go for the **Chiaha Harvest Fair,** *706-235-4542,* held on the banks of the Coosa River downtown; Chiaha is an Indian word meaning "meeting of the hills and the waters." The fair promotes the work of local craftspersons.

Accommodations
Days Inn, *706-295-0400, 840 Turner McCall Blvd;* **Holiday Inn,** *706-295-1100, Hwy 411E;* **Chandler Arms Bed & Breakfast,** *800-438-9492, 2 Coral Ave;* 1902 Victorian mansion, English breakfast, afternoon high tea, fireplaces in bedrooms; **The Claremont House Bed & Breakfast,** *800-254-4797, 906 E 2nd Ave;* Victorian mansion built in 1882, listed on National Historic Register, nostalgic charm.

Summerville, GA
pop 5,025
Eastern Time
Chattooga County Chamber of Commerce 706-857-4033

To See and Do
One of the South's best known visionary artists, **Howard Finster,** lives in Summerville. You can visit **Paradise Gardens,** *800-FINSTER, Hwy U27N, turn on Rena Street, then Knox;* browse **Finster Folk Art Gallery** too. The Gardens are a maze of abstract, symbolic sculptures and structures; scripture adorns each creation. Finster's art has been shown in the Smithsonian; a Finster Folk Art Festival is held each May.
Just outside of Summerville is **James H. Floyd State Park,** *706-857-0826, off Hwy U27,* with picnic areas and hiking trails.

LaFayette, GA
pop 6,313
Eastern Time
Walker County Chamber of Commerce, 706-375-7702

To See and Do
Good access to **Pigeon Mountain** from here, 706-375-7702, Hwy S193, 2.5 miles to Chamberlain Rd, left 3 miles to Rocky Lane Rd, right 1 mile on gravel road, where you'll find some of the deepest caves in the world. There's a check-in station for the 16,000-acre **Crockford-Pigeon Mountain Wildlife Management Area.** Here are primitive areas for hunting, fishing, and camping; hiking, biking and horseback riding trails; rock cliffs and outcrops for novice or experienced climbers; and the **Hood Overlook** for hang gliding for experienced pilots. **Rock Town**, a 150-acre maze of sandstone, crowns the mountain.

Chickamauga, GA
pop 2,149
Eastern Time
Walker County Chamber of Commerce 706-375-7702

To See and Do
Historic downtown offers pleasant walking, and out at **Hidden Hollow Farm**, 706-539-2372, 463 Hidden Hollow Lane, off Hwy S136, there is folk dancing, hiking and fishing.
Accommodations
Gordon-Lee Mansion Bed & Breakfast, 706-375-4728, 217 Cove Rd, is an 1847 plantation house; private baths, gardens, museum; **Hidden Hollow Resort**, 706-539-2372, 463 Hidden Hollow Ln, rustic cabins.

National Battlefield Park
Eastern Time
Chickamauga Battlefield, 706-866-9241, Hwy U27 south of Ft Oglethorpe; the Battlefield is part of the Chickamauga and

Chattanooga National Military Park, the oldest and largest military park in the nation, dedicated in 1895. Watch a 26-minute multi-media show in the Visitor Center's Centennial Theatre about the fierce Battle of September 19 and 20, 1863. There are other demonstrations, displays and exhibits, including the 355 weapons of the **Fuller Gun Collection**; a well-stocked book store and facilities for doing research.

In the park are monuments, historical tablets, hiking trails, and horse trails. Pick up a map to guide you and explain the 8 stops on the 7-mile auto tour; rent a special tape tour produced by the Eastern National Park & Monument Association.

Fort Oglethorpe, GA
pop 5,880
Eastern Time
Catoosa County Chamber of Commerce 706-965-5201

To See and Do

The Fort was built in 1904 and became a post for the Sixth U. S. Cavalry in 1919. When the Cavalry left, in 1942, it became a WAC training center. The **6th Cavalry Museum**, *706-861-2860, Barnhardt Circle,* showcases the life of the Cavalryman and is located on the former parade field; parade field is listed on the National Register of Historic Places.

Accommodations

Captain's Quarters Bed & Breakfast, *706-858-0624, 13 Barnhardt Circle,* is near the battlefield, house was once officers' quarters.

Rossville, GA
pop 3,601
Eastern Time
Walker County Chamber of Commerce 706-375-7702

To See and Do

The **John Ross House**, *706-375-7702, Spring Street, Rossville, GA,* is open during summer months. Also a stop on the **Chieftains**

Trail, this 1797 log cabin was home to the Cherokee Nation Chief, John Ross. Ross was born in 1790 in Indian Territory; one-eighth Cherokee, he was brought up among the Cherokee and called Tsan-usdi, or Little John. This two-story log house was built by John McDonald, Ross's maternal grandfather, and was the first school in north Georgia. Ross lived here as a child, and came back after completing his education, operating the supply depot and warehouse at Ross's Landing on the river five miles away; the river settlement grew into the city of Chattanooga. The house was one of the first post offices in the area; Ross was appointed postmaster in 1817.

The original house is a National Historic Landmark and contains Ross's furniture; next to **Poplar Spring**, there is a pond and small park. Donations welcome.

Great family entertainment at **Lake Winnepesaukah**, *706-866-5681, 1115 Lakeview Dr,* where summertimes offer amusement park pleasures and music on Sunday afternoons. The lake has an interesting history; the earthen dam was built by Native Americans; during the Civil War thirsty troops fought over the water supply. Purchased by the Dixons in the 1920's, Carl Dixon designed the boat chute, forerunner of the type you see in major parks today; the miniature golf course was the second ever built in the USA, just after Fairyland's Tom Thumb course on Lookout Mountain.

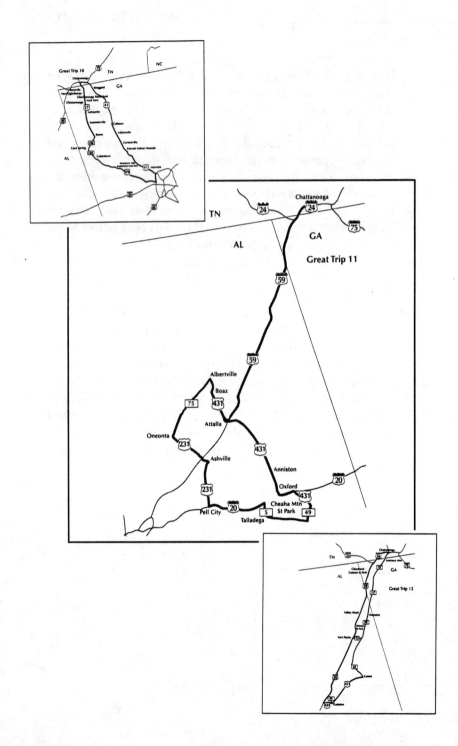

Great Trip 10

TN

NC

GA

AL

Chattanooga

Fort Oglethorpe
Chickamauga Battlefield Natl Park
Chickamauga

27

41

Lafayette

Summerville

Calhoun

Adairsville

Cave Spring

Rome

136

Cartersville

Cedartown

Etowah Indian Mounds

Marietta

41

278

Jasper

20

85

TN

AL

Chattanooga

24

24

75

GA

Great Trip 11

59

59

Albertville

Boaz

75

431

Attalla

Oneonta

231

Ashville

431

Anniston

Oxford

20

231

431

Cheaha Mtn
St Park

Pell City

20

5

49

Talladega

Great Trip 12

TN

Chattanooga

24

75

Cloudland Canyon St Park

AL

GA

Valley Head

Desoto
St Park

Fort Payne

Collinsville

Canoe

411

431

Gadsden

Great Trip 11

Chattanooga to Cheaha Mountain, AL
the mountain topping and shopping route
*via Anniston, Oxford, Cheaha Mtn St Pk, Talladega, Oneonta,
Boaz, Attalla, and returning to Chattanooga
approximately 415 miles round-trip, 8 hours driving time*

Why Go
Highest Point in Alabama, Cheaha Mountain at 2,407 ft
Seven Angels & Military Museums & Golf Trail & Antiques &
Baseball Cards & Quilts & Covered Bridges & Odum Scout Trail &
Inspiration Point & Silk Stocking District &
World's Fastest Speedway & Shoppers Paradise &
Lost Luggage & Flea Markets

Suggested route with approximate mileages

Instruction	Road	Dir	Miles
Chattanooga to Anniston	I-24 & I-59 & U431	S	129
Anniston to Oxford	U21	S	6
Oxford to Cheaha Mtn St Pk	I-20 & S281	E & S	31
Cheaha Mtn St Pk to Talladega	S281 & I-20 & S21	W & S	57
Talladega to Oneonta	U231 & I-20 & S75	N & W	55
Oneonta to Boaz	S75 & U431	N	33
Boaz to Attalla	U431	S	13
Attalla to Chattanooga	I-59 & I-24	N	90
Total Mileage			414

This is a kick-off-your-shoes trip. Get casual and get comfortable. We're going for flea markets, antique malls, and outlet malls; for car racing and fishing and camping. We're going to the mountain tops. The "loop" doesn't begin until you've traversed **Lookout Valley** and **Big Wills Valley** alongside Lookout Mountain on I-59 for 90 miles south to Gadsden. Then you're off the freeway on U431S, headed for Anniston, nestled between **Coldwater Mountain** and **Skeleton Mountain**, and founded as a "model" private company town in 1872. Next door is the US Army Military Reservation that houses **Ft. McClellan.** You can visit a number of military museums there.

Your first big shopping opportunity comes at the **Olde Mill Antique Mall** in Oxford, the southeast's largest; your first opportunity for mountain-topping comes at **Cheaha State Park**, where you can drive to Alabama's highest point, **Cheaha Mountain.** Great views at 2,407 feet from the observation tower built by the Civilian Conservation Corps back in the 30's. Take time to relax with a meal in the mountaintop restaurant; get a room or pitch your tent and stay a few days. There's a nice swimming beach at **Cheaha Lake**, and many wood rambles on easy trails through the park. Ten-mile **Odum Scout Trail** will appeal to more experienced hikers. You'll want to plan at least one trip to enjoy the fall color in the **Talladega National Forest.**

If you're a NASCAR fan you already know the schedule for the **Talladega Superspeedway**; if you're not, treat yourself to a bus ride around the track so you can talk racing to someone who is.

Cross Canoe Creek Valley to ascend **Sand Mountain** on the way to Oneonta. Slow down and explore this area; find the **three historic covered bridges.**

Warm up your shopping muscles and hit the **shoppers paradise** in Boaz. How long will it take you to peruse 140 outlet stores? After that, are you ready for the state's largest flea market? The every-Sunday event at the **Mountain Top Flea Market & Country Mall** near Attalla draws 1,500 dealers; come ahead in your camper so you can be there when it opens at 5 AM. You're back where the loop began now; head for home with the merchandise piled high in back.

Anniston, AL
pop 26,623
Central Time
Visitors Bureau 205-237-3536

To See and Do

Progressive industrialist Samuel Noble founded Anniston as "a model city" in 1872, establishing textile mills and blast furnaces to help the South recover from the Civil War's devastation. Renowned architect Stanford White was hired to design a modern "company" town; it remained private until 1883 when it was opened to the public.

You'll find many historic churches and homes; Noble contributed to construction of the **Church of St Michael's and All Angels**; *205-237-4011, W 18th St and Cobb Ave;* this Episcopal Church has a 95-foot bell tower with 12 bells, the largest weighing 4,350 pounds; the handcarved ceiling is an exact replica of a ship's ribs. The 1888 Romantic Romanesque church is made entirely of Alabama stone and has a 12-foot-long white Carrara marble altar; the ornamental screen behind the altar is surmounted by seven angels; open daily.

Museum of Natural History, *205-237-6766, 800 Museum Dr,* displays include dinosaurs and fossils, African and North American mammals in open dioramas, a 400-species bird collection that includes extinct and endangered birds, two authentic Egyptian mummies, and a walk-through replica of an Alabama cave; located in the **John B. Lagarde Environmental Interpretive Center**, there are nature trails and picnic areas.

US Army Fort McClellan, *Hwy S21,* is a center for basic combat training and houses the US Army Chemical School, US Army Military Police School, and DOD Polygraph Institute. Three museums are open to the public; all are free. **US Army Chemical Corps Museum**, *205-848-3355, Bldg 2299 Fort McClellan,* features more than 4,000 chemical warfare artifacts from Biblical times to the Nuclear Age. **US Army Military Police Corps Regimental Museum**, *205-848-3522, Bldg 3182 Fort McClellan,* has a collection of firearms and period uniforms, military vehicles, combat art from WWI to Vietnam. **Women's**

Army Corp Museum, 205-848-3512, Bldg 1077, Fort McClellan, depicts women's roles in the US Army from the Revolutionary War to the present.

North of Anniston at Glencoe is **Silver Lakes,** 205-892-3268, 730 Lake Dr, Glencoe, on the **Robert Trent Jones Golf Trail,** a 36-hole facility at the edge of the Talladega National Forest; public.

Accommodations

Holiday Inn, 800-HOLIDAY, Hwy U78 & Hwy S21S. The **Victoria Country Inn & Restaurant,** 800-260-8781, 1604 Quintard; built in 1888, listed on National Register of Historic Places, original home with **full-service restaurant** and suites plus annex, brick courtyard, swimming pool, 3-story turret, conservatory, colonnaded verandas, valet parking, welcoming cocktail.

Oxford, AL
pop 9,362
Central Time
Chamber of Commerce 205-237-3536

To See and Do

Olde Mill Antique Mall, 205-835-0599, 100 Mill St; inside a cotton mill that's over 100 years old you'll find the southeast's largest antique mall; antiques and collectibles from more than 150 dealers; there's more down Mill Street; find baseball cards, books, crafts and quilts in 10 village cottages which formerly housed mill workers.

Coldwater Covered Bridge, off I-20 at Oxford; bridge was moved to Oxford Lake and Civic Center in 1990 and restored to its original condition; paved walking trail.

Alabama State Park
Central Time
Cheaha State Park, 205-488-5111, off I-20 on Hwy S281; the 2,799-acre park is where you'll find **Cheaha Mountain;** Cheaha is a Choctaw Indian word for high, and the mountain is

Alabama's highest point at 2,407 feet; climb the observation tower at the top for a panoramic view of the surrounding **Talladega National Forest.** Roads, cabins, cottages, lodges, picnic shelters, hiking trails and swimming areas were developed under the Civilian Conservation Corp in the 30's; many park trails are short, easy wood rambles; experienced hikers may want the ten-mile **Odum Scout Trail,** part of the **Pinhoti Trail System** maintained by the National Forest Service. **Cheaha Lake** has a swimming beach.

Accommodations

Cheaha Resort Hotel, *800-846-2654,* has 30 guest rooms designed to take advantage of the spectacular views; restaurant adjacent with country inn atmosphere is open daily, year round; group lodge, 15 cottages, and 73 campsites; campstore and chapel.

Talladega, AL
pop 18,175
Central Time
Chamber of Commerce 205-362-9075

To See and Do

Heritage Hall, *205-761-1364, 200 South St E,* houses the Talladega and Alabama Heritage historic photograph collection; exhibits show the history of east central Alabama. Hall is located in the **Silk Stocking District,** where antebellum and turn-of-the-century houses grace tree-lined streets; the area is bounded by East Street South, Court Street South, and South Street East. The **Talladega County Courthouse,** oldest courthouse still in use in the state, is in historic **Talladega Square.**

Near the freeway is **Talladega Superspeedway,** *205-362-2261, I-20 exits 168 and 173;* home of the Winston Select 500 and the Diehard 500. It's said to be one of the fastest speedways in the world with 33 degree banks in the turns; you can ride the track in a bus any day but race days. The **International Motorsports Hall of Fame,** *205-362-5002, by the speedway,* houses a collection of racing vehicles and memorabilia; ride in the Richard Petty race car simulator; open year round.

Two districts of the **Talladega National Forest** are near; the **Talladega Ranger District**, 205-362-2909, 1001 North St and the **Shoal Creek Ranger District**, 205-463-2273, 450 Hwy S46, Heflin. Hiking trails, water recreation, and scenic drives are plentiful in the forest; there is fall color from the oaks, maples, hickories and persimmons; dogwoods and redbuds show off in the spring.

Accommodations

Oakwood Bed & Breakfast, 205-362-0662, 715 E North St; four rooms in 1847 antebellum home, period furnishings; full breakfast; horseshoes, badminton. **Orangevale Plantation**, 205-362-3052, 1400 Whiting Rd; three rooms, continental breakfast; country setting with farm animals, shady lanes.

Oneonta, AL
pop 4,844
Central Time
Blount County Chamber of Commerce
205-274-2153

To See and Do

Blount County Memorial Museum, 205-625-6905, 204 2nd St N; genealogical research material and county history; the Edison Foundation's Collection of Edisonia for the State of Alabama is here too. Go out of town to **Palisades Park**, 205-274-0017, atop Ebell Mountain, Off Hwy U231, N of Oneonta; located on Mt Ebell on Stone Bluff are two pioneer cabins, a schoolhouse, and a farm museum. "Inspiration Point" allows visitors to overlook eastern Blount County into St Clair County; nature study, classroom, arboretum, nature trails, pavilions, conference halls; nationally acclaimed for its design; 1,300-foot elevation.

Scattered around the county are three of the state's historic covered bridges; all are open to public traffic and are used daily. They are **Easley Covered Bridge**, off Hwy U231, SE of Rosa; **Horton Mill Covered Bridge**, off Hwy S75, N of Oneonta; **Swann Covered Bridge**, off Hwy S79, NW of Cleveland.

Boaz, AL
pop 6,928
Central Time
Chamber of Commerce 205-593-8154

To See and Do
They call it "A Shopper's Paradise" and if it's shopping you want, then shopping you can do, at **Boaz Outlet Shopping,** 205-593-8154, *off Hwy U431 on Billy B Dyar Blvd and Hwy S68.* The largest outlet center in the South, there are more than 140 stores here, including direct factory outlets, off-price and discount retailers, discount department stores, and outlet boutiques; discounts up to 70%. Look for fine china, running shoes, home furnishings, lingerie, and jeans; there is even an **Unclaimed Baggage Center,** *205-593-4393, 101 E Bartlett;* lost luggage winds up here! Buy for a fraction of original cost.

Accommodations
Best Western, *800-528-1234, 751 Hwy U431S;* **Days Inn,** *205-593-0000, 12960 Hwy U431S;* **Boaz Bed & Breakfast Inn,** *205-593-8031, 200 Thomas St,* 5 rooms, fireplace. **Barclay RV Park,** *205-593-8769, 104 S Main St.*

Attalla, AL
pop 6,859
Central Time
Etowah Tourism Board 205-549-0351

To See and Do
Keep shopping. **Mountain Top Flea Market & Country Mall,** *800-535-2286, 11301 Hwy U278W,* is Alabama's largest flea market. Open at 5 AM 52 Sundays a year, over 1,500 dealers display their wares on these 97 acres; sellers, dealers and overnight camping welcome; it's BYOT -- bring your own table for a 10x22 space; all on one level; concessions, restrooms.

Accommodations
Econo Lodge, *800-424-4777, 507 Cherry St;* **Holiday Inn Express,** *800-HOLIDAY, 801 Cleveland Ave.*

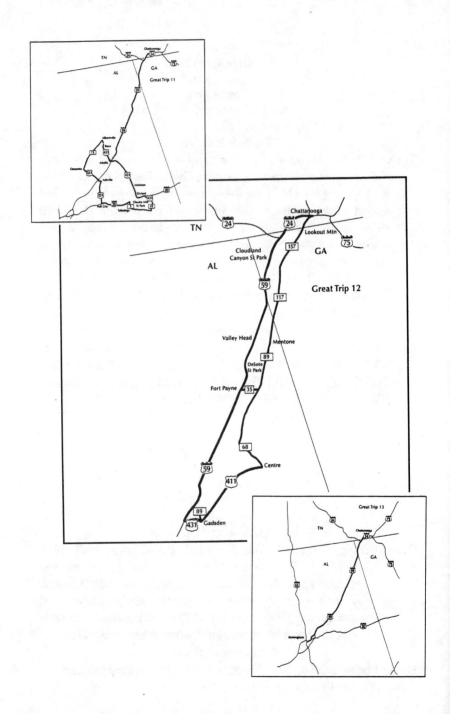

Great Trip 12

Chattanooga to Little River Canyon, AL
the mountain falls and canyons route

*via GA - Lookout Mtn, Cloudland Canyon State Park; AL - Mentone,
Valley Head, DeSoto State Park, Fort Payne, Little River Canyon, Centre,
Gadsden, Noccalula Falls Park, returning to Chattanooga
approximately 240 miles round-trip, 5 hours driving time*

Why Go

Hang Gliding & Sitton Gulch & Wedding Chapel & Dude Ranch &
Ski Slopes & Canyon Drives & Rock Village & Crappie Capital &
ALABAMA Museum & Alabama Princess & Green Corn Festival &
Rainbow Falls & DeSoto Falls & Noccalula Falls

Suggested route with approximate mileages

Instruction	Road	Dir	Miles
Chattanooga to Lookout Mtn	S58 & S189	S	3
Lookout Mtn to Cloudland Canyon St Pk	S189 & S136	S	19
Cloudland Canyon St Pk to Mentone	S136 & S157 & S117	S	41
Mentone to Valley Head	S117	S	3
Valley Head to DeSoto St Pk	S117 & S165	S	10
DeSoto St Pk to Ft Payne	S165 & S35	W	6
Ft Payne to Centre via Little River Canyon	S35 & S176 & S68	S	43
Centre to Gadsden	U411	W	20
Gadsden to Chattanooga	U431 & I-59 & I-24	N	96
Total Mileage			241

Chattanooga sits at one end of Lookout Mountain and Gadsden is 90 miles away at the other. This tour explores the mountain, with drives along the top and up and down both sides, digging into the mountain's secrets and delights.

This is a three-state, two-time-zone Trip; with two state's parks, and a national preserve. Just how big is this mountain anyhow? It stretches 83 miles in a southwesterly direction from Chattanooga, rising to a highest point of 2,393 feet. Its broad top ranges from a mile in width to almost ten. The **Tennessee River** shapes its northernmost point, the **Coosa River** defines the south end, and the **Little River** flows along the top. Can you guess how many scenic vistas, how many caves, how many rock formations, how many species of plants are to be found on such a mountain? Hard to do. The fun will be in making your own memories.

Drive past **Covenant College**; its Carter Hall is a former resort hotel and is visible from the valleys below. Stop at **McCarty's Bluff** and watch people step off the side of the mountain, hang gliding of course, at **Lookout Mountain Flight Park.**

On to Georgia's **Cloudland Canyon State Park**, where even non-hikers are treated to royal canyon views at the overlooks. The gorgeous scenery has you so relaxed you won't notice when you cross the state line into Alabama and the time zone into central on your way to **Mentone**, where shops and restaurants vie for your attention. It's just a short drive off the mountain to **Valley Head.**

Cloudmont Resort and Alabama's **DeSoto State Park** are next; and **Fort Payne** is close by in the valley. How many days do you have to explore DeSoto Park? Stay as long as you can and drive the 20-mile canyon drive, stopping along the way to admire one of the deepest gorges in the country, cut by **Little River**, which is formed and flows entirely on the mountain.

You are surrounded by farmland as you drive towards **Cherokee Rock Village**; then off the mountain to **Weiss Lake** for an admiring look back up at the mountain, or a fishing stop at the crappie capital of the world.

Enjoy a ride on the riverboat in **Gadsden** before you go back up the mountain to **Noccalula Falls**, and see the Princess poised at the edge. Return on Lookout Mountain Parkway or take the faster route on I-59.

Lookout Mtn, GA
pop 1,636
Eastern Time

To See and Do
Lookout Mountain Flight Park, *706-398-3541, 800-688-LMFP, Hwy S189;* a hang glider's heaven perched on the western edge of Lookout Mountain. Non-flyers gather round to watch the brave; this training facility is USHGA certified, has been around more than 15 years, offers tandem training, a completely stocked pro shop, and repair facilities. There's aero towing from the 2,200 foot runway below.

Accommodations
Lookout Inn, *706-820-2000, Hwy S189,* 16 motel rooms and cabins, some with porch offering view east towards Chattanooga Valley and city; pool; complimentary continental breakfast; Covenant College across street.

Georgia State Park
Eastern Time

Cloudland Canyon State Park, *706-657-4050, Hwy S136;* this 2,219-acre park straddles a deep gorge cut into Lookout Mountain by Sitton Gulch Creek. Elevation goes from 800 feet to 1,980 feet; ridges and valley offer rugged geology and beautiful vistas. West Rim and Waterfalls Trail; backcountry backpacking trail; pool, bathhouse, tennis courts, bike rentals.

Accommodations
Cloudland Canyon State Park, *706-657-4050,* has 16 cabins, both 2 and 3 bedroom; a 40-bed group camp; 75 tent/trailer sites, 30 walk-in campsites, four pioneer campsites.

Note time change from Eastern to Central when you cross the state line from Georgia into Alabama.

Mentone, AL
pop 474
Central Time
DeKalb County Tourist Association
205-845-2741

To See and Do

Mentone means "musical mountain spring," but here you can add the sound of fiddles and church chimes too, with year-round festivals and a Musical Mountain Christmas; the Mentone Wedding Chapel is a lovely spot for getting married. The little town has a number of craft shops, many artists and craftspersons live on the mountain. Thousands of boys and girls get their summer camp experience in the Mentone area.

The southernmost ski resort in the country is the **Cloudmont Ski and Golf Resort**, 205-634-4344, Co Rd 164; when there is snow, or weather cold enough to make snow, the thousand-foot hills above **Saddle Rock Golf Course** are used for skiing; the rest of the year you can putt. The Resort is open year round for housing, horseback, trails, fishing, and either golf or skiing. **Shady Grove Dude and Guest Ranch**, Alabama's only dude ranch, is situated on 1,000 acres near Cloudmont, the entire area offers hiking trails and river and wilderness adventure; horseback and wagon rides, square dancing.

Accommodations

Shady Grove Dude Ranch, 205-634-4344, Co Rd 164, Bunk House has 10 singles; Farm House has 5 bedrooms; Roundup Lodge has motel rooms and continental breakfast. Beds & breakfasts at **Mentone Inn**, 800-455-7470, Hwy 117, 12 rooms, full breakfast; **Madaperca Bed & Breakfast**, 205-634-4792, Hwy 117, riverside view, stone fireplace, private patio; **Blossom Hill Bed & Breakfast & Herb Farm**, 800-889-4244, 624 Rd 948, separate guest house, herbal gardens; **Raven Haven**, 205-634-4310, 651 Co Rd 644; **Valhalla**, 205-634-4006, 672 Co Rd 626. Restaurants include **Cragsmere Mana Restaurant**, 205-634-4677, **Dessie's Kountry Chef**, 205-634-4232, and **Log Cabin Restaurant & Deli**, 205-634-4560.

Valley Head, AL
pop 577
Central Time
DeKalb County Tourist Association
205-845-2741

To See and Do

Sequoyah Caverns, 205-635-0024, *off I-59, 6 miles north of Valley Head,* are named for Sequoyah, the Indian who developed the Cherokee alphabet in the "Will's Town" settlement near Fort Payne; dramatically-lit looking-glass lakes, Rainbow Falls, towering stalagmites give appearance of underground palace; cave temperature stays at about 60 degrees year-round. **Fox Mountain Trout Farm,** 205-632-3194, *north of Valley Head, 2 miles off I-59, Rising Fawn exit, turn west,* open March to November, call for hours; trout raised here, charge per pound of fish caught; fishing poles, bait, bagging, icing included in the fee.

Accommodations

Winston Place Bed & Breakfast, 205-635-6381, *one block off 117 in the heart of town;* antebellum mansion is on National Historic Register; served as headquarters for Civil War soldiers; original furnishings; 6 rooms and suites have private access to sprawling verandas. **Woodhaven Bed & Breakfast,** 205-635-6438, *Lowry Rd;* 3 rooms, full breakfast, Victorian-style house, verandas, 10-acre park-like wooded setting, a working farm.

Alabama State Park
Central Time

DeSoto State Park/DeSoto Falls/Little River Canyon; *800-ALA-PARK, 205-845-5380; off Hwy 35, Ft Payne.* One of the deepest gorges east of the Mississippi River is 27-mile Little River Canyon in 5,067-acre DeSoto State Park on Lookout Mountain. The Little River is the only river in the US that forms and flows almost entirely on a mountain and DeSoto Falls plunges 110 feet from a mile-long lake. A 20-mile drive along the canyon's edge has many scenic overlook areas where you can pull off the road for incredible views; the park has dense woodlands, wildflowers and miles of hiking trails -- mountaintop and in the gorge. A Nature Center has a trained park naturalist to help identify new-found wonders of the woods.

Accommodations

DeSoto Resort Inn, 205-845-5380, 25 rooms in lodge and 22 rustic family cabins; restaurant in lodge, wooded setting; 78 campsites; hiking trails, swimming pool.

Fort Payne, AL

pop 11,838
Central Time
DeKalb County Tourist Association
205-845-2741

To See and Do

ALABAMA Fan Club and Museum, 205-845-1646, Hwy S35, photographs, awards, and personal items showcase the history of the homegrown country group ALABAMA; the annual June Jam brings in nationally known performers. The **Fort Payne Opera House**, 205-845-3957, 510 N Gault Ave, is open by appointment only, built in 1889, it's the oldest theater in Alabama still in use; the 1891 **Fort Payne Depot**, 205-845-5714, 5th St NE, is an excellent example of Richardsonian Romanesque architecture with its turrets, arched windows, and heavy stone facade; inside are artifacts from several Indian tribes, farm equipment, photographs, artwork, and railroad memorabilia.

Accommodations

Best Western, 800-528-1234, 1828 Gault Ave; **Quality Inn**, 205-845-4013, I-59 at Hwy S35.

Centre, AL

pop 2,893
Central Time
Cherokee County Chamber of Commerce
205-927-8455

To See and Do

Cherokee Rock Village, *205-927-8455, atop Lookout Mountain;* gives you a 30-mile panoramic view overlooking Weiss Lake. The giant boulders of all shapes and sizes date back 300 million years to the Pennsylvanian Period; some are 200 feet high. There is a natural arch in the park, eight mountain springs, and miles of crevices, cracks, caves and trails for rock climbers to enjoy.

More out-of-state fishing licenses are issued for **Weiss Lake** than any other site in Alabama, lending credence to its claim as "Crapple Capital of the World;" the record is 5 lb 1 oz. The 30,200-acre lake offers 447 miles of shoreline, shallow flats, underwater dropoffs, deep channels, and large coves; bream, shad, and crawfish are abundant in the lake's stump flats, sloping points, weed beds, and strong feeder creeks. Many fishing guide services in the area; call the Chamber for a listing.

Of historical interest in the area is **Cornwall Furnace Park,** *205-927-8455, Hwy S9, 2 miles east of Cedar Bluff;* this 1862 cold blast furnace was the first in the country to be powered by water and was an important part of the Confederate's ironworks; the 5-1/2-acre park contains a 3,000-foot nature trail; it's a National Historic Site. **Cherokee County Historical Museum,** *205-927-7835, 101 E Main St, Centre,* has housewares, farm tools, blacksmith shop, newspapers, pictures, and records dating to mid-1800's; nearly 5000 items pertaining to area history.

Accommodations

Muffins Cafe, *205-927-2233, Hwy U411,* is a full service restaurant with a 50's atmosphere, restored cars, lots of memorabilia; gift shop with 50's and 60's collectibles. Call the Chamber for a listing of campgrounds and marinas in the area.

Gadsden, AL
pop 42,523
Central Time
Chamber of Commerce 205-549-0351

To See and Do

Downtown visit the **Center for Cultural Arts,** 205-543-2787, 5th &
Broad, for traveling exhibits as well as works by local and regional
artists; **Imagination Place** is a hands-on museum, special activities
and events include dinner theater, concerts, recitals, dance;
restaurant at lunchtime. The **Museum of Fine Arts,** 205-546-
7365, 2829 W Meighan Blvd, has a permanent collection of
paintings, sculpture, prints; monthly changing exhibits feature
local and regional artists.

This city on the Coosa makes good use of its river with the **Alabama
Princess,** 205-549-1111, Riverside Boardwalk, 300 Albert Rains
Blvd S in downtown Gadsden; it's an authentic replica of the
picturesque stern-wheeler excursion boats of America's last
century; the main deck is completely enclosed, the second deck is
covered; excursions, dinner cruises and charters available year-
round.

Legend has it that Indian Princess Noccalula threw herself over the 90-
foot waterfall rather than marry the neighboring Chief her father
had chosen; a statue is perched on the spot in **Noccalula Falls
Park,** 205-549-4663, Noccalula Rd, Hwy S211; also in the park
are botanical gardens, hiking trails lined with rock formations, and
picnic areas; camping is available.

In nearby **Turkeytown Ceremonial Grounds,** 205-549-0351, Hwy
U411, 5 miles north of Hwy U278, the Annual Cherokee Indian
PowWow and Green Corn Festival is held on the third week-end
of August each year; features traditional, inter-tribal and
competition dancing, lifestyle demonstrations, story-telling,
special music and song; Indian Traders with tribal foods, face
painting, arts and crafts, literature. Turkeytown Association of
the Cherokee, PO Box 1517, Gadsden, AL 35902.

Accommodations

Econo Lodge, 800-424-4777, 507 Cherry St; Attalla; **Holiday Inn
Express,** 800-HOLIDAY, 801 Cleveland Ave, Attalla.

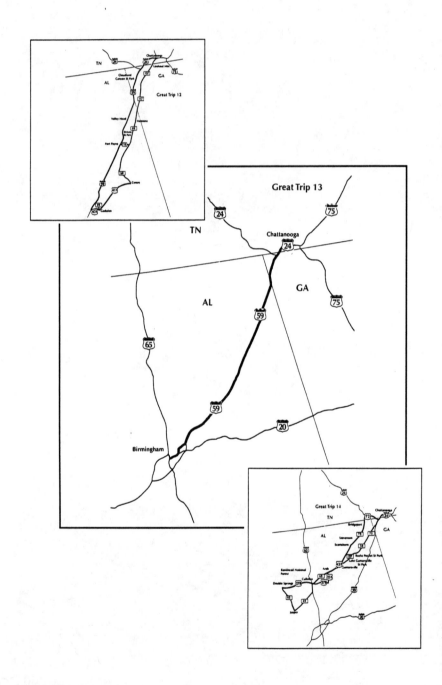

Great Trip 13

Chattanooga to Birmingham, AL
the steel magnolias route
via Birmingham and Bessemer, AL, returning to Chattanooga
approximately 350 miles round-trip, 6.5 hours driving time

Why Go

Grand Prize Vulcan Statue & Steel Furnaces & Iron Ore Mining &
Civil Rights Institute & Jazz Hall of Fame & Sports Hall of Fame &
Magnolia Trees & Wedgwood & Rucker Agee Maps &
City Stages & Linn Park & Red Mountain Cut & Peavine Falls &
Temple of Sibyl & Golf Trail & Social Animals &
International Medical Center & WWII Link Trainer &
Greyhound Racing & Fried Green Tomatoes

Suggested route with approximate mileages

Instruction	Road	Dir	Miles
Chattanooga to Birmingham	I-24 & I-59	S	150
Birmingham to Chattanooga	I-59 & I-24	N	150
Total Mileage			300

Rolling hills, green trees, an internationally known medical center, a tall iron statue watching over everything -- that's Birmingham, an easy, pleasant drive away on I-59. Visit the **Heart of Dixie**, and explore quaint neighborhoods on the side of several mountains, three wonderful downtown public spots, and a visit to the **Civil Rights Institute**, one of the most thoughtfully designed historical exhibits you will ever see.

Downtown, park and walk. Get information at the **Visitor Center**, *2200 9th, near the Sheraton;* it's just a few blocks under the freeway to the magnificent **Art Museum**, which is free. Stroll across the street to historic **Linn Park**, named after Charles Linn, one of the city's developers and promoters, who once threw a Calico Ball, inviting folks to the opening of his huge new bank which had been dubbed "Linn's Folly." People came from around the state; the women in calico gowns and the men in calico formal suits; the bank was saved! Fountains and tree-shaded benches invite you to rest in this area that serves as a greenway bridge between the governmental buildings and other downtown offices. Access the **Linn-Henley Research Library** from the Park; the **Atrium** section of the library is on the other side of the block.

Facing **Kelly Ingram Park**, at *5th Ave & 16th St*, is the **Civil Rights Institute**. A film introduces what you are about to see; then the screen lifts and invites you to walk through time, listening to voices and standing inside events as racial conflicts and resolutions evolve to present times. The fabulous **UAB Medical Center**, part of the 70-block campus area just south of downtown, is home to 17,000 students and has over 17,000 employees.

Drive on 20th to **Five Points South**, another park-and-walk spot. Beautiful churches, more fountains, outdoor dining, and interesting shops; pull up a chair and relax. A few blocks away **Cobb Lane** is nestled against the mountainside, outdoor dining is the norm.

You've almost reached **Vulcan Park** now, so drive up the mountain and stop to enjoy the view from the top of the town. Buy yourself a little Vulcan statue in the gift shop to take home for a souvenir. After all, the only statue in the country that's taller, or more famous, is the Statue of Liberty!

Birmingham, AL

pop 265,968
metro pop 907,810
Central Time
Visitors Bureau 205-252-9825

To See and Do

The Iron Man atop Red Mountain has been watching over the city of Birmingham since 1939. Start your visit with a stop at **Vulcan Statue and Park**, *205-328-6198, atop Red Mountain with entrance at corner of 20th St and Valley Ave.* There are fountains and picnic areas in the park, and from the observation deck there is a breathtaking view of the city's landmarks and the greater Birmingham area. Vulcan is one of the largest iron figures ever cast; standing on a pedestal 124 feet high, he's 55 feet tall and weighs 60 tons. And he's a prizewinner! Made of Birmingham iron and cast locally, he was designed and made as an exhibit for the 1904 St Louis World's Fair, and won the Grand Prize. He's named, of course, after the Roman mythical god of the forge, so is a symbol of the city's years as a "steel city."

For nearly 90 years Birmingham's foundries and mills were in operation; the giant furnaces which produced the pig iron they needed have been preserved for today's visitor to explore at **Sloss Furnaces National Historic Landmark**, *205-324-1911, beside First Ave N viaduct, entrance on 32nd St N.* The massive web of pipes and smokestacks tells the story of Birmingham's dramatic rise to prominence as the South's foremost industrial city; they also serve as a backdrop for concerts, dramas and other events regularly scheduled here.

Art and Museums

Gain a greater understanding of Birmingham, and the South, at the **Birmingham Civil Rights Institute**, *205-328-9696, 520 16th St N;* you go on a journey through time, with walk-through exhibits of life-sized people in the places they occupied during racial separation, struggle, and success; from post WWI to present-day. Sounds and speeches surround as you move from one scene to the next, creating an in-the-moment experience for the visitor. The Institute promotes on-going research on human rights issues through its educational programs. The Civil Rights District includes Kelly Ingram Park and the historic 16th St Baptist Church where much activity of the Civil Rights Movement took place.

The **Birmingham Museum of Art**, 205-254-2565, 2000 8th Ave N, has an outstanding permanent collection of over 17,000 works of art, including the largest collection of Wedgwood outside of England. See Renaissance, Asian and American art; Remington bronzes, pre-Columbian artifacts, and outdoors, a multi-level sculpture garden. There is no admission charge except for special events.

The **Birmingham Public Library**, 205-226-3600, 2100 Park Place, is one of the largest in the Southeast. The main library in the City Center has two buildings; the East Building has a dramatic atrium; the 1927 Linn-Henley Research Library has beautiful wall murals, the Tutwiler Collection of Southern History, and the historic Rucker Agee Map Collection. There are 19 branches.

Sports are bigtime in Alabama, and legendary figures such as Paul "Bear" Bryant are showcased in the **Alabama Sports Hall of Fame**, 205-323-6665, 2150 Civic Center Blvd in Birmingham-Jefferson Civic Center. Others so honored are Heisman Trophy winner Pat Sullivan, and boxer Joe Louis; there are outstanding displays on football, baseball, archery, and marksmanship.

Children and families can have fun learning at **Discovery 2000**, 205-933-4142, 14212 22nd St S. Most kids prefer hands-on learning, and there is plenty of it here; explore technology, the sciences, and the arts. More to experience at **Red Mountain Museum**, 205-933-4142, 1421 22nd St S, where a walkway carved into the face of the mountain exposes 150 million years of geologic history. The **Red Mountain Road Cut** is a National Natural Landmark. In the museum see fossils of dinosaurs and Ice Age mammals; geologic history displays and exhibits.

Alabama Theatre for the Performing Arts, 205-ALA-BAMA, 1817 Third Ave N, hosts more than 250 evenings of entertainment a year, such as Broadway shows, ballet, opera, fashion shows and beauty pageants. A summer film series features classic films, with a prelude by the Mighty Wurlitzer organ. Opened in 1927 and renovated in 1987, tours are available for the historic theater.

Who wrote the jazz standard *Tuxedo Junction*? Erskine Hawkins, any jazz-lover will answer. Hawkins is a Birmingham native; the "junction" was a streetcar crossing in nearby Ensley. Learn about other jazz greats at the **Alabama Jazz Hall of Fame**, *205-254-2731, 1631 Fourth Ave N*; displays feature Lionel Hampton, Erskine Hawkins, Sun Ra and more; from the beginning of jazz to present day.

In nearby Bessemer is the **Hall of History Museum**, *205-426-1633, 1905 Alabama Ave*; it's in a 1916 Southern Railway Terminal and displays fossils, Indian mound excavations, and Pioneer and Civil War relics. **Pioneer Homes** are open for tours by appointment; they are original structures dating back to 1817, furnished with period pieces; all on the National Register of Historic Places. The **Sadler Plantation**, 1838, is considered one of Alabama's finest examples of plantation architecture.

Alabama Museum of the Health Sciences and Reynolds Historical Library, *205-934-4475, 1700 University Blvd*, has displays relating to the history of medicine and health professions; ivory anatomical mannequins; collection of rare books representing the history of health sciences.

At the **Southern Museum of Flight**, *205-833-8226, 4343 73rd St N*, you'll find 15 restored aircraft, vintage 1912 to 1990, and hundreds of models; a WWII Link trainer used to teach pilots to fly "blind," and mementos from the notorious WWI Red Baron.

Robert R Meyer Planetarium, *205-226-4770, on Birmingham-Southern College campus*; presentations are open to the public the first and third weekends of each month; if your interest is astronomy, you'll enjoy the feeling of being on a giant space platform where celestial bodies seem almost within reach.

Historical Homes and Gardens

A glimpse of the old South at **Arlington Antebellum Home and Gardens**, *205-780-5656, 331 Cotton Ave SW*; this Greek Revival mansion was built in 1842 and is authentically furnished with period furnishings; includes a diverse collection of 19th century American decorative art. Set in lovely gardens on a sloping hill in Elyton, the house is surrounded by oak and magnolia trees. Call about the special Thursday lunches.

The **Birmingham Botanical Gardens**, *205-879-1227, 2612 Lane Park Rd*, are a living museum; thousands of flowers, trees, and shrubs are displayed on 68 acres with specialized plant collections, a Japanese garden and bonsai complex, and one of the largest glass conservatories in the Southeast. Also 230 species of native birds, an arboretum of rare plants and trees, and a Touch and See Trail for the disabled.

For tremendous views of Shades Valley and the Samford University campus, stop at the **Temple of Sibyl**, *Hwy 31 at entrance to city of Vestavia Hills*, on top of Shades Mountain. A replica of the temple of Sibyl at Tivoli near Rome, it's listed on the Alabama Register of Landmarks and Heritage.

Entertainment and Tours

Bird lovers will enjoy the aviary at the **Birmingham Zoo**, *205-879-0408, 2630 Cahaba Rd;* the 100-acre parkland offers natural outdoor settings for many animals; there is also a Predators Building, Social Animals Building, and a Cheetah exhibit. Watch them feed the sea lions. Guides for the blind upon request.

Ruffner Mountain Nature Center, *205-833-8264, 1214 S 81st St,* is only eight miles from downtown, but this 538-acre urban forest is one of the last undeveloped sections of the Appalachian Mountains. It offers an unusual view of the city skyline as well as unusual geological formations. Exhibits depict the mountain's natural and iron-ore-mining history; there are more than seven miles of hiking trails in this wildlife refuge; maps are available, and environmental programs offered.

Sports fans, follow the Southern League with the **Birmingham Barons Baseball Club**, *205-988-3200, 100 Ben Chapman Dr,* they play at Hoover Metropolitan Stadium; or try your hand at picking the winners at the **Birmingham Race Course**, *205-838-7500, and 1-800-998-UBET, between Hwy U11 and I-20 near I-459 on 100 John Rogers Dr;* the year-round greyhound racing is live; horse racing from tracks all over the country is simulcast; track level accommodates 2,500. Alabama-Auburn still duke it out in **Legion Field**, a Big Event at the end of November, for those who love the taste of SEC football.

For golf, **Oxmoor Valley**, *205-942-1177, 100 Sunbelt Pkwy,* is on Alabama's **Robert Trent Jones Golf Trail**; a 54-hole facility; Ridge Course has heavy tree cover and 150-foot elevation changes, the Valley Course is dotted with lakes; public.

Events

City Stages, a Birmingham Cultural & Heritage Festival, 3-day music festival centered in downtown's Linn Park, covers 12 city blocks, mid June; **Birmingham Oktoberfest**, 205-923-6564, *Sloss Furnaces, 2nd Ave N and 32nd St N, late September;* **Alabama State Fair**, 205-786-8100, *Fairgrounds,* mid-October.

Accommodations

Downtown hotels include the **Sheraton Civic Center**, 800-325-3535, *2101 Civic Center Blvd;* **Holiday Inn Redmont**, 800-HOLIDAY, *2101 5th Ave N;* **Best Western Civic Center Inn**, 800-528-1234, *2230 Civic Center Blvd;* all near the **Birmingham-Jefferson Civic Center & Coliseum**. Enjoy outdoor dining and strolling at Five Points South and at Cobb Lane; some interesting spots are **Cobb Lane Restaurant**, 205-933-0462, *1 Cobb Lane;* with garden courtyard dining; **Highland Bar & Grill**, 205-939-1400, *2011 11th Ave S;* **Hot and Hot Fish Club**, 205-933-5474, *2180 11th Ct S;* and **The Mill Bakery, Eatery, Brewery**, 205-939-3001, *1035 20th St S,* where outdoor tables face the fountain. For a picnic in the park, stop at **Savage's Bakery & Restaurant**, 205-871-4901, *2916 18th St S* for box lunches; a downtown tradition is **John's Restaurant**, 205-322-6014, *112 21st St N;* out in Irondale get your Fried Green Tomatoes right where the train stopped at the original **Whistle Stop Cafe**, 205-956-5258, *1906 1st Ave N.*

Alabama State Parks
Central Time

Oak Mountain State Park, 205-620-2524, *15 mi S on I-65, exit 246;* Peavine Falls and Gorge and two lakes sit amidst 9,940 acres of the state's most rugged mountains. Swimming, hiking, backpacking, bridle trails, camping and a demonstration farm.

Rickwood Caverns State Park, 205-647-9692, *20 mi N on I-65, exit 284;* this 380-acre park offers swimming and hiking. One-hour tours of cave with 260-million-year-old limestone formations.

Accommodations

Oak Mountain State Park, *Office* 205-620-2520, *Campground* 205-620-2527, 10 cabins, 93 campsites. **Rickwood Caverns State Park**, 205-647-9692, 13 campsites.

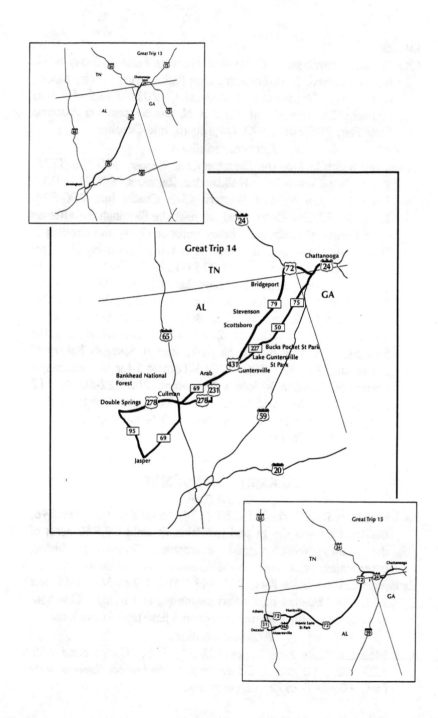

Great Trip 14

Chattanooga to Double Springs, AL
the rivers and forests route
*via Bridgeport, Stevenson, Scottsboro, Cullman, Double Springs,
Bankhead National Forest, Jasper, Smith Lake, Guntersville, Lake
Guntersville St Pk, Bucks Pocket St Pk, returning to Chattanooga
approximately 350 miles round-trip, 7 hours driving time*

Why Go
Russell Cave & Prehistoric Relics & Tater Knob & Goose Pond &
Little Jerusalem & Looney's Tavern Park & Free State of Winston &
Smith Lake & Bankhead National Forest & Sipsey Wilderness &
Black Warrior River & Swift Streams & Limestone Bluffs &
500-Year-Old Poplar & Fishing & Canoeing & Coal-Miner Statue &
Tennessee River & Lake Guntersville & Bucks Pocket

Suggested route with approximate mileages

Instruction	Road	Dir	Miles
Chattanooga to Bridgeport	I-24 & U72	S	38
Bridgeport to Stevenson	U72	S	18
Stevenson to Scottsboro	U72	S	20
Scottsboro to Cullman	U72 & S79 & S69 & U231 & U278	S	43
Cullman to Double Springs	U278	W	37
Double Springs to Jasper	S195	S	24
Jasper to Guntersville	S69	N	73
Guntersville to Lake Guntersville St Pk	S227	N	11
Lake Guntersville St Pk to Bucks Pocket St Pk	S227	N	13
Bucks Pocket St Pk to Chattanooga	S75 & I-59 & I-24	N	70
Total Mileage			347

Don't get dizzy with all the highway changes. You'll be glad you ventured off the main roads for a while into a landscape that shapes the towns and the lifestyles of the people who live there.

Follow the path of the mighty **Tennessee River** as it moves in a southerly direction in the valley between Sand Mountain and mountains named Crow, Poorhouse, July, and Tater Knob. You are treated to many magnificent river views as you ride. Learn the history of early Alabama in museums along the way, beginning with **Russell Cave National Monument** near Bridgeport.

Stay a while in Cullman, a town with a heavy German influence, and visit unique **Ave Maria Grotto**, a miniature Jerusalem on the grounds of St Bernard Abbey. The drive from Cullman literally "loops" around **Lewis Smith Lake**, a 21,000-acre lake with 500 miles of shoreline, made from the **Sipsey River**, which becomes the **Black Warrior** at the dam. You are now in the **Bankhead National Forest.**

Before you get into Double Springs, you will arrive at **Looney's Tavern Amphitheater and Park.** If it is summertime, make sure you called ahead for tickets to the **"Free State of Winston" Civil War drama** and a ride on Smith Lake aboard the **Free State Lady riverboat.**

South to Jasper through the Bankhead Forest; explore the many recreation areas for adventure-level wilderness hiking or couch-potato picnicking just a few feet from the car. Jasper is **coal-mining country**; there is a museum about mining just east in Dora, and you're likely to see coal-hauling trucks on the road. Scenic Highway 69 between Jasper and Cullman brings you around the south side of Smith Lake; a short drive will take you to the Dam, or a bit farther to **Duskin Point**, where you can pop right into fishing mode; make sure you've brought your fishing gear.

Continue north on Highway 69 to Guntersville, this time to stay a while. The fishing gear gets double duty on this Trip! Perhaps you'll want to stay at **Lake Guntersville State Park**; maybe you prefer more seclusion at **Buck's Pocket**. You're on top of Sand Mountain now, a pleasant drive ahead on its broad flat top to bring you home.

Bridgeport, AL
pop 2,936
Central Time
Jackson County Chamber of Commerce
205-259-5500

To See and Do
The railroad bridge in Bridgeport was a major supply route during the Civil War; wagons and then cars crossed the Tennessee River on "the Bridgeport Ferry" for over a hundred years, and many people still prefer the charm of a water crossing to the speedier highway route. North of town is **Russell Cave National Monument**, 205-495-2672, 7 *mi* NE of Bridgeport off Hwy U72. The archaeological cave shelter has record of human habitation from 7000 BC to 1000 AD; prehistoric relics are on display in the visitor center and programs are held inside the cave and on the nature trails. The tours are self-guided, though guided tours are available for groups with reservations and living history demonstrations will be made upon request; also picnic facilities in this 310-acre park.

Stevenson, AL
pop 2,046
Central Time
Jackson County Chamber of Commerce
205-259-5500

To See and Do
You'll find more Civil War artifacts, railroading history, and displays of Native American heritage at the **Railroad Depot**, 205-437-3012, *off Hwy U72;* built in the 1850's, the depot was an important junction during the Civil War and showcases the past.

Scottsboro, AL
pop 13,786
Central Time
Jackson County Chamber of Commerce
205-259-5500

To See and Do
More of the past is preserved at the **Scottsboro-Jackson Heritage Center**, *205-259-2122, 208 S Houston St*. The centerpiece of the downtown complex is the 1880's Greek Revival Brown-Proctor house; "Sage Town," a collection of pioneer log structures, houses year-round exhibits, classes, and demonstrations of early north Alabama life.

Goose Pond Colony Recreation Complex, *800-268-2884, 417 Ed Hembree Dr, off Hwy S79, on Lake Guntersville*, is a sprawling 360-acre peninsula park bounded on three sides by the Guntersville reservoir of the Tennessee River. A 1,500-seat amphitheater overlooks the river; there are 5 miles of walking trails, an 18-hole championship golf course, an Olympic-size pool with bath house, and a marina with pontoon boats available for rent.

Accommodations
Days Inn, *800-329-7466, 1106 John T Reid Pkwy*; **Goose Pond Colony**, *800-268-2884, Hwy 79S*; cottages with kitchens and screened porch or deck, 117 campsites, playground; **Crawdaddy's Restaurant**, *205-574-3071*, in the complex.

Cullman, AL
pop 13,367
Central Time
Cullman County Visitors Bureau
205-734-0454

To See and Do
In 1873 Col John G Cullman, a German refugee, established a colony in north Alabama that was called "Die Duetsche Kolonie Von Nord Alabama." You can see a replica of Cullman's home in the **Cullman County Museum**, *205-739-1258, 211 2nd Ave NE*, as

well as a replica of a city street of the 1800's. The Cullman Archaeological Society has displays here too. One of the most loved, most unique attractions in Cullman is **Ave Maria Grotto**, *205-734-4110, 1600 St Bernard Dr SE, off Hwy U278*, located on the grounds of St Bernard Abbey. St Bernard is Alabama's only Benedictine Abbey; the Grotto was built by Brother Joseph Zoettl, who came to the abbey in 1892 from Bavaria. It's known as Little Jerusalem, a miniature fairyland consisting of 125 small stone and cement structures -- reproductions of famous churches, buildings and shrines. The creation was a hobby for Brother Joseph, who used materials sent from all over the world; he was 80 when he built his last model, the Basilica in Lourdes, in 1958. He died in 1961 and is buried in the Abbey cemetery.

Outside of town you'll find **Hurricane Creek Park**, *205-734-2125, Hwy U31, 7 miles north of Cullman*; in the rustic park is a swinging bridge over a waterfall, a natural spiral staircase, and nature trails speckled with stone sculptures; return from your hike by small cable car; and **Clarkson Covered Bridge**, *Hwy U278*; named to the National Register of Historic Places, it is Alabama's largest covered truss bridge; hiking trails and picnic grounds.

Accommodations
Days Inn, *800-325-2525, 1841 4th St SW*; **Holiday Inn Express**, *800-HOLIDAY, I65 Exit 304*; **Howard Johnson Lodge**, *800-446-4656, I65 Exit 308*; **Ramada Inn**, *205-734-8484, I65 Exit 304*. A number of restaurant choices in town, join the crowd that comes from miles around to the **All Steak House**, *205-734-4322, 414 2nd Ave SW*; known for vegetables and desserts too.

Double Springs, AL
pop 1,138
Central Time
Tourist Assistance 205-489-5000

To See and Do
Go for the show at **Looney's Tavern Amphitheater and Park**, *800-566-6397, 205-489-5000, Hwy U278E, 6 miles east of Double Springs*; but make your reservations ahead of time. The 1,500-seat amphitheatre is in a complex of restaurants, stores, an indoor

theater, and even miniature golf, all in a beautiful setting in the **Sipsey Wilderness** area of the **Bankhead National Forest**. The Confederate flag hangs alongside the Union flag here as a reminder of the struggle in Winston County, which voted not to secede from the Union. The play, *"Free State of Winston,"* tells the story of schoolteacher Christopher Sheats, who was elected to go to Montgomery's secession convention and was ultimately imprisoned for his stand against secession; it's told entertainingly with music, dance and humor in this summertime production. A variety of musical productions indoors in the **Dual Destiny Showcase Theater**, call for schedule.

While you're there, cruise the waters of **Smith Lake** on the *"Free State Lady,"* 800-566-6397, a paddlewheel-style **riverboat**; and enjoy yarns spun by master storytellers in hill-country hospitality style. Part legend? Part history? Part tall-tale? You guess! Early dinner and moonlight dinner cruises are available on showdate weekends; reservations are required.

Accommodations

Sister Sara's Kitchen, *800-566-6397, in the complex;* is open year round and is known for its mountain "fixins," the hill-country buffet includes chicken 'n dumplins, ham and beans, and even cracklin' cornbread and buttermilk; enjoy the spectacular view of the Bankhead Forest.

National Forest
Central Time

The **Bankhead National Forest**, *205-489-5111, Ranger District Office Hwy S33N of Double Springs,* is Alabama's largest national forest, with 180,000 acres; in the forest is the nationally designated Wild and Scenic River, the Sipsey. Called the **Land of a Thousand Waterfalls**, the area is ideal for hiking, horseback riding, hunting, boating, fishing, swimming, canoeing, and more. You'll see rare birds, mammals, an abundance of swift streams, limestone bluffs, wildlife, wildflowers and the states largest tree, a 500-year-old 150-foot tall poplar. Indian relics abound in the Bankhead, one of the southeast's premier sites for petroglyphs, prehistoric drawings and rock carvings.

Brushy Creek Lake Recreation Area, *15 miles S of Moulton off Hwy S33,* a remote environment, has 400 acres for recreation, and a 33-acre manmade lake; boating, canoeing, fishing, boat launch; swimming, camping, nature and hiking trails, ball field.

Clear Creek Recreation Area, *13.5 miles N of Jasper off Hwy S195;* has 425 acres adjacent to **Lewis Smith Lake;** waterfalls, high bluffs, sandy white beach, boating, canoeing, fishing, boat launch, swimming, camping, nature and hiking trails.

Houston Recreation Area, *12 mi E of Double Springs off Hwy U278,* adjacent to **Lewis Smith Lake,** with 3 camping loops; swimming, picnicking, boating, canoeing, boat launch, nature trails.

Sipsey Wilderness Area, *8.5 miles NE of Haleyville off Hwy S195,* has 26,000 acres of wildland, diverse topography, plant and wildlife; sandstone bluffs, flowing streams, canyons and gorges combined with pine and hardwood and native wildlife; one of most unique areas in southeast. Fishing, camping, nature trails, hiking. Open year round, it's a real paradise for hikers and canoe enthusiasts, with gorges, cool, moist canyons, virgin timber, exotic plants, and rare birds and mammals; fish in the **Sipsey Branch** of the **Black Warrior River;** if you hike along **Bee Branch** from Forest Rd 208, you'll encounter a rock-rimmed box canyon with sheer vertical walls rising 100 feet.

Accommodations

Get camping information from the **Bankhead Ranger District Office,** *205-489-5111, Hwy S33 north of Double Springs.*

Jasper, AL
pop 13,553
Central Time
Chamber of Commerce 205-384-4571

To See and Do

A hundred years ago there were six coal mines and four hundred coke ovens operating in **Jasper;** today a branch of the **University of Alabama** is located here on a 37-acre campus in a town with lovely residential areas; people still talk about President Franklin Roosevelt's visit when he attended Speaker Bankhead's funeral in the downtown **Methodist Church;** a special ramp was built to accommodate his wheelchair; a plaque marks where he sat.

In nearby Dora, you can learn more of the history of mining at the **Alabama Mining Museum**, *205-648-2442, 120 East St, off Hwy U78W*, which depicts the **coal mines** and their development from 1890 to 1940. Lots of interesting pictures and memorabilia; plus you'll see a **coal car**, **mining tools**, and rooms set up to show the miner's life -- the doctor's office, post office, time office, and the company store, where small coins called **"clackers"** were used as money. More than five mines are operating in that area of the state today though not open for touring.

In the other direction is **Old York USA Heritage Park**, *205-622-3951, Hwy S69S in Oakman*. It's a western theme town that takes you back 100 years, they have special events each month, call for hours.

Accommodations

Old Harbin Hotel, *205-697-5652, 3rd St at McDaniel Ave, Nauvoo*; historic hotel has four rooms, full breakfast; **William Cook House**, *205-272-1972, William Cook Pkwy, Nauvoo*; 4 rooms in house built by Scottish immigrants, reflects old-country setting. **Quigley's Tearoom**, *205-384-1963, 401 E 19th St*, serves lunch and dinner in a beautifully decorated house; make dinner reservations in advance. **Uncle Mort's Country Store, Smokehouse & Restaurant**, *205-483-7614, Hwy U78*, serves inhouse-cured ham, bacon and porkchops; served with sorghum syrup, biscuits and redeye gravy. Check out the store for a coal-miner statue carved of southern bituminous coal, or buy smokehouse meat by the pound.

Guntersville, AL
pop 7,038
Central Time
Marshall County Tourism 205-582-7015
Lake Guntersville Chamber of Commerce
205-582-3612

To See and Do

Recreation here is centered on 30-mile-long, 69,000-square mile **Guntersville Lake**; with 949 miles of winding shoreline it seems to surround the town and is loved for wonderful swimming, skiing, boating and sailing, and not the least for its bass and crappie fishing. December's Parade of Lights is a water-lit delight. An interesting non-water spot to visit is **Ryder's Replica Fighter Museum,** *205-582-4309, Hwy U431N,* where you'll see the world's largest collection of replica aircraft from 1916-18 and meticulous examples of most significant fighter aircraft. Also antique automobiles.

Accommodations

Days Inn, *800-DAYSINN, 14040 Hwy U431S;* **Holiday Inn,** *800-HOLIDAY, 2140 Gunter Ave.*

Alabama State Parks
Central Time

Lake Guntersville State Park; *800-ALA-PARK, 205-571-5444,* off *Hwy S227,* resort facility offering lodge accommodations, cottages, chalets and campground; swimming, boating, fishing, golf, tennis, picnic area, nature center, hiking trails, overlooking majestic 66,470-acre Guntersville Reservoir; park sits on Little Mountain, ranges over 5,909 acres of ridge tops and meadows. American bald eagles winter in the park.

Bucks Pocket State Park, *800-ALA-PARK, 205-659-2000, 2 mi off Hwy 227, NE of Grove Oak,* secluded in natural pocket of Appalachian Mountain chain, this 2,000-acre park is a naturalist's dream. Mountain vistas, serenity; boat launch, fishing area, picnicking, playground, hiking, campground.

Accommodations

Lake Guntersville State Park Lodge, *800-548-4553, 1155 Lodge Dr;* 100 rooms, fireplaces, on 500-ft bluff overlooking lake, park also has 15 lakeview cottages, 322 campsites; restaurant, golf, tennis. **Bucks Pocket State Park,** *205-659-2000,* 48 campsites.

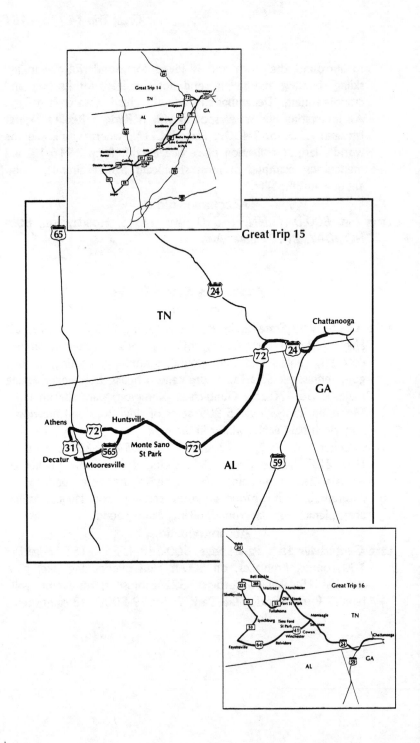

Great Trip 14

TN

GA

AL

Chattanooga
Bridgeport

Stevenson

Scottsboro

Buck Pocket St Park
Lake Guntersville
St Park
Guntersville

Bankhead National
Forest

Double Springs

Cullman

Jasper

Great Trip 15

TN

Chattanooga

72   24

GA

AL

Athens   Huntsville

Decatur

Mooresville

Monte Sano
St Park

72

65

24

31   72

565

72

59

Great Trip 16

TN

Chattanooga

Bell Buckle

Manchester

Wartrace

Shelbyville

Tullahoma

Lynchburg

Fayetteville

Tims Ford
St Park

Old Stone
Fort St Park

Monteagle

Sewanee

Winchester   Cowan

Belvidere

GA

AL

24

231   269

82

55

50

64

41

24

59

Great Trip 15

Chattanooga to Huntsville, AL
the back to the future route
via Huntsville, Athens, Decatur, and Mooresville,
returning to Chattanooga
approximately 285 miles round-trip, 5.5 hours driving time

Why Go
Rocket Center & Saturn V & Space Shuttle & Space Camp &
Spacedome & Constitution Village & Costumed Guides &
Twickenham & Civil War Poet & Burritt Mansion & 1860 Depot &
Golf Trail & Monte Sano Park & Wheeler Wildlife Refuge &
Beaverdam Peninsula & 1819 Post Office & Stagecoach Inn &
Old Time Fiddlers Convention

Suggested route with approximate mileages

Instruction	Road	Dir	Miles
Chattanooga to Huntsville	I-24 & U72	SW	109
Huntsville to Athens	U72	W	24
Athens to Decatur	U31 & U72	S	15
Decatur to Mooresville	U72	E	8
Mooresville to Chattanooga	U72 & I-565 & I-24	NE	129
Total Mileage			285

Of course you're going to plan a trip to Huntsville. The drive is pleasant, the city is interesting, and your patriotic spirit calls you to go. Patriotic? Well yes. A visit to the **US Space and Rocket Center** is your ticket to accompanying our astronauts into outer space through the medium of film. The real-live spacecraft that have "been there" sit proudly in **Rocket Park**. Even more exciting is a visit to the **Marshall Space Flight Center**, where work on our future space shuttle is underway. And kids can set their sights on the stars with a week at **US Space Camp**.

Patriotic too because Huntsville is filled with carefully recreated scenes from the past, such as **Constitution Village**, where costumed guides show you the way things used to be. Alabama's statehood began here, at the Constitutional Convention of 1819. The nearby town of **Mooresville** also takes you back; the entire village is on the National Historic Register; the state's oldest post office is here, with original pre-Civil War call boxes.

So much history on this tour! In Huntsville's **Twickenham Historic District**, which you can self-tour or request a guide, some of the antebellum homes are occupied by descendants of the original owners! The **Huntsville Depot** is one of America's oldest railroad structures; inside you'll enjoy the HO-gauge recreation of Huntsville in the 1860's.

In nearby Athens, on the campus of Alabama's oldest institute of higher learning, admire the altar in **Founders Hall**. It was built in 1842, and the elegant wood carvings tell the story of the New Testament. **Athens State College** lays claim to another "preservation;" that of our musical heritage, as it hosts the "Granddaddy of Midsouth Fiddlers Conventions," the **Tennessee Valley Old Time Fiddlers Convention**, every year.

And, at the **Wheeler National Wildlife Refuge** in Decatur, you can be proud of the fine area that has been set aside for wintering migratory birds. "Wintering" means, of course, that you need to visit in the wintertime to see the great variety of birds. Toss a warm jacket in the car along with the binoculars, for some of the finest **Wildlife Viewing** you'll ever experience.

Huntsville, AL
pop 159,789
Central Time
Visitors Bureau 205-551-2230

To See and Do

Huntsville is an amazing blend of the past and the future. Space exploration is the mind-boggler at the **US Space and Rocket Center and NASA Visitor Center**, *205-837-3400 or 800-63-SPACE, One Tranquility Base, I-565.* You see the rockets as you approach, poised and looking ready to do it again, an impressive sight. Parked in **Rocket Park** are a full-size shuttle and a Saturn V moon rocket; part of the collection of NASA rockets developed in Huntsville. Inside, get into the action in the **Spacedome Theater;** it has a 67-foot screen and shows films photographed by astronauts; because it's actual shuttle footage, it gives the sense of being aboard space missions; effects are heightened by use of Super 70mm Omnimax and multi-speaker stereophonic sound; films are about 45 minutes each. Yes, there is a **US Space Camp;** know anyone with astronaut aspirations? They offer one-week programs for children from 4th grade up. Visit the camp training center and watch trainees experience weightlessness on a Zero-G machine, guide spacecraft by computer, fire a rocket engine, or go on a simulated Shuttle flight. NASA bus tours escort you through the **Marshall Space Flight Center**, Mission Control; there you'll see various Space Shuttle components; it's where scientists are designing portions of the space station.

The modern **Von Braun Civic Center**, *700 Monroe St, downtown,* is named for space pioneer Dr. Werner von Braun and has a 9,000-seat arena, a 2,171-seat concert hall, and a 502-seat theater.

After the excitement of technology, slow down and review the beginnings at **Alabama Constitution Village**, *800-678-1819, 109 Gates Ave E, downtown Huntsville.* It is a living history museum, portraying a view of life as it was 175 years ago and recreated on original sites. The park commemorates the place where the 1819 Constitutional Convention was held and the document was written that prepared the way for Alabama's statehood. Today costumed guides lead you on a tour of a working village (1805-1819), complete with a cabinetmaker's shop, print shop, confectionery shop, theater, library, and post office. The museum offers exhibits and special events too.

Continue your reflections of the past in **The Twickenham Historic District**, south and east of courthouse square, where you'll see the largest collection of antebellum houses in the state. Some of the homes are occupied by descendants of the original owners. Groups can request guided tours from the **Visitors Bureau**, 205-551-2230. Otherwise, enjoy a self-guided drive or walk through the area.

The **Weeden House Museum**, 205-536-7718, 300 Gates Ave SE, is the former home of noted artist and poet Maria Howard Weeden, who supported her family after the Civil War by teaching art and writing poems about ex-slaves and masters. The home features handcarved woodwork and mantles and original glass.

Another home open to the public is at **Burritt Museum and Park**, 205-536-2882, 3101 Burritt Dr, off Hwy U431. The 167-acre Park contains the **Burritt Mansion** and a collection of 19th century historic rural structures. The 11-room mansion, one of the city's most unusual architectural landmarks, was built in the shape of a cross, and contains exhibitions on southern women, archaeology, and antiques. Many special events are held here throughout the year, such as Earth Day, Indian Heritage Festival, and Candlelight Christmas. There are nature trails and picnic facilities on the grounds.

More Huntsville history and some fun at the **Huntsville Depot Museum**, 205-531-1860, 320 Church St. Take a trolley for a tour of downtown, or go on a guided tour of the depot; see an HO-gauge recreation of the city in the 1860's, the roundhouse, a working turntable, and a steam locomotive. The depot, built in 1860, is one of America's oldest railroad structures.

Indoor enjoyment at the **Huntsville Museum of Art**, 205-535-4350, 700 Monroe St, which has a variety of visual art, with traditional traveling exhibitions, and one-person shows by

Alabama artists. The museum's permanent collection emphasizes 19th and 20th century American paintings and graphics; there is an art education gallery and tours, talks and films during year.

Outdoor pleasures at **Huntsville/Madison County Botanical Gardens,** *205-830-4447, 4747 Bob Wallace Ave,* which provide 112 acres of woodland paths, grassy meadows, and colorful flower gardens in the middle of the city.

Big Spring International Park, *Spragins St W of Courthouse Square,* is the best example of the city's past and present. Truly where Huntsville began, the town grew around the spring and it's still Huntsville's water supply, producing 24 million gallons a day.

Alabama's **Robert Trent Jones Golf Trail** begins at **Hampton Cove,** *205-551-1818, 450 Old Hwy U431S,* a 54-hole facility with Highlands Course and River Course; public.

Accommodations

Courtyard by Marriott, *800-321-2211, 4804 University Dr;* **Days Inn North,** *800-325-2525, 2201 N Memorial Pkwy;* **Hampton Inn,** *800-426-7866, 4815 University Dr;* **Holiday Inn Space Center,** *800-HOLIDAY, 3810 University Dr;* **Hilton,** *800-HILTONS, 401 Williams Ave;* **Radisson Suite,** *800-333-3333, 6000 Memorial Pkwy;* **Ramada,** *800-228-2828, 3502 S Memorial Pkwy.* **Wandlers Inn,** *205-837-6694, 101 Shawnee Dr NW,* is a one-bedroom apartment in a restored antebellum barn, full breakfast, country setting.

Alabama State Park
Central Time

Monte Sano State Park, *800-ALA-PARK, 205-534-3757, atop Monte Sano Mountain;* this 2,140-acre state park is almost in the city, with a mountaintop perch 1,000 feet above the eastern edge. Opened in 1935, it provides wonderful scenic views, trees, and wildflowers; picnic areas and hiking trails.

Accommodations

Monte Sano State Park , *205-534-3757,* has rustic cottages with views from atop the mountain; playground.

Athens, AL
pop 16,901
Central Time
Chamber of Commerce 205-232-2600

To See and Do
Athens State College, 205-233-8100, 300 N Beaty St, off Hwy U31, is Alabama's oldest institute of higher learning. Greek Revival Founders Hall was built in 1842; its altar consists of elegant wood carvings telling the story of the New Testament. Over 12,000 people gather on the campus each year for the **Tennessee Valley Old Time Fiddlers Convention**, 205-233-8100; it's been around since 1957, and is known as the "Granddaddy of Midsouth Fiddlers Conventions" for its role in reviving the tradition of competition in old time music.

Accommodations
Days Inn, 800-DAYS INN, 1322 Hwy U72E; **Travelodge**, 800-578-7878, 1325 Hwy U72E.

Decatur, AL
pop 48,761
Central Time
Chamber of Commerce 205-353-5312

To See and Do
Wheeler National Wildlife Refuge, 205-350-6639, off I-65; is a wintering area for migratory birds; the Refuge is one of the South's largest educational and viewing areas for wildlife. It sits on an island created by Wheeler Dam; from the observation platform on **Beaverdam Peninsula** you can observe flights of migratory waterfowl from September through May. In the **Givens Wildlife Interpretive Center** are displays of native animals and a program on the hour; hiking trails, nature study.

More study of nature at **Cook's Natural Science Museum**, 205-350-9347, 412 13th St E, where exhibits feature beautiful and exotic animals in their natural habitats; also rocks and minerals, seashells, and coral.

Accommodations

Days Inn, 800-325-2525, 810 6th Ave NE; **Holiday Inn,** 800-HOLIDAY, 1101 6th Ave; **Ramada Limited,** 800-228-2828, 1317 E Hwy S67. Bed and breakfasts include **Dancy-Polk House,** 205-353-3579, 901 Railroad St NW, 1829 Palladian-style house, furnished with antiques, 2 rooms, upper porch; **Hearts & Treasures Bed & Breakfast,** 205-353-9562, 911 7th Ave SE, 1920's home, antiques, fireplace. **Point Mallard Campground,** 205-350-3000, 1800 Point Mallard Dr SE, 175 campsites.

Mooresville, AL
Central Time
Historic Mooresville 800-648-5381
Limestone County Chamber of Commerce 205-232-2600

This entire picturesque village, incorporated in 1818, is listed on the National Register of Historic Places. The one-mile-square community once was home to Andrew Johnson, our 17th President. The **Mooresville post office** has been in continual operation since 1819, and features original call boxes built prior to the Civil War. Other points of interest are the 1839 community brick church with a slave balcony, the old tavern, and the 1825 stagecoach inn.

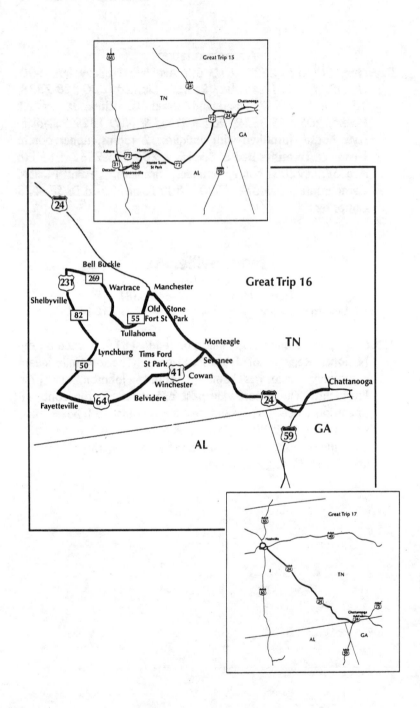

Great Trip 16

Chattanooga to Shelbyville, TN
the high stepping slow sipping route
*via Manchester, Tullahoma, Wartrace, Bell Buckle, Shelbyville, Lynchburg,
Fayetteville, Belvidere, Winchester, Cowan, Sewanee, Monteagle,
returning to Chattanooga
approximately 245 miles round-trip, 5 hours driving time*

Why Go
Tennessee Walking Horses & National Celebration & Horse Farms &
Tipsy Cake & Tennessee Whiskey & Cave Spring Water & Trout Farm &
Elk River & Falls Mill & Mountain Tunnel & Wind Tunnels &
Baseball Bats & Custom Guitars & Strolling Jim & Quilt Walk &
Moon Pie Festival & Fishing & Boating & Sewanee Summer Music

Suggested route with approximate mileages

Instruction	Road	Dir	Miles
Chattanooga to Manchester	I-24	N	68
Manchester to Tullahoma	U41	W	12
Tullahoma to Wartrace	S269	N	18
Wartrace to Bell Buckle	S269	N	6
Bell Buckle to Shelbyville	S82 & U231	W & S	13
Shelbyville to Lynchburg	S82 & S55	S	17
Lynchburg to Fayetteville	S50	S	15
Fayetteville to Belvidere	U64	E	27
Belvidere to Winchester	U64	E	5
Winchester to Cowan	U64	E	4
Cowan to Sewanee	U64	E	4
Sewanee to Monteagle	U64	E	10
Monteagle to Chattanooga	I-24	S	46
Total Mileage			245

Tennessee Sour Mash Whiskey and **Tennessee Walking Horses** -- famous around the world and uniquely situated in middle Tennessee, the background for this Trip. The pure cave-spring water is the reason the distilleries are here; the rolling hills are perfect for grazing horses.

A number of places invite you to stop and tour; some of them require advance notice. One of those is the **Arnold Engineering Development Center** at the Air Force Base. If missiles and space systems are of interest to you, it's worth the effort, they have over 50 test facilities. Other places on this Trip have regularly scheduled tours you are welcome to join, some will let you tour on an informal basis; check ahead to be sure.

Pull off the freeway along about **Manchester**, and don't get in a hurry again till you've looped your way back to **Monteagle**. The countryside is so pretty you'll run out of film long before you get home.

Stop at **Old Stone Fort Archaeological State Park**; the earth and stone enclosure is over 2,000 years old; walk the wall and cliff perimeter. Watch for bats in **Tullahoma**, baseballs too; millions are manufactured annually at the family-run Worth business. North of Tullahoma is the first distillery tour at **George Dickel**; more cave-water at **Nut Cave Trout Farm**. Follow the country roads to **Wartrace**, and **Bell Buckle**; soak in the countryside.

Visit some of the more than 40 horse farms here; Shelbyville's Chamber will give you a map; always call ahead, of course. Two big annual events in **Shelbyville** draw horse-lovers from everywhere; the **Tennessee Walking Horse National Celebration** in August and a 3-day show in May. Anytime of year you can see the Celebration Grounds and the Museum.

Buy a **Tennessee Tipsy Cake** from a store on the town square in Lynchburg, after you've toured **Jack Daniels** place. Canoe the beautiful **Elk River** or fish in **Tims Ford Lake**; sit by the giant water wheel at **Falls Mill**; buy fresh bread at the **Swiss Pantry**; now drive towards the looming plateau. It's awesome! Climb to an elevation of 1,900 feet and visit the magnificent campus of the **University of the South** at Sewanee. At Monteagle, it's back to the freeway, and trucks downshifting the mountain cut.

Manchester, TN
pop 7,709
Central Time
Chamber of Commerce 615-728-7635

To See and Do
Arrowheads/Aerospace Museum, 615-723-1323, 24 Campground Rd, Exit 114 off I-24, has everything from Lionel trains to Indian artifacts, and Civil War to WWII exhibits; old country store, covers 5 acres; playground. **Foothills Crafts**, 615-728-9236, 418 Woodbury Hwy; this non-profit craft association of more than 600 members displays works of its juried craftsmen in wood, clay, metal, glass and fiber; offers classes. **Parnassus Theatre**, 615-723-ARTS, 800-767-2480, 909 Hillsboro Hwy, dinner theater and arts activity center; art gallery open daily.

Accommodations
Ambassador Inn & Suites, 800-237-9228, Exit 110 off I-24; **Comfort Inn**, 800-221-2222, Exit 114 off I-24; **Holiday Inn**, 800-465-4329, Exit 114 off I-24. **My Grandmother's House B & B**, 615-728-6293, 704 Hickory Grove Rd, 3 rooms, full breakfast, 1837 log home on quiet country road, high tea at 4, country walks, bicycling.

Tennessee State Park
Central Time
Old Stone Fort Archaeological State Park, 615-723-5073, Hwy U41 off I-24. The Old Stone Fort is a 2,000-year-old earth and stone enclosure built as a sacred site by prehistoric Woodland Indians; other visible ruins in the park are the remains of 19th century industries that built on both forks of the Duck River. A 1.25-mile walk with an interpretive booklet follows the wall and cliff perimeter; interpretive tours available. May Prairie is nearby, and contains dozens of rare plants.

Accommodations
Old Stone Fort Archaeological State Park, 615-723-5073, 51 campsites in this 760-acre park.

Tullahoma, TN
pop 16,761
Central Time
Chamber of Commerce 615-455-5497

To See and Do

The drive from the freeway to Tullahoma takes you past **Arnold Engineering Development Center**, *615-454-5655, Arnold Air Force Base;* since its dedication in 1951 AEDC has been involved in the development of all high performance military jet aircraft, missiles and space systems; over **50 test facilities ranging from wind tunnels to space chambers;** group tours are available but MUST be scheduled at least 7 working days in advance. Call for registration packet and instructions. Tour includes video presentation and major facilities; approximately 3 hours. Individuals interested in touring should submit name and request inclusion with a group; tours usually limited to age 13 and older although a 6th grade class tour is available; anyone not a US Citizen must be cleared through their embassy before visiting.

In Tullahoma, arts and sports lovers will enjoy the **Tullahoma Fine Arts Center/Regional Art Museum**, *615-455-1234, 401 S Jackson St,* where southern artists are showcased, the regional collection rotates and they have national exhibits, workshops, classes and an annual Fine Arts Festival; and a visit to **Worth, Inc**, *615-455-0691, 2100 N Jackson St,* call ahead for tour schedule. If you play ball, you know the name; 6 million baseballs and 300,000 aluminum bats are manufactured here each year; see how cores are made, covers sewn on, and aluminum bats come into being. Relax at the peaceful **Nut Cave Trout Farm**, *615-857-3315, 340 Shippmans Creek Rd, 8 miles N of Tullahoma off Hwy U41A;* where a catch is guaranteed; a family spot, no license or poles required. **Granny Fishes' House** restaurant serves trout fresh from the farm.

Drive towards Normandy on S269 and watch for signs to Cascade Hollow. Cascade Hollow is on the highland rim of the Cumberland Plateau, and hidden in the Hollow is the **George A. Dickel Distillery**, *615-857-3124, 1950 Cascade Hollow Rd,*

Normandy. Guided tours show how Tennessee Sour Mash Whisky is still made the way George Dickel made it over 100 years ago. Water for the whiskey comes from Cascade Spring, still the same quality as when George found it in 1870. Signs will tell you there "Ain't Nothin' Better" than this Tennessee Sippin' Whiskey; shop in the General Store and collect some unusual middle-Tennessee recipes; mail your postcards back home from their very own post office.

Accommodations
Steeplechase Inn, *615-455-4501, 1410 N Jackson St;* **Holly Berry Inn**, *615-455-4445, 302 N Atlantic,* turn of the century setting. For food, **The Stuffed Goose**, *615-455-6673, 115 N Collins St;* lunch weekdays, dinner by reservation; collectors items for sale; **Alexanders**, *615-455-2194, 122 W Lincoln St,* steaks & seafood, live entertainment; **Granny Fishes'**, *615-857-4025, 340 Shippmans Creek Rd, 8 mi N of Tullahoma on U41A,* fresh trout from Nut Cave Trout Farm, catfish, frog legs, homemade desserts, open Thursday-Saturday.

Wartrace, TN
Central Time
Bedford County Chamber of Commerce
615-684-3482

To See and Do
Wartrace is known as the Cradle of the Tennessee Walking Horse; the first **World Champion, Strolling Jim,** was raised here and today is buried behind the Walking Horse Hotel; the stop sign out front cautions you to "Whoa." The world-known **Gallagher Guitars**, *615-389-6455, 7 Main St,* are handmade in Wartrace; while they are not set up for group tours, individual visitors are welcome to drop in and see the work in progress, as Brazilian rosewood, African mahogany, Indian ebony and other beautiful woods are shaped into musical instruments.

Accommodations
Log Cabin Bed & Breakfast, *615-389-6713, 171 Loop Rd,* just outside of town, relaxing view, country breakfast. **Our House**

Restaurant, 800-876-6616, 1059 Haley Rd; fine dining in 1920's era home; fresh seafoods, luncheon buffet, homemade desserts.

Bell Buckle, TN
A Governor's Three-Star Community
Central Time
Bedford County Chamber of Commerce
615-684-3482

To See and Do

Bell Buckle is home to Tennessee's Poet Laureate Maggie Vaughn and a number of sculptors; downtown boasts craft and antique stores; the town is home of **Webb School**, 615-389-6045, a college prep school founded in 1870, which has produced ten Rhodes Scholars and the governors of three states. **Bell Buckle Crafts**, 615-389-9371, 14 Railroad Sq, sells handmade arts and crafts from the Middle Tennessee area, stoneware pottery; in a 100-year-old former bank building. **Downtown Antique & Crafts Center**, S82; business section of this 19th-century village has 14 shops and 2 malls of craft and antique stores; over 30 dealers in the 1899 **Livery Stable Antique Mall**; over 50 dealers in **Bell Buckle Antique Mall**. Many festivals throughout the year including Daffodil Day in March, a Moon Pie festival in June, Blues to Bluegrass in August, and the Quilt Walk in September.

Accommodations

Liberty Pike Inn, 615-389-9328, 110 Liberty Pike, 2 rooms, shared bath, continental breakfast, 2 blocks from downtown, quaint house, porch swing. Check out the **Bell Buckle Cafe**, 615-389-9693, open daily, bar-b-q and fresh-squeezed lemonade, live country music weekend nights and Sunday afternoons; Thursday night is songwriters night; J. Gregory Jamboree is live every Saturday afternoon from 1-3 PM on WLIJ 1580 AM.

Shelbyville, TN
pop 14,049
Central Time
Chamber of Commerce 615-684-3482

To See and Do

Shelbyville is known as the Walking Horse Capital of the World, and every August people come from all over the world to the **Tennessee Walking Horse National Celebration**, *615-684-5915, corner of Calhoun & Evans St, on The Celebration Grounds*. The 100-acre showgrounds have 650 permanent barns with 1,650 stalls, an outdoor arena which seats 30,000; and the indoor Calsonic Arena, which seats 4,500. The weekend event which was first held in 1939 has grown to a 10-day show attracting a quarter of a million people today; there is a 3-day show on Memorial Day weekend too. If you've just come to town for a visit, see **The Tennessee Walking Horse Museum**, *615-684-0314, in Calsonic Arena, 721 Whitthorne St*, where the only horse named for its state is featured; you'll find interactive video, Walking Horse artifacts, and 3-D displays, it's open weekdays. There are more than 40 farms in the greater area; call the **Chamber**, *615-684-3482*, for a **Visitor's Guide to Area Horse Farms**; always call ahead before you visit.

Shelbyville Town Square was laid out in 1810 as the prototype for town squares in the South and Midwest; today it houses thriving businesses while retaining its old-time atmosphere, listed on National Register of Historic Places.

Accommodations

Best Western, *615-684-2378, 724 Madison St*; **Shelbyville Inn**, *615-684-6050, 317 N Cannon Blvd*; **Cinnamon Ridge Bed & Breakfast**, *615-685-9200, 799 Whitthorne St*, 5 rooms, private baths, full breakfast, colonial home, walking distance to National Walking Horse Celebration grounds; **Taylor House Bed & Breakfast**, *615-684-3894, 300 E Lane St*, 5 rooms, private baths, full breakfast, minutes from Calsonic Arena & TWHNC grounds. **The Old Gore House**, *615-685-0636, 410 Belmont Ave*, Colonial style home, double parlors, fireplace in dining room. **Rebecca's Restaurant,** *615-684-6050, 317 N Cannon Blvd,* family restaurant, homestyle breakfast, lunch buffet, dinner specials; **Pope's Cafe,** *615-684-7933, 120 East Side Sq,* country ham and home cooking.

Lynchburg, TN
pop 668
Central Time
Chamber of Commerce 615-759-4111

To See and Do
Stop first at the **Welcome Center,** *615-759-4111,* on the edge of the square and gather information on the sights to see. A prime sight is **Jack Daniel's Distillery,** *615-759-6180,* the nations oldest distillery, registered No. 1 with the U. S. Government in 1866; daily tours begin in the barrelhouse and wind up at the cave where the iron-free spring water used for this famous Tennessee whiskey pours forth; watch out when you are allowed a whiff of the fermenting process! Though you are given a bus-ride for parts of the tour, be prepared for climbing as you wander over the barrelhouse-dotted knob hills. Walk through the original office, where a plaque designates the distillery a National Historic Place.

Check out the **Moore County Courthouse,** built in 1855 with bricks made right in Lynchburg, and the now-just-for-photographs **Moore County Jail,** operated by the Moore County Historical Society, donations appreciated. The **Lynchburg Square** is the county's social center; sit and gossip with the whittlers; shop the stores around the square; many have Jack Daniels souvenirs; get your Jack Daniels Tennessee Tipsy Cake at the **Pepper Patch Bakery,** they ship all over the country. The famous **Miss Mary Bobo's Boarding House** is a landmark dating back to 1866; make reservations ahead for their wonderful southern-style mid-day dinners.

Accommodations
Lynchburg Bed & Breakfast, *615-759-7158,* restored 1877 home one block off the square, private bath, quaint atmosphere;

Goose Branch Farm Bed & Breakfast, 615-759-5919, 140 Goose Branch Rd, continental breakfast, 2 rooms with private bath and private entrance, 1899 farm; **Tucker's Inn,** 615-759-5922, 5 miles from downtown, 2-story historical home, 15-mile overlook, furnished with antiques, 3 bedrooms with private baths. Restaurants include **The Countryside,** 615-759-4430, 3 meals a day and tour buses welcome; **Iron Kettle Restaurant,** 615-759-4274, featuring plate lunches and their "Whiskey Topper," and **Miss Mary Bobo's Boarding House,** 615-759-7394, for mid-day meals, reservations required.

Fayetteville, TN
pop 6,921
Central Time
Chamber of Commerce 615-433-1234

To See and Do
Historic Downtown Fayetteville has many traditional and unusual folk art shops, **Pastime Cafe** with live country music every Thursday, **Cahoots,** an old jail and firehouse turned restaurant, the Southeast's largest fabric store, and antebellum homes. **Lincoln County Museum,** 615-438-0339, located in Old Borden Milk Plant, exhibits show long-ago examples of industry, pastimes, education, military, and people.
Elk River Plantation, 615-433-9757, 77 Eldad Rd, a working farm, features exotic animals, tours for schoolchildren; fall festival has Pumpkin Patch and various events each weekend in October. **Elk River Canoe Rental,** 615-937-6886, 90 Smithland Rd, lets you float this Class I river in beautiful Old Town Discovery canoes, everything provided; changing rooms and primitive campgrounds; first-timers welcome.

Accommodations
Best Western, 800-528-1234, 3021 Thornton Taylor Pkwy; **Days Inn,** 800-DAYSINN, 1651 Huntsville Hwy. **Heritage House,** 615-433-9238, 315 E College St, 3 rooms, private bath, continental breakfast, antebellum brick colonial home, walking distance of downtown; **Old Cowan Plantation,** 615-433-0225,

126 Old Boonshill Rd, 2 rooms, continental breakfast, large porch and country atmosphere in 1886 Colonial home.

Belvidere, TN
Central Time
Franklin County Chamber of Commerce
615-967-6788

To See and Do
Falls Mill & Country Store, 615-469-7161, *134 Falls Mill Road,* water-powered grain mill powered by 32-foot overshot water wheel, museum; built in 1873, produces stone-ground flour and meal; self-guided tours or group tours with reservations.

Accommodations
Falls Mill Bed & Breakfast Log Cabin, 615-469-7161, *134 Falls Mill Road,* cabin built in 1895 with fireplace, tin roof, full kitchen, sleeps 5; continental breakfast. **Swiss Pantry,** 615-962-0567, *7970 David Crockett Hwy,* homemade baked goods, breads, cheeses and desserts.

Winchester, TN
pop 6,305
Central Time
Franklin County Chamber of Commerce
615-967-6788

To See and Do
Franklin County Old Jail Museum, 615-967-0524, *400 Dinah Shore Blvd,* 6 rooms show artifacts of Franklin County's history. **Rainbow Row,** 615-967-8844, *101-115 Second Ave NW;* restored 19th-century building houses shops featuring antiques, folk art, gifts, gourmet foods; open daily.

Accommodations
Antebellum Inn Bed & Breakfast, 615-967-5550, *974 Lynchburg Rd,* 3 rooms, private bath, continental breakfast, panoramic view of Tims Ford Lake. **Tims Ford Marina & Resort,** 800-

722-1164, 175 Marina Lane, 15 cabins, kitchens, pontoon rentals, restaurant, guide service. **Hawk's Steak & Pizza**, *615-967-1111, 1106 Dinah Shore Blvd*, daily buffets, daily specials; **The Brick Cafe**, *615-962-2233, 103 2nd Ave NW*, fresh breads, unique salads, homemade desserts.

Tennessee State Park
Central Time

Tims Ford State Park, *800-421-6683, 615-967-4457, 570 Tims Ford Drive, off TN50*, 413-acre park located on 10,700-acre Tims Ford Reservoir, in shadows of Cumberland Plateau. Marina, fishing, water recreation, biking and hiking trails; large pool, playgrounds, playfields.

Accommodations
Tims Ford State Park, *615-967-4457, 570 Tims Ford Drive*, 20 cabin units, fireplaces; 50 campsites.

Cowan, TN
pop 1,738
Central Time
Franklin County Chamber of Commerce
615-967-6788

To See and Do
Cowan Railroad Museum, *615-967-7365, off Hwy U64/41A*; restored depot, rare Columbia-type steam locomotive and caboose on display; many railroad articles plus model railroad; learn about the Cumberland Mountain Tunnel built in mid 1800's. Open summers, weekends. Free, but donations appreciated.

Accommodations
Corner House, *615-967-3910, 400 E Cumberland*, luncheon in Victorian tea house, fresh-baked breads and "Rich & Famous" desserts.

Sewanee, TN

pop 2,128
Central Time
Franklin County Chamber of Commerce
615-967-6788

To See and Do

University of the South, *tours 615-598-1286, 735 University Avenue,* 10,000-acre campus in gorgeous mountain setting atop Cumberland Plateau; independent liberal arts university; native sandstone used for gothic buildings Oxford/Cambridge style; be sure to see All Saints' Chapel, the Memorial Cross, Green's View overlook, and the Abbott Martin Ravine Gardens, tours are available. **Sewanee Summer Music Center,** *615-598-1225;* for over 40 years summers have been graced with concerts; include faculty recitals, the Sewanee Symphony and Cumberland Orchestra, and guest conductors and soloists of international fame; season tickets available.

Accommodations

Clouds Rest, *615-598-0993, 400 Rattlesnake Spring Lane,* B&B with 4 rooms, gourmet breakfast, lake. **4-Seasons Restaurant,** *615-598-5544, between Sewanee and Monteagle,* all-you-can-eat buffet.

Monteagle, TN

pop 1,138
Central Time
Grundy County Chamber of Commerce
615-779-3462

To See and Do

Monteagle Wine Cellars, *615-924-2120, Hwy U64,* these vineyards and cellars are on the Cumberland Plateau; tastings, free tours, gift shop. **Wonder Cave,** *615-467-3060, off Hwy U41 at Pelham,* open daily May-October. One of oldest commercial caves in the country; explore passages with hand-held lanterns; or make appointment for wild-cave tour.

Accommodations

Days Inn, *800-325-2525, Exit 135 and US41;* **DuBose Conference Center,** *800-537-9968, Hwy U41 at College Street,* 75 rooms, meeting facilities, restaurant. **Jim Oliver's Smoke House Lodge,** *800-489-2091 or 615-924-2268, Exit 134 off I-24,* motel and cabins, some with hot tubs, fireplaces, kitchens, front porches with mountain view, rocking chairs; banquet and recreational facilities, group rates. Country cooking restaurant, trading post on premises. B&B's include **Adams Edgeworth Inn,** *615-924-4000, Monteagle Assembly,* listed on National Historic Register, 14 rooms, located in Victorian Village, 200-foot porches, breakfast, dinner; **North Gate Inn,** *615-924-2799, 103 Monteagle Assembly,* 7 guest rooms with private baths, full breakfasts, open all year; **Wonder Cave Bed & Breakfast,** *615-467-3060, Pelham;* 6 rooms, shared bath, spacious grounds.

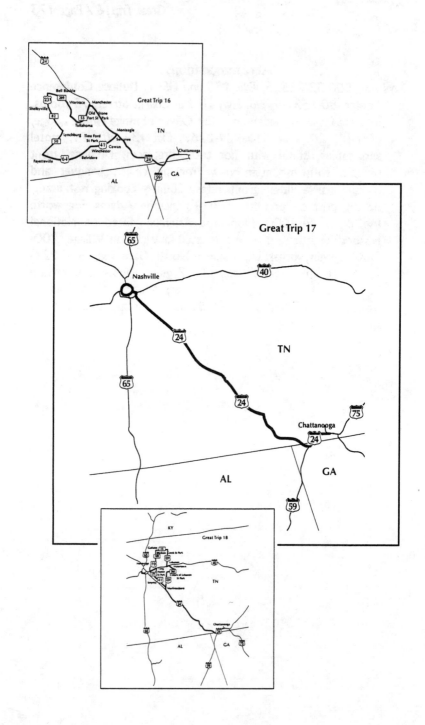

Great Trip 17

Chattanooga to Nashville, TN
the music and mansions route
via I-24
approximately 270 miles round-trip, 5 hours driving time

Why Go
State Capitol & Bicentennial Mall Park & Pioneer Fort &
Carnegie Hall of South & Tootsies & Wildhorses & Guitar Stores &
Music Row & Country Music Hall of Fame & Recording Stars &
World's Largest Indoor Sculpture & Picasso & Parthenon &
Queen of Plantations & Lapis Lazuli Mantle & Toy Museum &
Old Mill Scream & Oldest Radio Show & Largest Broadcast Studio &
Showboats & Riverboats & River Taxis & Wildlife Park & Red Pandas &
Southern Festival of Books & Bluebird Cafe

Suggested route with approximate mileages

Instruction	Road	Dir	Miles
Chattanooga to Nashville	I-24	N	134
Nashville to Chattanooga	I-24	S	134
Total Mileage			268

It's just plain fun to go to Nashville. A spirit-lifting trip. Maybe it's the **Music City** title; maybe it's the use of the word Grand with the word Opry. Can you hear the banjos playing? Rise up so early in the morn! This music and mansions tour shows you historic mansions of days gone by, present-day mansions of the stars, and music shows everywhere. But, that's not all.

When you think of Nashville, what comes to mind? It's the **Heartland of Tennessee**. It's the **state capital**. It's first in the nation in **country music recording**. It's a city of **publishing firms** and **colleges**, including Vanderbilt. It's a city with green trees, vista hills, the **Cumberland River**, great places to eat, and many historic and interesting places to see.

Nashville is big; spread out and circled by freeways; but the downtown area is a manageable walking size; from the cluster of governmental buildings in the capitol area to the riverfront and The District you can travel on foot. The Visitors Bureau has prepared a nice map with your "trail" clearly marked. Visit the capitol early in the day and hang out in The District in the evening; catch a show at the **Ryman**, drop in at old-time **Tootsie's Orchid Lounge** or the new family-style dance hall known as the **Wildhorse Saloon**. The converted warehouses facing the river are filled with restaurants and shops; the area will be buzzing with activity. At the River Dock, you can board a riverboat or a train and have dinner while you ride.

Drive to **Centennial Park** and visit the **Parthenon**; you'll enjoy browsing the art galleries inside and be awed by the design of the building itself. Nearby is **Music Row** where more than a hundred record companies, publishing houses and recording studios increase the chance that you'll spot your favorite recording artist walking by.

Are you ready for the **Grand Ole Opry** now? You can be a part of WSN's live radio show; it's located in **Opryland**, as are many music shows and attractions. Organized bus tours offer packages that include the mansions of the stars as part of the itinerary.

If historic mansions are what you prefer, visit the magnificent **Belmont** and **Cheekwood Mansions** or the sprawling plantation of **Belle Meade** at your leisure, relaxing with a glimpse into the past.

Nashville, TN
pop 488,374
metro pop 965,026
Central Time
Chamber of Commerce 615- 259-4755
Tourist Information Center 615-259-4747

Tennessee State Park

A perfect beginning for your visit to this state capital city is the **Bicentennial Capitol Mall State Park**, 615-741-5280, downtown, a 19-acre park designed as a lasting monument to the 1996 Bicentennial celebration. Tennessee history is portrayed in the park, and from here you have a wonderful view of the capitol.

The City

The **State Capitol**, 615-741-1621, 6th & Charlotte Ave, is open weekdays. You'll hear some interesting stories as you tour this antebellum building high on a hill overlooking the city. Some other state capitols have historic bullet holes in their walls, but none because the lawmakers were trying to flee! That's part of the story you're told while touring this 1859 building, as the guide points to the chipped place in the curved marble stair. The guard fired from above to "persuade" them to come back. They tromped to their seats and ratified the 14th Amendment that momentous day in 1866, allowing Tennessee to become the first Confederate state to be readmitted to the Union.

Another momentous event occurred on August 18, 1920, when Rep. Harry Burn, at 24 the youngest member of the legislature, cast the deciding ballot that gave women across the country the right to vote. The 19th Amendment needed ratification by 36 states; Tennessee's approval did the trick. As the story goes, Rep. Burn had voted "no" on first roll call; upon receiving a note from his mother advising him that she, as a landowner, paid taxes and should therefore be allowed to vote; he changed to "yes" for the final count.

In the capitol area are the **Tennessee State Museum**, 615-741-2692, James K. Polk State Bldg., 5th & Deaderick; with exhibits on life in Tennessee from early man through the early 1900's; and the **Tennessee State Library and Archives**, 615-741-2764, 403 7th

Ave N. This research center has extensive holdings on Tennessee, southern, and US history; and diverse material for genealogical research in Tennessee and other states. Government information, news sources, and law collections too; open Monday-Saturday.

Fort Nashborough, *170 1st Ave N, north end of Riverfront Park,* overlooking the Cumberland River, is a reconstruction of the original settlement of Nashville. A self-guided tour within the stockaded walls shows the lifestyle of pioneers in the late 1700's.

Also in Downtown Area

The famous **Ryman Auditorium & Museum,** *615-889-6611, 116 5th Ave N* was used in the early part of century for religious revivals; then showcased such acts as W.C.Fields, Harpo Marx, Mae West, Ziegfeld Follies, Will Rogers, Enrico Caruso, John Philip Sousa, Isadora Duncan, Charlie Chaplin, Katherine Hepburn; and legendary country musicians including Hank Williams, Marty Robbins, Patsy Cline and Roy Acuff. Once called the **Carnegie Hall of the South,** it now is a museum with memorabilia and photos of Opry notables. The shows go on; performances today include a tribute to Pasty Cline, bluegrass, and inspirational music.

Around the corner from the Ryman is **Tootsies Orchid Lounge,** *615-726-0463, 422 Broadway;* its walls covered with autographs from performers who have stopped by over the years; on the corner is **Gruhn Guitar,** *615-256-2033,* a busy place in a music town. Nearer the river is the **Wildhorse Saloon,** *615-251-1000, 120 2nd Ave N;* a country music dance club that's fun for watching, learning how to dance, or showing off your fancy western garb. Sit at a balcony table; order dinner and watch the scene below; buy your own boots in the on-premises shops and scoot onto the floor. It's a family place; the kids are dancing too. Many restaurants and shops in this area known as **The District.**

Go by boat or train; have dinner either way. From Riverfront Park, board the **Broadway Dinner Train,** *615-254-8000,* for a four-course dinner in restored dining cars; the **Belle Carol Riverboats,** *615-244-3430,* Music City Queen or Captain Ann have narrated sightseeing, entertainment dinner, or latenight party cruises. Opryland River Taxis are boarded here too.

Music Row Area & Centennial Park Area

Music Row, the area along Music Square East and West, Music Circle, and Demonbreun Street, is home to more than 100 of the music industry's most well-known record companies, publishing houses and recording studios. Park and **Stroll the Row.** Souvenir stops and shops are there for your favorite country western star. In the **Country Music Hall of Fame and Museum,** *615-255-5333, 4 Music Square E,* you are treated to a behind-the-scenes look at the music industry with a focus on performers, songwriters, movie clips and memorabilia.

Picnic in Centennial Park, and visit Nashville's famous landmark, the **Parthenon,** *615-862-8431, Centennial Park, W End Ave & 25th Ave N.* Intended to duplicate the original in Greece, a "temporary" Parthenon was built in 1897 to house the international art exhibition for the Centennial Exposition. Redone with permanent materials in 1931, today it contains the East and West art galleries, with changing exhibits; and the **Cowan Gallery,** which houses a permanent collection of American art. The **Naos,** on the upper level, houses the 42-foot high statue of the goddess Athena, the largest piece of indoor sculpture in the western world. Nike, the winged goddess of victory, is in her right palm; her left hand and arm support a 17-ft shield and a 36-ft spear. At **Van Vechten Gallery at Fisk University,** *615-329-8720, Jackson St & D.B. Todd Blvd,* is a permanent collection of more than 100 pieces including works by Picasso, Renoir, Cezanne and O'Keefe.

Opryland Area

Opryland, *615-889-6611, 10 mi E on I-40, 4 mi N on Briley Pkwy, exit 11,* is a 120-acre entertainment park filled with music shows and plenty of rides; try the Old Mill Scream, or a coaster. Open daily through the summer, weekends after Labor Day.

The Grand Ole Opry, *615-889-3060, 2804 Opryland Dr; weekends all year,* has moved to Opryland now. The nation's oldest radio show, it occupies the world's largest broadcast studio, the **Opry House,** which seats 4,424. More than 60 acts are members of the Opry. You can be a part of the live radio show on weekends; check ahead of time for schedules and seat availability.

TNN: The Nashville Network, *615-883-7000, 2806 Opryland Dr;* is a cable network producing county shows with studio audiences; call for schedule; *615-889-6611 for reservations.* **Nashville On Stage,** *615-889-6611, 2802 Opryland Dr,* is a concert series at the

Theater by the Lake. The **General Jackson,** *615-889-6611, Cumberland River,* a 300-foot paddlewheel showboat with a musical stage show, cruises breakfast through dinner. And don't forget the **Opryland River Taxis** that will carry you back and forth between Opryland and downtown.

Grand Ole Opry Tours, *615-889-9490,* guides you to houses of country music stars, Music Row, recording studios, and backstage at the Grand Ole Opry.

Historical Homes and Gardens

Belle Meade, *615-356-0501, 5025 Harding Rd,* is called the Queen of Tennessee Plantations, and once was considered the greatest thoroughbred breeding farm in the country. The 1853 mansion was part of a 5,300-acre working plantation; the 1890 Carriage House is filled with antique carriages; the 1790 log cabin is one of the oldest houses in Tennessee; six more original outbuildings; tour guides in period costume. Open daily.

Belmont Mansion, *615-269-9537, 1900 Belmont Blvd,* features a fine collection of original and period furnishings, artwork and statues; the Italian-style villa was built in 1850 by Adelicia Acklen, one of America's wealthiest women. Open daily.

Cheekwood, Tennessee Botanical Gardens and Museum of Art, *615-356-8000, 1200 Forrest Park Dr, 8 mi SW on Forrest Park Dr.* This 3-story Georgian mansion, with beautiful mahogany and fruitwood doors, an Adam mantel of lapis lazuli, and a unique spiral staircase, now houses a permanent collection of American art of the 19th and 20th centuries. The cultural center sits on a 55-acre hilltop site, with lawns, woodlands, wildflowers, roses, display gardens, Japanese garden, herb study garden, and greenhouses. The **Pineapple Room Restaurant** is in the Reception Center; come in December for the **Trees of Christmas** display. Open daily.

Travellers Rest, *615-832-2962, 636 Farrell Pkwy,* Judge John Overton's restored 1799 home has a large collection of pre-1840 Tennessee-made furniture. Overton was Tennessee's first Supreme Court Judge, and was Andrew Jackson's campaign manager when Jackson ran for president. As the name implies, this once was a stop for travelers passing through. Open daily.

Other Interesting Places

Cumberland Science Museum, *615-862-5160, 800 Ft Negley Blvd;* a

Planetarium here, and discovery adventures for the whole family with live animal and science programs, changing exhibits, and the Curiosity Corner. Open daily summer, Tuesday-Sunday rest of year.

Nashville Toy Museum, *615-883-8870, 2613-B McGavock Pike.* This collection of antique toys, china dolls, lead soldiers, and 250 toy and model locomotives spans more than 150 years. Open daily.

Grassmere Wildlife Park, *615-833-1534, 3777 Nolensville Rd.* A zoological park featuring animals indigenous to the Tennessee area. Call for hours.

Nashville Zoo, *615-370-3333, 761 Old Hickory Blvd, I-24 West Exit 31.* A natural environment zoo on 100 acres in the country, with more than 800 animals representing more than 150 species; see snow and clouded leopards, red pandas, white tigers, Vietnamese pot bellied pigs, binturongs, pythons, llamas, giraffe, and zebra.

Events

Tennessee State Fair, *615-862-8980, Fairgrounds, Wedgewood Ave & Rains;* mid-September. **Southern Festival of Books**, sponsored by Tennessee Humanities Council, *615-320-7001, held on Legislative Plaza and surrounding buildings;* mid-October.

Accommodations

Downtown hotels **Doubletree**, *615-244-8200, 315 4th Ave N;* **Holiday Inn Crowne Plaza**, *800-HOLIDAY, 623 Union St;* **Loew's Vanderbilt Plaza**, *615-320-1700, 2100 West End Ave;* **Renaissance National**, *615-255-8400, 611 Commerce St;* **Union Station**, *800-331-2123, 1001 Broadway.* Opryland area: **Opryland Hotel**, *615-889-1000, 2800 Opryland Dr;* two atriums with tropical plants, fountains, ponds, and pathways; shopping concourse. Check with your favorite chain for accommodations in other areas; if you're looking for a B&B, call **About Tennessee Bed & Breakfast Reservation Service**, *615-331-5244.* You'll be eating your way along the entertainment route, with dinner cruises, dinner shows, and restaurants right under your nose. Unique to Nashville is the **Bluebird Cafe**, *615-383-1461, 4104 Hillsboro Rd*, a showcase club featuring songwriters, and original country, blues, and acoustic music; such greats as Garth Brooks and Mary Chapin Carpenter performed here.

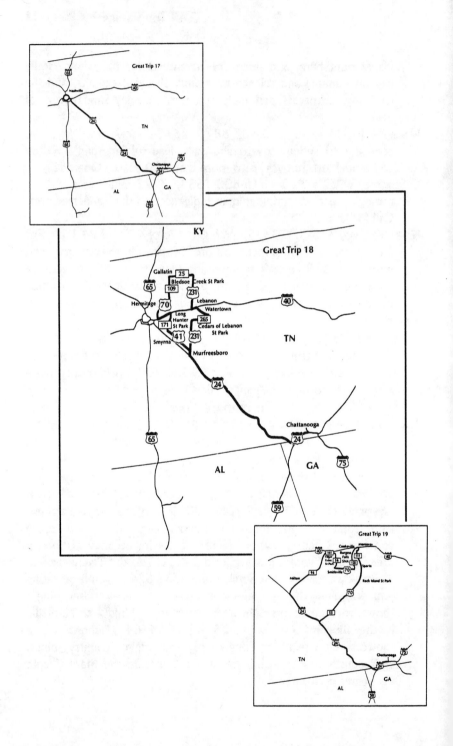

Great Trip 17

Great Trip 18

Great Trip 19

Great Trip 18

Chattanooga to Lebanon, TN
the cedars and squares route
via Murfreesboro, Cedars of Lebanon St Pk, Watertown, Lebanon, Gallatin, Hermitage, Long Hunter St Pk, Smyrna, returning to Chattanooga approximately 330 miles round-trip, 6 hours driving time

Why Go
Town Squares & Cedar Glades & Rolling Hills & Winding Rivers & Civil War Battlefield & National Cemetery & President's Homes & Cannonsburgh & Fiddlers Grove & Time Capsule Town & Antiquer's Heaven & Dimple of the Universe & Avery Trace & Horseback Riding & Backpacking & Fishing & Boating & Camping & Teddy Bears & Yard Sales

Suggested route with approximate mileages

Instruction	Road	Dir	Miles
Chattanooga to Murfreesboro	I-24	N	101
Murfreesboro to Watertown	U231 & S265 & U70	N & E	26
Watertown to Lebanon	U70	N	17
Lebanon to Gallatin	U231 & S25	N & W	24
Gallatin to Hermitage	S109 & U70	S & W	23
Hermitage to Smyrna	I-40 & S171 & U41	S	25
Smyrna to Chattanooga	S102 & I-24	S	113
Total Mileage			329

Don't want to mess with traffic and hurry-up? Need some time to slow down and wipe out agendas? Small-town squares with benches for sitting and fragrant cedar glades with paths for walking may be just what the doctor ordered.

Before this Trip ends, you'll experience the warmth and good-naturedness of town-square living, stroll through historical villages, and visit the homes of former Presidents, Governors, and Confederate heroes. You are treated to the pleasures of scenic highways, rolling hills, the winding **Cumberland River, J. Percy Priest and Old Hickory Lakes**, and **Cedars of Lebanon, Long Hunter, and Bledsoe Creek State Parks**.

Maybe you'll go on a horseback ride through a cedar forest, or backpacking on the lookout for deer. Perhaps you'll fish in Old Hickory Lake, and rent a cabin with a kitchen to cook your catch. When trading and talking are on your mind, the antique stores will welcome you with treasures galore; and be sure to get the dates for the mile-long yard sales twice a year in **Watertown**.

Murfreesboro is the geographic center of Tennessee, an obelisk identifies the exact spot, which nearby residents nicknamed "the **dimple of the universe**." **Stones River National Battlefield** was the site of a crucial Civil War battle; one of the nation's oldest **National Cemeteries** is here too. The largest red cedar forest remaining the country is found at Cedars of Lebanon State Park; in April you'll see more than 20 native wildflowers growing in the glades. Barrier-free trails and fishing piers at Long Hunter State Park make the outdoor experience available to everyone.

It looks like a party's about to happen in **Lebanon's Town Square**; flags are flying, flowers are blooming, and people stop to chat. If you don't see the whittlers, you'll see evidence of their presence by the pile of shavings in front of the bench. Over at **Fiddlers Grove**, walk through 20 structures including a replica of Sam Houston's law office and an original general store from the mid-1800's. More history at **Wynnewood**, near Castalian Springs; the former stagecoach inn is the largest log structure ever built in the state and dates to 1828. A view of plantation living is yours at the 600-acre estate of **President Andrew Jackson, The Hermitage**; audio-tape tours offer insights and information about the lifestyles and the times.

Murfreesboro, TN
pop 44,922
Central Time
Chamber of Commerce 615-893-6565

To See and Do

Find your way to Front Street for a stop at the **Chamber of Commerce** building located right beside Cannonsburgh. Plenty of information about the area, and then time for your stroll around the Pioneer Village. **Cannonsburgh**, *615-890-0355, South Front Street, is a* rural Southern village, circa 1800-1925, that was assembled in 1974 as an American Revolution Bicentennial project. Enjoy the one-room schoolhouse, several residences, a beautiful chapel, general store, blacksmith shop, and more.

Then drive to the pretty downtown square; park and walk, the **Rutherford County Courthouse** is one of only six pre-Civil war buildings still operating in the state; along the flower-dotted streets you'll find bookstores, shops, and restaurants. Visit the **Children's Discovery House Museum**, *615-890-2300, 503 N Maple St,* a hands-on science and nature museum for the kids. A drive down tree-lined Main Street leads to **Middle Tennessee State University;** five basic undergraduate schools here, plus the **Tennessee Livestock Center**, which is home to the **International Grand Champion Walking Horse Show**, *615-890-9120,* each August; over 150 classes and 20 championships in the week-long competition.

A mile beyond the downtown area you'll find a stone obelisk identifying the **Geographic Center of Tennessee**, *Old Luscassas Pike;* residents nicknamed the spot "The Dimple of the Universe." Tour **Oaklands Historic House Museum**, *615-893-0022, 900 N Maney Ave,* at its peak the center of a 1,500-acre plantation, occupied by both Northern and Southern armies during the Civil War; on the National Register of Historic Places.

Accommodations

Hampton Inn, *800-HAMPTON, 2230 Old Fort Pkwy;* **Holiday Inn Holidome**, *800-HOLIDAY, 2227 Old Fort Pkwy;* **Howard Johnson Lodge**, *800-446-4656, 2424 S Church St;* **Clardy's Guest House Bed & Breakfast**, *615-893-6030, 435 E Main St,* 1898 Victorian house located in city's Historic District, unusual ornate features.

National Battlefield Site
Central Time
Stones River National Battlefield, *615-893-9501, 3501 Old Nashville Hwy;* 350-acre national park was the site of a crucial battle involving more than 80,000 soldiers. Living history demonstrations during summer months; audio tape tours are available from the visitor center. One of the nation's oldest National Cemeteries here, open daily.

Tennessee State Park
Central Time
Cedars of Lebanon State Park, *615-443-2769, 328 Cedar Forest Rd, South of I-40 on Hwy U231;* nine cabins, 117 campsites, and in April more than 20 native wildflowers in the cedar glades; this 830-acre park was named for the cedars that grew in the land of King Solomon and has the largest red cedar forest remaining in the country; for recreation an Olympic-sized pool and playground, hiking trails, and horseback riding trails, overnight guests may reserve stalls at the park stables.

Watertown, TN
pop 1,250
Central Time
Chamber of Commerce 800-789-1327

To See and Do
Historic Watertown, *615-237-9999, 116 Depot St;* known as one of the premier "time capsule" attractions in the state, Watertown is the destination several times each year for excursionists on Nashville's Broadway Dinner Train. Step back in time in the town's original square; visit antique shops or just relax in the gazebo. There's a **Mile-Long Yard Sale** each April and October, and **Christmas in the Country** with a **Tour of Homes** the first week-end in December. **Tour Groups** are welcome, call *615-237-3976.*
Accommodations
Watertown Bed & Breakfast, *615-237-9999, 116 Depot St,* restored

19th-century railroad hotel, library, verandas with swings, four rooms, full breakfast, 1 suite with Jacuzzi, one block from square. **Depot Junction Cafe**, *615-237-3976, 108 Depot St,* train photos and a 240-foot G-scale train track around the top of the dining rooms in this former livery stable built in the late 1800's; country cooking, steaks, seafood, open 5 AM through dinnertime except closes 3 PM on Sundays.

Lebanon, TN
pop 15,208
Central Time
Chamber of Commerce 800-789-1327

To See and Do
Square off on the square and get info from the **Chamber of Commerce,** *149 Public Square;* **downtown Lebanon** is an antiquer's heaven, from dolls to stained glass, tea sets to teddy bears, Indian artifacts to quilts; browse and shop where Lebanon first began; the town square was built over the spring by which Neddy Jacobs, a Revolutionary War veteran, built the area's first home in 1780. The square maintains a festive look with flags flying in front of every store, sidewalk planters overflowing with the season's brightest flowers, and benches inviting shoppers and whittlers to sit for a while. Learn more of the town's history at the **Wilson County Museum,** *615-444-5503, 236 W Main St;* this 1840's home, known as the Fessenden House, displays over 100 years of history, open Saturday afternoons or by appointment.
Drive through the campus of **Cumberland University,** *800-467-0562, South Greenwood Street;* founded in 1842, it counts among its alumni 16 state governors, 32 U.S. senators, two U. S. Supreme Court Justices, and Secretary of State Cordell Hull, who received the Nobel Peace Prize for his role in organizing the United Nations.
Fiddlers Grove Historical Village, *615-443-2626, 945 Baddour Pkwy, in Ward Agricultural Center,* has 20 historical structures, some original, some replicated; the original Stringtown General Store as it was in the mid-to-late 1800's, a replica of Sam Houston's Law Office as he would have used in pre-Civil War times, a newspaper

and print shop, school house, doctor's office, bank, jail, post office, blacksmith shop and more; also a petting barn; open year round, guided tours available, free but donations appreciated.

Annual events in Lebanon include mid-July's **Cedarfest** with competitions in square dancing, buck dancing and clogging as well as fiddlin', whittlin', checkers and horseshoes.

Accommodations

Best Western, *800-528-1234, 631 S Cumberland;* **Comfort Inn**, *800-228-5150, I-40 and U231S;* **Days Inn**, *800-325-2525, 231 Murfreesboro Rd;* **Hampton Inn**, *800-HAMPTON, 704 S Cumberland;* **Holiday Inn**, *800-HOLIDAY, 641 S Cumberland St,* **Hamblen House Bed & Breakfast**, *615-443-0327, 126 S Tarver St,* Victorian furnishings, country breakfast served in sunroom, patio, parlor, adjacent to Cumberland University campus in residential neighborhood. **Natureview Inn Bed & Breakfast**, *800-758-7972, 3354 Old Lebanon Dirt Rd,* located on old stagecoach road, pool, decks, stalls for horses, croquet, badminton, 4 rooms, fireplace, full breakfast, children welcome. Start your antique browsing with an espresso or a light lunch from **The Perfect Cup**, *615-449-7939, 104 N Maple St;* enjoy home-cooked meals mid-day Sunday through Friday at **New City Cafe**, *615-444-7117, 115 E Main,* just half a block off the square. Lebanon is home to **Cracker Barrel Old Country Stores**, now found in 25 states.

Tennessee State Parks
Central Time

Bledsoe Creek State Park, *615-452-3706, 400 Zieglers Fort Rd;* good boating, skiing and fishing at Old Hickory Lake, the 164-acre park is situated on the Bledsoe Creek embayment, boat-launching ramps, hiking trails; 110 campsites, year-round.

Bledsoe Fort Historic Park, *615-452-5463, Hwy S25, Castalian Springs,* 80-acres encompassing the archaeological site of the 1780's fort and portion of Avery Trace, walking trail with descriptive signage, open year-round by appointment.

Gallatin, TN

pop 18,794
Central Time
Chamber of Commerce 615-452-4000

To See and Do

Before you get into Gallatin, while you are driving on beautiful Scenic
Highway 25 near Castalian Springs, watch for the signs to
Wynnewood, *615-452-5463, Castalian Springs,* a log structure
built in 1828. It's two stories tall and 142 feet long, and is said to
be the largest log structure ever built in the state. It was a
stagecoach inn and then a mineral springs resort; furnished in
period furniture and open daily.

Watch carefully for the turn to **Cragfont**, *615-452-7070, Castalian
Springs,* a beautifully restored example of Federal period
architecture in a lovely setting far off the highway. It was built in
1798 by Gen James Winchester, one of the founders of Memphis;
open hours vary.

Many of the 25 restored buildings in **Historic Downtown Gallatin**, *615-
452-5692, 112 Public Square,* predate the Civil War. Now they
house shops and restaurants; take a self-guided tour. See also
Trousdale Place, *615-452-5648, 183 W Main St,* home of William
Trousdale, governor of Tennessee from 1849-1851; it has
authentic furniture and a small Confederate library. In the **Sumner
County Museum**, *615-451-3738, 183 W Main St,* exhibits range
from fossils to Native American, pioneers, and early settlers goods
and tools; there are over 250,000 artifacts. Group and school
tours by appointment.

Accommodations

Shoney's Inn, *800-222-2222, 221 W Main St.* The **Hancock House**,
615-452-8431, 2144 Nashville Pike; 5 rooms, private baths, full
country breakfast in colonial log inn, built before 1878 as a
stagecoach stop on the Avery Trail.

Hermitage, TN
Central Time
Chamber of Commerce 615-883-7896

To See and Do
A tour of the **Hermitage**, *615-889-2941, 4580 Rachel's Lane, 12 mi E off I-40 exit 221A*, is a true walk back in time. It was the residence of Andrew Jackson, the seventh president of the United States, and his beloved wife Rachel. They are buried in the corner of her garden. Now a 600-acre estate, it was 1,000 acres when Jackson died in 1845; cotton was the chief cash crop and about 150 slaves worked the farm. You can rent a tape for the walking tour; there is a museum, restaurant and gift shop. Other buildings on the property are Tulip Grove, where Jackson's nephew resided, the Old Hermitage Church, and original cabins. Open daily.

Tennessee State Park
Central Time
Long Hunter State Park, *615-885-2422, 2910 Hobson Pk, Hwy S171*; many day-use recreational opportunities in this 2,315-acre park, located on the shores of Percy Priest Reservoir. There are no campsites, but 28 miles of day hiking and overnight backpacking trails, and unique fauna and flora, including a cedar glade. The Couchville Lake Area is totally barrier free; programs for the handicapped and elderly.

Smyrna, TN
pop 13,647
Central Time
Chamber of Commerce 615-893-6565

To See and Do
Visit one more historical spot, the **Sam Davis Home**, *615-459-2341, 1399 Sam Davis Rd*, a 168-acre plantation with the fully furnished home of the Boy Hero of the Confederacy, who was captured and executed as a spy at age 21; then get back to the present and

ready for freeway driving. And cars. **Nissan Motor Manufacturing Corporation,** *615-459-1444, Hwy U41/70 south of Smyrna,* is the largest automotive manufacturing facility under one roof in the U. S.; interesting to watch the robots and people working together in the production line; advance reservations are required for their Tuesday and Thursday tours.

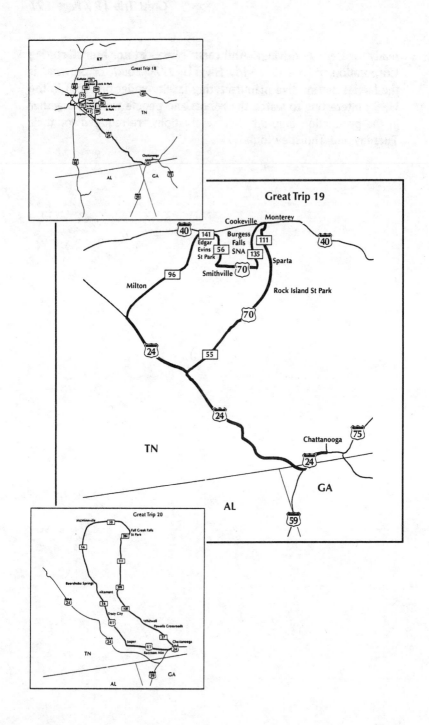

Great Trip 19

Chattanooga to Smithville, TN
the crafts and creeks scenic route

*via Rock Island St Pk, Sparta, Monterey, Cookeville, Burgess Falls St
Natural Area, Smithville, Silver Point, Edgar Evins St Pk,
returning to Chattanooga
approximately 360 miles round-trip, 7 hours driving time*

Why Go

Limestone Gorge & Blue Hole & Big Bone Cave & Sunset Rock &
Forested Hills & Clear-water Coves & Virgin Falls &
Rock House Shrine & Waterwheels & Handmade Furniture &
Appalachian Crafts & Artists Studios &
Fiddlers Jamboree & Fishing & More Fishing

Suggested route with approximate mileages

Instruction	Road	Dir	Miles
Chattanooga to Sparta	I-24 & S55 & U70S	N	122
Sparta to Monterey	S111 & U70N	N & E	30
Monterey to Cookeville	I-40	W	12
Cookeville to Smithville	S135 & U70	S & W	32
Smithville to Silver Point	S56N	N	14
Silver Point to Chattanooga	S141 & S96 & I-24	S	149
Total Mileage			359

The fishing is good and the living is easy. Quality of life and appreciation of the simple things are the keywords in the towns you'll visit on this Trip.

You'll see evidence of quality at **The Sparta Spoke Factory**; even their address is One Quality Lane. They've been in business since 1896, and today you can select the custom finish for your handmade rocker, or side table, and have it numbered for authenticity; the only one of its kind.

At the **Joe L. Evins Appalachian Craft Center**, you can study in a professional crafts school, or admire the work done by others. The gallery displays crafts from artisans in the 13 Appalachian states; the classes offer training in fiber, metal, wood, glass and clay. From a degreed program through Tennessee Tech to summer workshops, children's classes, Elderhostel, or simply visiting the studio of a working artist, you can develop your appreciation of fine craftsmanship.

In **Smithville** every July, people come together to hone the craft of fiddle playing at one of the top 100 tourism events in North America, the **Smithville Fiddlers Jamboree**. The **National Championship Country Musician Beginners** category of the event was designed to preserve the country music tradition by encouraging young people to compete.

Perhaps the natural beauty of this area increases the "appreciation" factor of anyone who lives here, or visits. It's easy to stop at **Sunset Rock** and gaze out over the **Central Basin**, enjoying a 50-mile view. It's awesome to hike to **Virgin Falls** in **Scott Gulf**; an 8-mile trek to see a stream emerge from a cave, plunge 110 feet, and disappear again in a cave at the bottom. It's calming to walk the lush woodlands and sit beside the cascading **Falling Water River** in **Burgess Falls Natural Area**.

Did somebody mention fishing? It's no secret that **The Blue Hole** in **Center Hill Lake** is considered one of the finest fishing places in the state; it's adjacent to the shore in **Rock Island State Rustic Park**. Center Hill Lake is blessed with two state parks, nine recreation areas, and eight commercial marinas that offer boat rentals and fishing supplies. **Edgar Evins State Park** has cabins and campsites. Come in the fall for the 50-mile cruise up the lake. Ah yes, the fishing is good, and the living is easy.

Tennessee State Park
Central Time

To See and Do

Rock Island State Rustic Park, *615-686-2471, Hwy U70S.* Great Falls on the Caney Fork River creates an imposing limestone gorge with plenty of scenic overlooks; good fishing and exploring; and there's a natural sand beach on Center Hill Lake. The Blue Hole, adjacent to the shore, is considered one of the finest fishing places in the state. This 883-acre wooded park is located at the confluence of the Collins and Caney Fork Rivers and even has several historic sites -- a 19th century textile mill and an early hydroelectric plant. Tours of nearby Big Bone Cave available on request. 10 Cabins, 60 Campsites available year-round, *restaurant* seasonal, 615-686-2471.

Sparta, TN
pop 4,681
Central Time
Chamber of Commerce 615-836-3552

To See and Do

Rock House Shrine, *615-836-3552, Hwy U70,* Andrew Jackson slept here as he traveled between Nashville and Washington, President James K. Polk stopped here too; this former stagecoach inn was constructed in 1835 along the Wilderness Trail and is listed today on the National Register of Historic Sites; call for hours.

Virgin Falls, *615-836-3552, Hwy U70 on Scott Gulf Rd;* formed by an underground stream as it emerges from a cave, it plunges 110 feet and goes back into a cave at the bottom; allow 6-8 hours for the complete 8-mile hike. **Sunset Rock,** *Hwy U70 east of Sparta,* is a scenic overlook that gives a 50-mile view of the Central Basin on clear days.

In downtown Sparta's Liberty Square, check out the **Sparta Amphitheater,** *615-836-3248;* it seats 500 and is used for concerts and programs; gazebo concession area. **The Sparta Spoke Factory,** *800-736-1896, One Quality Lane,* began making spokes for wagon wheels in 1896; today they produce hardwood furniture parts and a fine line of handmade furniture that is custom finished and numbered for authenticity; order red oak rockers, walnut candlesticks.

Accommodations
Royal Inn, 615-738-8585, Hwy 111 Bypass.

Monterey, TN
pop 2,559
Central Time
Chamber of Commerce 615-526-2211

To See and Do
Stop in the City Park to see **Standing Stone Monument**, 615-839-2323, E Commercial Ave; now sitting atop a pedestal, this ancient stone monolith was once the focus of Cherokee cultural activities and today is the center of the annual **Standing Stone Native American celebration.**

Wilson's North American Wildlife Museum, 615-839-3230, 914 N Chestnut, has over 150 scenes, under glass, of wildlife -- buffalo, moose, beaver, lynx, bear, bobcat and more.

Visit in the fall to watch molasses being made the old-time way in the **Muddy Pond Mennonite Community**, Hanging Limb Community; craftspeople, including buggy and harness maker, reside here; open daily.

Cookeville, TN
pop 21,744
Central Time
Chamber of Commerce 800-264-5541

To See and Do
Tennessee Technological University, 615-372-3101, N Dixie Ave, is here, and its **Bryan Fine Arts Center**, 615-372-3161, N Dixie Ave, on campus, has year-round exhibits of local and national artists, also performances by the Bryan Symphony Orchestra.

Cookeville Drama Center, *615-528-1313, 10 E Broad St*, is a 462-seat performing arts center located in the heart of Cookeville; many theatrical and musical productions hosted each year including touring Broadway productions; call for schedules.

The Cookeville Depot Museum, *615-528-8570, Corner of Cedar & Broad*, was built in 1909 by the Tennessee Central Railroad; today it's surrounded by a park plaza; its permanent holdings include railway artifacts, old photos, and two cabooses with original interiors, call for hours, or by appointment.

You'll find plenty of outdoor opportunities at a number of nearby parks. **Cane Creek Park**, *615-526-9591, 3 mi off I-40, exit 286*, is a 260-acre park with a 56-acre recreational lake; it's the largest municipal park in the Upper Cumberland Region; picnic shelters, biking/hiking trails, paddleboats, fishing piers, playgrounds, concession stand; year-round. **Golden Mountain Park**, *615-526-5253, 1555 Interstate Dr*, has picnic areas and pavilions for up to 800; volleyball & basketball courts, a softball complex, and miniature golf, go-carts, and bumper boats. **City Lake Natural Area**, *615-526-9591, Bridgeway Rd, just off Hwy U70 at I-40 exit 290*, is a 40-acre natural park bordering Old City Cave, with a fishing pier, hiking trail, waterfall with overlook, boat ramp, and for a little history, preserved water treatment buildings from the '20's At **Hidden Hollow Park**, *615-526-4038, 1901 Mt Pleasant Rd, Exit 290 on I-40*, you'll find a mill house with a 19 foot water wheel and a 35-foot waterfall; a covered bridge, 50-ft cross, and small chapel; a multi-colored fountain, lakes, canal, sandy beach with kiddie pool, swimming, hiking, fishing, volleyball, horseshoes, picnic shelters, unusual playgrounds, and even a petting zoo. The 86-acre park is open year round. **Upper Cumberland Sporting Clays**, *615-484-1624, on Brotherton Mountain 3 miles east of Algood*, is open weekends; it's Tennessee's first National Sporting Clays Association range.

Accommodations

Comfort Inn, *800-221-2222, 1100 S Jefferson Ave*; **Days Inn**, *800-325-2525, 1292 Bunker Hill Rd*; **Hampton Inn**, *800-426-7866, 1025 Interstate Dr*; **Howard Johnson Lodge**, *800-*

213-2016, 2021 E Spring St. Bed and breakfast at **Scarecrow Country Inn**, 615-526-3431, 644 Whitson Chapel Rd, 4 rooms, private bath, full breakfast, old log building with stained glass windows, full porch; lunch/dinner served in restaurant.

Tennessee State Park
Central Time

Burgess Falls State Natural Area, 615-432-5312, 4000 Burgess Falls Dr, just off Hwy S135; Falling Water River has beautiful cascades and the plunging Burgess Falls; historic waterworks, lush woodlands, scenic limestone cliffs, nature trail, picnic facilities in 155-acre setting; fishing in Burgess Falls Lake and the river.

Smithville, TN
pop 3,791
Central Time
Chamber of Commerce 615-597-4163

To See and Do

In downtown Smithville once a year, you can attend one of the top 100 tourism events in North America, the **Smithville Fiddlers Jamboree, Crafts Festival, and National Championship Country Musician Beginners**, 615-597-4163; it may hold the record as the festival with the longest name, too. Held in the square on the weekend nearest July 4, this country and bluegrass contest has been going on since 1972, with prizes for the best fiddle band, flat top guitar, dulcimer, gospel singing, folksinging, clogging and more; there is even a novelty event for spoon clacking, jug blowing, or washboard, and of course, the Grand Champion Fiddle-Off. The National Championship Country Musician Beginners category was added in 1984, in an effort to further preserve the country music tradition by encouraging young people to compete.

The address is officially Smithville, but the **Joe L. Evins Appalachian Craft Center**, 615- 597-6801, 1560 Craft Center Dr, I-40 Exit

273, Hwy S56, is spectacularly located on 180 acres overlooking Center Hill Lake, near Hurricane Bridge. Fine Appalachian crafts are taught and exhibited at this professional crafts school, with teaching programs in fiber, metal, wood, glass, and clay. A component of Tennessee Technological University, it has unsurpassed facilities and a nationally recognized faculty; summer workshops, evening classes, child-oriented and Elderhostel programs are offered too. It is the home of one of the finest craft galleries in the southeast, with a wide selection of items on sale from faculty and students at the center, as well as artisans from the 13 Appalachian states. It boasts 50,000 sq ft of studio space, 4,000 sq ft of exhibition and gallery space, conference and classrooms, a library, modern housing and a cafeteria.

Accommodations

Evins Mill Retreat, *615-597-2088, 1535 Evins Mill Rd;* 14 rooms, private baths, full breakfast, 90-foot waterfall, operational gristmill, fishing pond, hiking trails, conference center. **Wind in the Trees,** *800-852-4681,* 5 rooms, hot tub, view of Center Hill Lake. **Hidden Harbor Marina at Holmes Creek,** *615-597-8800, Holmes Creek Rd,* 5 units with kitchens; **Lakeside Resort & Educational Complex,** *615-597-4298,* 12 units with kitchens, meeting facilities.

Tennessee State Park
Central Time

Edgar Evins State Park, *615-858-2446, S of I-40, Hwy S96,* north of Smithville on the shores of Center Hill Reservoir; 6,280-acre park has steep forested hills and clear-water coves, Caney Fork River Valley; attracts boaters and fishermen. A fall cruise goes upstream for 50 miles to Rock Island State Park. Picnicking areas and shelters, marina, paddle boat rental.

Accommodations

Edgar Evins State Park, *615-858-2114, Silver Point,* village complex of 34 cabins with pool for guests; 60 campsites and bathhouse.

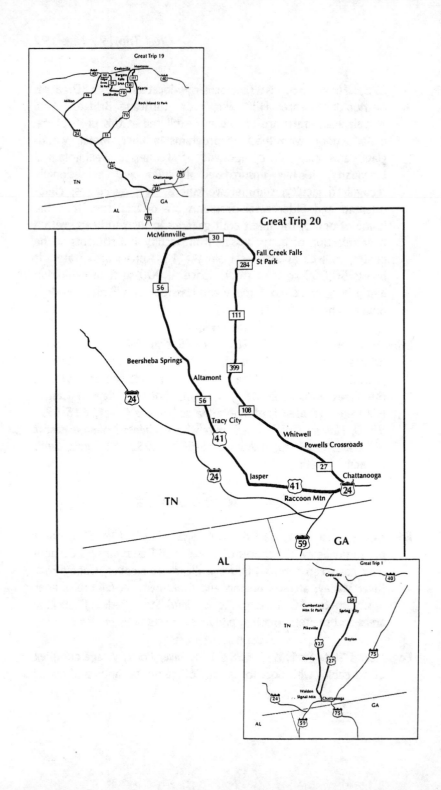

Great Trip 20

Chattanooga to Fall Creek Falls, TN
the gorges & gulfs & caves & coves route

*via Tennessee River Gorge, Jasper, Tracy City, South Cumberland
Recreation Area, Altamont, McMinnville, Fall Creek Falls St Pk,
Whitwell, Powells Crossroads, Prentice Cooper State Forest,
returning to Chattanooga
approximately 180 miles round-trip, 4 hours driving time*

Why Go

Savage Gulf & Lost Cove & Fiery Gizzard Trail & Stone Door &
River Gorge & Color Cruise & Country Fair & Country Cooking &
Wagon Rides & Clog Dancing & Applesauce Fruitcake &
Fall Creek Falls & Hall of Mountain King &
Natural Bridge & Backpacking & Bald Eagles & Peregrine Falcons

Suggested route with approximate mileage

Instruction	Road	Dir	Miles
Chattanooga to Jasper	I-24 & U41	S & N	28
Jasper to Tracy City	U41	N	19
Tracy City to Altamont	S56	N	15
Altamont to McMinnville	S56	N	28
McMinnville to Fall Creek Falls SP	S30 & S284	E	31
Fall Creek Falls SP to Whitwell	S111 & S399 & S108	S	36
Whitwell to Powells Crossroads	S283	E	2
Powells Crossroads to Chattanooga	S27	S	19
Total Mileage			178

Celebrate the scenery. In steep-walled narrow canyons, such as the Tennessee River Gorge, stretching 26 miles between Raccoon Mountain and Walden Ridge. In deep chasms, such as Savage Gulf in the South Cumberland Area. In small valleys in the mountain's side, such as Lost Cove in the Carter Natural Area. In underground chambers that open to the surface, such as Cumberland Caverns in McMinnville. This Trip is made of gorges and gulfs and coves and caves, and keeps you far from the madding crowd.

Except at **Color Cruise** time, of course. That's when everyone who has ever owned a boat gathers at Shellmound on Nickajack Lake and celebrates autumn, and boating, and music, and of course, the scenery. That's when the Gorge gets really gorgeous and the 1,000 varieties of trees and plants all turn a different color. And except during the **Ketner's Mill Country Fair** in the Sequatchie Valley, when country cooking and crafts mix it up with clog dancing and canoeing and anybody who has ever been can't stay away.

The rest of the year, the place is yours, to spend a lifetime exploring and camping in the seclusion of one of the most ruggedly beautiful places in the Southeast. The **Tennessee River Gorge** is 25,000 acres and home to endangered species such as the bald eagle and the peregrine falcon.

The **South Cumberland Recreation Area** sets aside 12,000 acres for your use; five natural areas with enticing names like Fiery Gizzard Trail, and Savage Gulf, and Stone Door.

Fall Creek Falls State Park is the largest in the state system, with half its 16,000 acres in wilderness. A fine resort hotel take full advantage of the spectacular scenery; cabins and campsites are spread among the trees and by the lake.

Prentice Cooper State Forest covers the south end of Walden Ridge; 26,800 acres of wilderness in Chattanooga's back door.

This part of the country has too many caves to count, but one of the largest open to the public is **Cumberland Caverns** near McMinnville. Only Mammoth Cave is larger! The Hall of the Mountain King is 600 by 150 feet, almost big enough to hold the Color Cruise crowd! Or, maybe you'll meet the neighborhood Scouts, getting ready for a wild cave tour.

Tennessee River Gorge
Eastern & Central Time

The Tennessee River Gorge is 25,000 acres carved through the Cumberland Mountains by a 26-mile stretch of the Tennessee River and serves as a habitat for more than 1,000 varieties of plants, trees, and flowers; endangered species such a mountain skullcap, bald eagle, and peregrine falcon live in the gorge. Raccoon Mountain makes up the south side of the Gorge, and a stop at TVA's **Raccoon Mountain Pumped Storage Reservoir,** *423-825-3100, Hwy U41,* allows spectacular views from the **Gorge Overlook.** Inside the building a guide will board the elevator with you for a descent deep into the mountain. Your tour underground shows how water is pumped to the manmade lake at the top of the mountain and stored for use as power demands require. The drive around the reservoir allows good views of neighboring Lookout Mountain and Walden Ridge; you're likely to see hawks and eagles soaring overhead. Picnic areas, hiking trails, and overlooks facing the city and Lookout Mountain too.

**Note time change from Eastern to Central
as you go into Marion County**

Jasper, TN
pop 2,780
Central Time
Marion County Chamber of Commerce 423-942-5103

To See and Do
When you come out of the Gorge, you reach the widest waters of TVA's **Nickajack Lake.** The 10,900-acre lake has a shoreline of 192 miles and offers an abundance of fishing and boating opportunities. Boating through the Gorge to the Nickajack Reservation is an autumn tradition on the **Fall Color Cruise & Folk Festival,** *423-892-0223 for info, Shellmound Recreation area, last two weekends in October;* since 1968 Tennessee's fall color has been celebrated here with music, dancing, crafts and food. This is one of the Top Twenty Annual events in the

southeastern United States.

Accommodations

Hales Bar Marina & Campground, 423-942-4040, houseboat and pontoon rental, covered storage, 42 campsites.

Tracy City, TN
pop 1,556
Central Time
Chamber of Commerce 615-779-3462

To See and Do

The Dutch Maid Bakery, 615-592-3171, 111 Main St, is Tennessee's oldest family-run bakery; it was established in 1902 by Swiss immigrants; most of the baking is done in a 1930's converted stoker oven and they are still turning out Old World recipe breads and their famous applesauce fruitcakes, informal tours are given on request, ask for a mail-order brochure so you can order such items as sugar plum cake or a sampler box of breads all year round. **Mountain Lakes Glassworks,** 615-592-5252, 340 Lake Rd, has lodging and classes available by appointment in a lakeside setting; hand-blown glassware, pottery and bronze casting.

Tennessee Recreation Area
Central Time

South Cumberland Recreation Area, 615-924-2980. Start at the **Visitors Center,** Hwy U41, between Tracy City and Monteagle; enjoy the interpretive exhibits and gather information on each component of the South Cumberland State Park Complex. There are seven separate areas spread over 12,000 acres. The five natural areas are Stone Door, Savage Gulf, Fiery Gizzard Trail, Carter Natural Area, and Sewanee Natural Bridge. **Stone Door and Savage Gulf** have forests, many miles of hiking and backpacking trails, waterfalls, and spectacular vistas. **Fiery Gizzard Trail** connects **Grundy Forest** and **Foster Falls;** hikers are treated to one of the nation's most outstanding trails, and may enjoy a swim in Fiery Gizzard Creek. **Carter Natural Area** is part of a unique enclosed valley sinkhole, **Lost Cove**, and has dense forests, clear streams, and an impressive cave entrance. **Sewanee Natural Bridge** is a sandstone arch overlooking Lost Cove. **Grundy Lakes** is a day-use area near Tracy City where you'll find swimming and picnicking areas and some historic 19th Century coke ovens.

Altamont, TN
pop 679
Central Time
Grundy County Chamber of Commerce
615-779-3462

To See and Do
Many artisans and craftspeople have settled in this area; **Cumberland Craftsman**, *615-692-3595*, *Greeters Mill*, *Hwy S56*, specializes in the work of woodcarver Ron Van Dyke and other local artists. Ask about the Hillbilly Chess Set.
Accommodations
The Manor, **1885**, *615-692-3153*, *Main St*, 5 rooms, full breakfast, 3 porches, children welcome, near Savage Gulf; **The Woodlee House**, *615-692-2368*, *10 Cumberland St*, 2 rooms, full breakfast, living room is pre-Civil War log cabin, on National Register of Historic Places.

McMinnville, TN
pop 11,194
Central Time
Chamber of Commerce 615-473-6611

To See and Do
The big draw here is **Cumberland Caverns**, *615-668-4396*, *Hwy S8, 7 mi SE*; second in size only to Kentucky's Mammoth Cave. This US National Landmark has great underground hallways and galleries; the Hall of the Mountain King room is the largest cave

room east of the Mississippi, at 600 feet long, 150 feet wide, and 140 feet high. In the underground dining room, which will seat 500 for a banquet, but is available by reservation only, hangs a half-ton crystal chandelier; there is a theatre pipe organ and a stage in the room too. "God of the Mountain," a dramatization, is shown on the cave tour.

Above ground, visit **Historic Falcon Manor**, *615-668-4444, 2645 Faulkner Springs Rd,* an 1890's Victorian mansion filled with museum-quality period antiques; once the home of Clay Faulkner, a wealthy entrepreneur; tours daily, group tours by appointment; also serves as a Bed & Breakfast.

Accommodations

Holiday Inn, *800-HOLIDAY, 809 Sparta St.* **Falcon Manor Bed & Breakfast**, *615-668-4444, 2645 Faulker Springs Rd,* 5 rooms in historic Victorian mansion, full breakfast, rocking chair verandas, tree-shaded lawn, daily tours.

Tennessee State Park
Central Time

Fall Creek Falls State Park, *423-881-5241, off Hwy S111 and S30,* is the largest park in the state system with over 16,000 acres. Here you'll find virgin timber, spectacular scenery, majestic cascades, and the striking Fall Creek Falls, which plunges 256 feet into a shaded pool. More than half the park is a natural area wilderness. A resort park, there is a 345-acre lake which has yielded record-size fish, an 18-hole championship golf course, and a Nature Center which provides exhibits on the geology, plants and animals of the area.

Accommodations

Fall Creek Falls Inn, *423-881-5241,* has a restaurant and 73 rooms; in the park are 20 cabins, a group lodge, a group camp, and 227 campsites. **Fall Creek Falls Bed & Breakfast**, *423-881-5494, 1 mile from north entrance to park;* a country manor home on forty acres of rolling hillside, 8 rooms, 2 sitting areas, view, full breakfast.

Whitwell / Powells Crossroads, TN

pop 1,622/pop 1,098
Central Time
Marion County Chamber of Commerce
423-942-5103

To See and Do

Ketner's Mill Fall Country Fair, *423-757-6232 for info, usually held middle weekend in October.* On the banks of the Sequatchie River in Marion County, parts of the mill date to 1824; the new addition 1882. It's still working, pick up some stone-ground cornmeal after you've admired the simplicity of this water-driven operation. The country fair has all the things you'd expect: country cooking, more than 150 artists and craftspersons, and music and dancing. You can catch a wagon ride around the place or canoe the peaceful Sequatchie waters.

Prentice Cooper State Forest, *423-658-5551, Hwy S27, Tower Dr,* is a 26,800-acre day-use area on the southern tip of Walden Ridge; hiking and mountain biking trails; rifle, archery, hunting allowed. Cumberland State Scenic Trail winds through forest; limited primitive camping.

**Note time change from Central to Eastern
as you return to Hamilton County**

Downtown Chattanooga

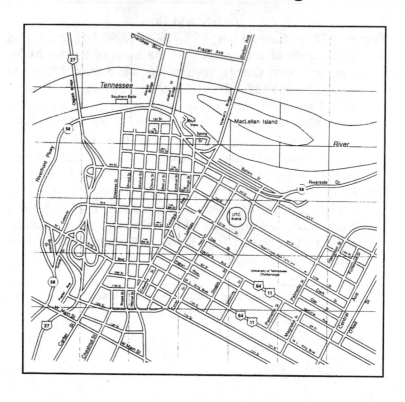

Great Trip 21

What to Do in Chattanooga If You Have A Day

To See and Do

Get a copy of *Chattanooga Great Places!* The one-and-only guidebook to Chattanooga will entice you to come back again and again!

Great Trips plus *Great Places!* A dynamite duo and the only guidebooks you need.

Great Trip 22

What to Do in Chattanooga
If You Have a Weekend

To See and Do

Spend a day at Lookout Mountain

Read the entire section on Chattanooga! Plan your next Weekend
    Trip with lots of new things to do.

And buy *Chattanooga Great Places*, the guidebook to the
    Chattanooga area, with over 700 listings of places to eat, go,
    shop, stay and use, so you can spend many delightful weekends
    in the Scenic City.

Great Trips plus *Great Places!* A dynamite duo and the only
    guidebooks you need.

Great Trip 23

What to Do in Chattanooga If You Have a Week

To See and Do

Spend Forever
Get *Chattanooga Great Places!*
If you live in Chattanooga or visit often, get the authoritative guidebook to the city. It has the lowdown on more than 700 places in the Chattanooga area to eat, go, shop, stay and use!
Great Trips plus *Great Places!* A dynamite duo and the only guidebooks you need.

Great Trip 24

What to Do in Chattanooga Rain or Shine

To See and Do

The Weather is Bad

Oh No! It's not just raining, the thunder is booming; or that Gulf air is making it so humid it's too hot to sweat; or that Arctic blast is freezing my mittens off.

The Weather is Great
Of course, you can do any bad-weather things on sunny days too, plus these.

And in all kinds of weather, browse your favorite bookstore!
You can have a delightful afternoon at any of the following places:
- Barrett & Company Booksellers, *423-267-2665, 16 Frazier Ave*
- Books A Million, *423-894-1690, 2020 Gunbarrel Rd*
- Books A Million, *423-874-0870, 5230 Hwy 153*
- Chattanooga State Bookstore, *423-697-4425, 4501 Amnicola Hwy, CSTCC Campus*
- Little Professor Book Center, *423-877-7080, 5450 Hwy 153*
- McKay Used Books, *423-892-0067, 6401 Lee Hwy*
- Media Play, *423-954-1855, 2132 Gunbarrel Rd*
- UTC Bookstore, *423-755-4107, 615 McCallie Ave, UTC Campus*
- Waldenbooks, *423-894-9406 & 894-6586, Hamilton Place; 423-265-2980, 700 Market St; 423-899-7557, Eastgate Mall; 423-875-0195, Northgate Mall*

Great Trip 25

What to Do in Chattanooga After Dark

To See and Do

Some of these you can do in the daytime, of course! But when you're looking for things to do after the sun goes down, try these.

Notes on My Own Favorite Things to Do in Chattanoga

I, _____ , owner of this book,
want/like to do these things in Chattanooga:

_____

_____

_____

_____

_____

_____

_____

_____

_____

_____

_____

_____

_____

_____

_____

_____

_____

_____

_____

_____

_____

Everything in Chattanooga is shaped by the mountains and the waters we have. **Lookout Mountain** stands like a sentinel over the city, holding memories of Civil War battles. It's the site of some of today's best-known attractions -- the **Incline**, **Point Park**, **Rock City**, **Ruby Falls** -- and gorgeous view homes.

Signal Mountain, on the other side of the river, served as a lookout post during Civil War times; today it's loved for its rugged beauty. **Prentice Cooper State Forest** takes up the south end, making it accessible to all; the **Tennessee Gorge**, also called the **Little Grand Canyon**, begins here.

Raccoon Mountain curves and twists to form the southern boundary of the Gorge, a 26-mile stretch that is home to over 1,000 varieties of plant life and endangered species such as the bald eagle and the peregrine falcon.

Missionary Ridge, in downtown Chattanooga, is graced with beautiful homes boasting Civil War cannons and historic markers in their yards; **Big Ridge** extends the same geologic formation across the river into the Hixson area. Beautiful mountains!

The mighty **Tennessee River** flows through the city, a TVA dam within the city limits forming 35,400-acre **Chickamauga Lake**, 59 miles long with a shoreline of 810 miles. That translates into unbelievable water recreation! Fishing, boating, skiing, sailing, swimming, and living water-side are the norm in Chattanooga. **North** and **South Chickamauga Creeks** and **Lookout Creek** add to the charm. Beautiful waters!

Have I mentioned downtown Chattanooga? The **world's largest freshest aquarium** is at **Ross's Landing!** The **Southern Belle Riverboat** is there too; and the **IMAX**, the **RiverWalk**, and the **Walnut Street Bridge**. A FREE state-of-the-art **electric shuttle** will take you throughout the downtown area, dropping you off at **Warehouse Row**, **museums**, unique downtown **restaurants**, your **hotel**, or the **Chattanooga ChooChoo!**

Yes, there is a choo-choo in Chattanooga. On the back cover of this book you can see the pretty red and green 1880 engine that sits in the ChooChoo complex today. You can climb on it, play "engineer" on it, or stand in front for souvenir pictures.

A visit to Chattanooga is a visit to everyplace you want to go. Unique and beautiful, it's a knock-your-socks-off **Great Place!**

Chattanooga, TN
pop 152,466; metro pop 433,210
Eastern Time
Chamber of Commerce 423-756-2121
Convention & Visitors Bureau 423-756-8687

To See and Do

Attractions Downtown

Chattanooga ChooChoo Complex, *423-266-5000, 1400 Market St;* 1880 ChooChoo engine and former 1909 train station with the highest dome of its kind in the world; a model railroad museum, an antique trolley with narrated ride; restaurants, shops, gardens, convention center and hotel. A route on the summer schedule of the Tennessee Valley Railroad Museum brings a passenger train into the ChooChoo for a ride to the Museum and back. The Shuttle bus runs from here through town to the Aquarium. The site is on the National Register of Historic Places. **Warehouse Row Factory Shops,** *423-267-1111, 1110 Market Street;* eight old railroad warehouses built in the early 1900's now house 45 outlet and factory stores; more shops in the Freight Depot across the street; don't miss **The J. Peterman Company!** Complimentary parking available in the 3-level garage, or catch the electric shuttle between the ChooChoo and the Aquarium.

The **Tennessee River** is 652 miles long and houses more species of fish than any river in North America. On its downtown banks is the **Tennessee Aquarium,** *423-265-0695, 1 Broad St, open daily 10-6, extended summer hours.* The largest freshwater aquarium in the world has two living forests and 7,000 animals made up of 400 species; a darkened canyon path takes you past huge, multi-storied bodies of water from a cove forest in the Appalachian highlands to flat Delta country and the Gulf. The Nickajack Lake exhibit depicts Tennessee River waters, see largemouth bass and catfish in the largest freshwater tank in the world -- 138,000 gallons, with windows 9 inches thick. World rivers have red-bellied piranhas from South America's Amazon, tiger fish from Africa's Zaire, sturgeon from Asia's Yenisy and North America's St Lawrence.

On the river and surrounding the aquarium are **Ross's Landing Park & Plaza** *423-266-7070, 100 Broad St;* Ross's Landing is the "beginning" of Chattanooga, site of a ferry and warehouse established about 1815 by John and Lewis Ross. A paved concrete path on the Plaza takes you from the formation of the first rivers to the bottling of the first Coca-Cola; from trading post days to the Chattanooga ChooChoo railroad era; park has stepping stones, waterfalls, benches.

Across the street is the **IMAX 3D Theater,** *423-266-4629, 201 Chestnut St;* one of only 14 in the world, the screen is six stories high and the images and sound are extraordinary.

At Ross's Landing is the **Southern Belle Riverboat,** *423-266-4488, 201 Riverfront Parkway, open daily, conditions permitting, schedules fluctuate seasonally;* two inside decks and a fresh-air upper deck for sightseeing-only trips, and breakfast, luncheon, and dinner cruises; accompanied by Dixieland, gospel, or country music.

Riverwalk extends from Ross's Landing to the **Bluff View Art District;** great river views and steps to the **Walnut Street Bridge,** an 1890's structure built for cars that's been preserved as a park; today claims the honor as longest pedestrian walkway over water in the world. Brightened by twinkling lights at night and flowerpots by day, it's a half-mile across and the best spot in town to watch the evening sunset, or walk to the artsy **North Shore.** Parking available on the street if you don't want steps.

Attractions Lookout Mountain

Incline Railway, *423-821-4224, 3917 St Elmo Ave (bottom), 827 E Brow Rd (top), open daily, 3-4 trips per hour;* "America's Most Amazing Mile" is the worlds steepest passenger railway; the grade is 72.7% as it nears the top of Lookout Mountain; glass-domed cars allow spectacular views of valley and city below. Originally built in 1895, it's a National Historic Site. Snack bars at each end and observation deck at the top.

From its perch on the northern tip of Lookout Mountain, **Point Park,** *423-821-7786, Visitor Center open daily 8-5:45 summer; closes 4:45 Sept-May; park open daylight hours;* is visible from all over the city and is the best spot from which to view the city. At the Visitor Center, watch an 8-minute slide program that gears you to what you'll find in the park; also see James Walker's 13x33-foot painting, *Battle Above the Clouds*. During summer months rangers give daily tours and talks; in the park three gun batteries mark a segment of the siege lines that encircled Chattanooga during the Civil War; on top of the 95-foot high **New York Peace Memorial**, Union and Confederate soldiers shake hands under one flag. Descend 500 feet down several tiers of steps to the **Ochs Overlook; Moccasin Bend** just below is where the Tennessee River changes direction from south to north, the only spot in the world you can see such a sight.

Rock City Gardens *706-820-2531, 1400 Patten Rd, Lookout Mountain, GA, open daily 8:30 am till sundown,* were built in 1932 among the boulders and waterfalls on top of the mountain; Lovers Leap and Fat Man's Squeeze are two well-known stops; spectacular views to "seven states;" swinging bridge, over 400 varieties of plants; Fairyland, Mother Goose Village and a real live Mother Goose dispensing Goosey hugs to the kiddies. Main half-mile trail has many steps and narrow passageways, allow one-two hours; benches and rest stops along the way and a special path wheelchair-accessible to view spots.

Ruby Falls Caverns, *423-821-2544, 1720 S Scenic Hwy, Lookout Mtn, open daily 8 am, closing varies from 6-9 pm during year,* For more than 60 years the elevator has carried people down inside the mountain to hike the crystal wonderlands to Ruby Falls. Named for the discoverer's wife, Ruby Lambert, floodlights now play on the 145-foot waterfall to turn it ruby red. Guides point out the stalactite-stalagmite formations you pass; the walk to the falls is four-fifths of a mile, generally flat except for 32 steps, allow about 70 minutes on an average day.

Raccoon Mountain Attractions, Alpine Slide, Grand Prix, *423-825-5666, 425 W Hills Dr, Hwy U41 off I-24 exit 174, open daily summer, limited hrs spring, fall, closed Dec-Feb, call for details;* chairlift to the top; 1/2-mile dry-slide descent down the mountain; car racing requires a driver's license for the Grand Prix; ten years and up can drive the Go Carts; there are Little Indys for the younger set; snack bar and picnic tables.

Raccoon Mountain Caverns, *423-821-9403, 319 W Hills Dr, Hwy*

U41 off I-24 exit 174; one of the most active caverns in the southeast, new growth continues to appear from season to season; cave coral, natural bridges, soda straws and an array of stalactites, stalagmites, columns and rimstone pools on the 45-minute walk. Wild Cave Tour for more experienced explorers.

Attractions Around Town

Tennessee Valley Railroad Museum, *423-894-8028, 4119 Cromwell Rd and 220 N Chamberlain Ave, Hours different summer/winter; BE SURE to call ahead for train schedules. Museum and parking free, fee for rides. Group reservations available.* The largest operating historic railroad in the south has a superb collection of engines and rail cars; from the Grand Junction Depot the train goes through the 986-foot Missionary Ridge tunnel, built in 1858. Two trips are available; the shorter trip goes to the East Chattanooga Depot and the shop area where engines are restored; your engine reverses directions on the turntable before reattaching itself to your railcar for a trip back through the tunnel. The other trip is offered in summer only, to the Chattanooga ChooChoo. **Lake Winnepesaukah Amusement Park,** *706-866-5681, 1115 Lakeview Dr, Rossville,* 32 rides, Cannonball coaster, miniature golf, 17 picnic shelters; music on Sunday afternoons in summer.

Museums, Galleries, Theater, Music Downtown

Tennessee Aquarium, *423-265-0695, 1 Broad St,* a living museum; also maps, schematics and photographs of the Tennessee River Valley as well as rivers of the world. **Creative Discovery Museum,** *423-756-2738, 4th & Chestnut St,* is a children's hands-on arts and sciences museum for children of all ages with an artist's studio, inventor's workshop, musician's workshop, and field scientist's lab; changing exhibits, theatre, observatory, science lab. **Chattanooga Regional History Museum,** *423-265-3247, 400 Chestnut St,* has more than 10,000 years of area history; changing exhibits include Civil War, sports history and period clothing; periodical quilt exhibitions. **International Towing & Recovery Hall of Fame & Museum,** *423-267-3132, 401 Broad St,* displays wreckers and towing equipment from 1916 when Chattanoogan Ernest Holmes began manufacturing.

Hunter Museum of American Art , *423-267-0968, 10 Bluff View;* permanent American art; touring shows in five galleries; exhibits, lectures, and films; 1906 mansion on National Register; 90 feet above the river on bluff used as a lookout and garrison during the Civil War. **Houston Museum of Decorative Arts,** *423-267-7176, 201 High Street,* dolls, toys, quilts, glassware; guided tour; groups welcome. **River Gallery,** *423-267-7353, 400 E 2nd St,* contemporary paintings, wood carvings, sculpture, basketry, ceramics, textiles, art furniture, art glass and handmade books. **River Gallery Sculpture Garden,** *423-267-7353, 214 Spring St,* outdoor gallery and park featuring regional, national, and international artists.

National Medal of Honor Museum, *423-267-1737, 400 Georgia;* military memorabilia; uniforms, videos, pictures, and weaponry recall the wars in which U. S. involved; unusual items include the first cannonball fired at Chattanooga during the Civil War. **Siskin Museum of Religious Artifacts,** *423-634-1700, 1 Siskin Plaza, Located in Siskin Rehabilitation Complex,* over 400 items from the 16th to 20th centuries in stone, wood, ivory, silver and porcelain; religions and philosophies represented include Judaism, Christianity, Confucianism, Islam, Buddhism, and Hindu; guided tours by appointment. **Oak Street Playhouse,** *423-756-2024, 419 McCallie Ave,* springtime play, Christmas dinner theatre show; fall puppet show in a 120-seat theatre.

Bessie Smith Hall, *423-757-0020, 200 M. L. King Boulevard,* exhibits about Chattanooga native Bessie Smith, legendary blues artist; special musical programs and performances; cabaret style; also in the hall is the **Chattanooga African-American Museum** *423-267-1076,* cultural and historical documents and artifacts portraying African-American contributions; art, original sculptures, musical recordings.

For music, catch the **Nightfall** at Miller Plaza, *423-265-0771, Chattanooga Downtown Partnership;* free performances on Fridays beginning at 7; great variety for families outdoors by the fountain from June through September; **Coffeehouse** free concerts inside the Pavilion on Tuesdays in January and February. At the **Sandbar,** *423-622-4432, 1011 Riverside Dr,* the Traveling Riverside Blues Caravan on Mondays; rock, pop, jazz, blues or folk also at **Boiled Frog**, 423-756-3764, 1269 Market St; **Brass Register**, 423-265-2175, 618 Georgia Ave, **Yesterdays**, 423-756-1978, 820 Georgia Ave, **Clearwater Cafe**, 423-266-0601,1301 Chestnut; **Stone Lion**, 423-266-5466, 418 High St; enjoy gospel, Dixieland, or country sounds during your dinner cruise on the **Southern Belle Riverboat**, 423-266-4488, 201 Riverfront Parkway.

Museums, Galleries, Theater, Music North Shore

Little Theatre of Chattanooga 423-267-8534, 400 River Street, has eight shows a season, and a Youth Theatre Program; dress rehearsals free. **In-Town Gallery** 423-267-9214, 26 Frazier Avenue, cooperative gallery, regional artists. **Plum Nelly Shop & Gallery**, 423-266-0585, 1101 Hixson Pike, 400 artists; pottery, baskets, handbound books, wind chimes, furniture, throws, metal works, bird carvings. Music at **Durty Nelly's**, 423-265-9970, 109 N Market; **Las Margaritas**, 423-756-3332, 1101 Hixson Pike.

Museums, Galleries Lookout Mountain

Clay Shop & Outlook Gallery, 423-821-5212, 3815 St Elmo Ave, 60 regional artists; pottery, jewelry, photography, hand-blown glass, weaving; Vaughan Greene at the potter's wheel. **Horsin' Around**, 423-825-5616, 3804 St Elmo Ave, the most unusual artists in town in a birthing-room for carousel animals; watch as they design, carve and paint. **Battles for Chattanooga Museum**, 423-821-2812, 3742 Tennessee Ave, 3-D electronic map, 5,000 miniature soldiers, 650 lights, sound effects; battles for Chattanooga changed the outcome of the Civil War; Sherman used Chattanooga as his base as he started his march to Atlanta and the sea.

Museums, Galleries, Theater, Music Around Town

All Around Town, Chattanooga State Technical Community College Sculpture Garden, 423-697-4400, 4501 Amnicola Hwy, twenty-five works on display on riverside campus, near Riverpark. **Tennessee Valley Railroad Museum**, 423-894-8028, 4119 Cromwell Rd, and 220 N Chamberlain Ave, collection of engines and rail cars in fixed position; shop area where volunteers restore locomotives, rail cars, push cars, and other rail memorabilia. **National Knife Museum**, 423-892-

5007, 7201 Shallowford Rd, collection of more than 5,000 knives, swords, razors and cutlery. **Back Stage Dinner Theatre,** *423-629-1565, 3264 Brainerd Rd,* musical comedies, mysteries, and dramas; Fri-Sat. **Barking Legs Theatre,** *423-624-5347, 1307 Dodds Ave;* intimate 80-seat house for music, theatre and dance. **Comedy Catch,** *423-622-CAFE, 3224 Brainerd Rd,* shows Wed -Sat, live comedy nightspot, dinner available in the Cafe Restaurant; smokefree show Friday. Music overlooking the lake at **Arts' Lakeshore,** *423-877-7068, 5600 Lake Resort Terrace.*

Country music at **Governors Lounge,** *423-624-2239, 4251 Bonny Oaks Dr;* **Palomino's,** *423-624-9274, 2620 Rossville Blvd;* **Rock and Country Club,** *423-894-9921, 6175 Airways Blvd.* **Mountain Opry,** *423-886-5897, Fairmount Rd, Signal Mtn,* old-time bluegrass in the Walden Ridge Civic Center every Friday night; free but donations appreciated.

Music Series includes **Chattanooga Symphony and Opera,** *423-267-8583, 630 Chestnut St,* seven symphony performances, three opera productions, and chamber music concerts. **Dorothy Patten Fine Arts Series,** *423-755-4269, Vine St at Palmetto, UTC Fine Arts Center on campus;* live performances by nationally recognized artists. **TAPA Series,** *423-757-5042, 399 McCallie Ave,* touring performances at Tivoli and Memorial Auditorium; **Eugene A. Anderson Organ Concert Series,** *423-238-2880, Collegedale SDA Church, College Dr off Apison Pike,* European and American artists, also organ and orchestra concerto with Southern College Symphony, annual week-long organ festival.

Recreation, Sports and the Great Outdoors

Baseball, AA Southern League, Chattanooga Lookouts, *423-267-2208, 1130 E 3rd St, Engel Stadium,* former Lookouts in the National Baseball Hall of Fame are Clark Griffith, Burleigh Grimes, Rogers Hornsby, Ferguson Jenkins, Harmon Killebrew, Willie Mays and Satchel Paige; the stadium went up in 1929; renovated in 1989, it's considered one of the finest in the Southern League.

Basketball, University of Tennessee at Chattanooga, *423-266-6627 for individual game tickets; 755-5285 for season tickets,* Men's

Basketball leads in Southern Conference Championships; the Roundhouse seats 11,200 for round ball; from November to March.

Billiards, Chattanooga Billiard Club, 423-267-7740, 725 Cherry St; East location 499-3883, 110 Jordan Dr; downtown location is home of Tennessee State 9-ball Championships; lessons and leagues available; restaurant and bar, late night. **Parkway Billiards,** 423-265-7665, 35 Patten Parkway, billiards, darts, lessons, leagues, restaurant and full bar, late night.

Bowling, Holiday Bowl, 423-894-0503, 5518 Brainerd Rd, 48 lanes with Brunswick automatic scoring; gameroom, snack bar, lounge, pro shop. **Holiday Bowl,** 423-843-2695, 5530 Hixson Pike, 24 lanes, same features as above. **Tri-State Lanes,** 423-867-2281, 3636 Ringgold Rd, 32 lanes with automatic scoring, snack bar, lounge, game room.

Canoeing, Lookout Creek, 423-821-1160, west side of Lookout Mountain, winds its way through the Chattanooga Nature Center; canoe explorations can be scheduled through Center. **North Chickamauga Creek,** OutVenture 423-842-6629, Greenway Farm departure for canoe trips; flows from Walden Ridge through Hixson Community. **South Chickamauga Creek,** OutVenture 423-842-6629., winds through Audubon Acres and the Brainerd levee. Get equipment and info at **Rock Creek Down Under,** 423-265-1836, 44 Frazier Avenue.

Climbing/Mountaineering, Sunset Rock on Lookout Mountain offers easy accessibility and 250 routes for experienced climbers; the Tennessee, or **T-Wall,** stretches two miles along the rim of the Gorge, and has more than 200 routes, ranging from intermediate to extreme in difficulty. **Adventure Guild,** 423-266-5709, 100 Cherokee Blvd, offers classes and organized trips. Get equipment and info at **Rock Creek Outfitters,** 423-265-5969, 100 Tremont Street.

Fishing, TVA Maps and Survey Information, 423-751-6277, 311 Broad St, TVA recreation maps show the fish attractor locations, boat launching sites, and other helpful information; navigation charts for all TVA waters. **TVA Lake Information Line,** 423-751-2264, gives latest information on lake levels and stream flows. **Osprey Trading Company,** 423-265-0306,

18 Frazier Ave; Orvis dealer, flies and tackle, guided trips, fly fishing schools. Good fishing piers along the river in **Tennessee Riverpark,** *Amnicola Hwy.*

Hiking, Bluff Trail *Point Park, Lookout Mountain;* get map at Visitor Center; main hiking trail from Point Park on Lookout Mountain; start at the metal steps left of the Ochs Museum, many trails lead away from the main one; Rifle Pits, Cravens House, Gum Springs, Skyuka, Jackson Gap, and Upper and Lower Truck Trail. **Cumberland State Scenic Trail,** *Signal Point, Signal Mountain,* from historic Signal Point see some of the most scenic areas in the state; Chattanooga section of trail begins in Prentice Cooper State Forest, winds along escarpments and stream valleys 20 miles northward to the rim of the Sequatchie Valley. **North Chickamauga Pocket Wilderness,** *Montlake Rd, Off Dayton Pike, Soddy-Daisy, TN,* 1,100-acre wilderness with waterfalls, interesting rock formations and breathtaking overlooks; Stevenson Trail runs along the north slope of the Creek for four miles, Hogskin Branch Loop is 1.5 miles from the parking lot.

Parks, Playgrounds & Greenways

Audubon Acres, *423-892-1499, I75 Exit 3A, right 2nd light to Gunbarrel Rd, 1 2/3 mi, follow signs,* is a 130-acre park with over 8 miles of walking and hiking trails, a swinging bridge to an area once populated by Native Americans and visited by DeSoto in the 1500's, and a cabin dating back to 1754. Cabin was first occupied by Cherokee naturalist Spring Frog, later by Robert Sparks Walker, who was nominated for Pulitzer Prize for his writings on nature and the Cherokee; park has eagle aviary and free-flight program; picnicking areas.

Chattanooga Nature Center, *423-821-1160, 400 Garden Rd, Lookout Mtn, some activities at Greenway Farm in Hixson,* is an environmental education facility featuring a crawl-in beaver lodge, a wildlife diorama, a 1,200-foot wetland walkway, and numerous wildlife exhibits on the western side of Lookout Mountain; some activities take place at the city-owned **Greenway Farm** in the Hixson area. **Reflection Riding** is a 300-acre botanic garden at the foot of Lookout Mountain; driving, biking and hiking trails; see Father Rock and the

legend of the dying Chief; spectacular wildflower gardens.
Chattanooga Parks & Recreation Department, 423-757-PLAY
for activities. Parks for Public Use include **Boynton Park,**
Cameron Hill, A one-acre park with civil war cannons, scenic
overlook of city; **Miller Park,** *423-697-9710 for reservations,*
10th & Market St. A one-acre park in the heart of downtown;
outdoor amphitheatre, large fountain, grassy areas and plants;
Montague Park, *1141 E 23rd St,* 45-acre park has 6
ballfields, concession stands, a playground, and grassy areas.
Ross's Landing Plaza, *Surrounds Tennessee Aquarium.* Outdoor
museum, paved history bands move back in time, stream
winds through regional history eras; benches, plants,
concessions. Connects to RiverWalk. **Walnut Street Bridge,**
Walnut Street at River. This half-mile linear park is the world's
longest pedestrian bridge; part of RiverWalk. **Warner Park,**
1254 3rd St. Largest of the city's major softball facilities; 53-
acres with 7 ballfields, 12 tennis courts, a paddle court,
playground, rose garden, horseshoe pits, picnic facilities,
public swimming pool, many grassy areas. Home to Power
House Fitness Center, ArtHaus, PAL and **Warner Park Zoo.**
Chester Frost County Park, 423-842-0177, *2318 Gold Point*
Circle, Hixson, on Chickamauga Lake's north side has boat
ramps, fishing, a lake swimming and beach area, showers,
snack bar, grills, a playground, and tennis courts..
Maclellan Island, *423-892-1499 for Audubon Society; island is*
near Walnut St & Veterans Bridges, 20-acre wildlife sanctuary
has meadows, wetlands, an observation deck, picnic shelter
and restrooms. A wildlife blind allows for observation of a
nesting colony of Great Blue Herons. Arrangements for
access must be made in advance.
Tennessee Riverpark, 423-493-9244, *4301 Amnicola Hwy,* all-
weather walking-jogging trail is two miles long, by the river,
with two launching facilities, five fishing piers, snack bar and
restrooms; picnic tables and pavilions; playground; large
meadow.
Rollerskating/Rollerblading, Roller Coaster Skate World 423-842-
6817, *5301 Hixson Pike;* **Skatin' Jakes,** *423-870-0000, 4300*
Access Rd.

Swimming, City and County parks (see Parks) have pools or lake swimming beaches; in summer there's a lifeguarded beach on the TVA reservation at the south side of Chickamauga Lake by the Dam.

Events & Festivals

Conference on Southern Literature, 423-267-1218, *Arts and Education Council biennially in odd years* brings distinguished southern authors to Chattanooga for lectures, informal discussions, book signings; includes films, dramas, music.

Hamilton County Fair, 423-842-0049. *Chester Frost Park, 4th weekend September;.* animals, exhibits, demonstrations, games and food; set in the trees along the lake in the county park.

Kaleidoscope, 423-265-4112, creative festival for children, with international, national and local performing arts; educational and interactive activities and displays.

Riverbend Festival, 423-265-4112 *info-line, held mid-June annually;* Over 100 artists from all over the country; the southeast's hottest festival takes place on the banks of the Tennessee River at Ross's Landing and spreads over five stages and nine days. Part of it is the free **Bessie Smith Strut** on Monday night; named after Chattanooga-born legendary blues singer Bessie Smith; it covers ten blocks along ML King Blvd, five stages of blues and jazz; barbecue tents and fish frys, and dancing.

Accommodations

Lodgings Downtown

ChooChoo **Holiday Inn,** *800-TRACK-29, 1400 Market St,* some train-car rooms; shopping arcade, gardens, restaurants; 1880 Chattanooga ChooChoo engine, trolley car. Shuttle through downtown to Aquarium.

Chattanooga Marriott at the Convention Center, *800-841-1674, 2 Carter Plaza,* indoor pool, restaurants, lounge, entertainment, adjacent to Convention and Trade Center, on Shuttle route.

Clarion Hotel, *800-252-7466, 407 Chestnut St,* restaurant and lounge, 2 blocks to Aquarium.

Marriott Residence Inn, *800-331-3131, 215 Chestnut St;* newest downtown hotel, rooms with kitchens, breakfast, indoor pool, convenient location between Creative Discovery Museum and IMAX Theater.

Radisson Read House Hotel, 800-333-3333, M L King & Broad Street, historic hotel listed on the National Register, Georgian style; terrazzo and marble floors, black-walnut paneling, carved woodwork. Central downtown location on shuttle route.

Bed and Breakfast at **Bluff View Inn,** 423-265-5033, 412 E 2nd St, two 1920's houses in the Bluff View Art District; parlors, suites with elegant kitchens; full gourmet breakfast; near RiverWalk.

Restaurants Downtown

Back Inn Cafe, 423-757-0108, 412 E 2nd, outside decks with river views; sculpture garden across the street; basement bistro in a 1920's home in Bluff View Art District.

Boiled Frog, 423-756-3764, 1269 Market St;; hop in for salads, samiches, and frog legs; cajun entrees include vegetable jambalaya, red beans and rice, mustard fried catfish.

Big River Grille, 423-267-2739, 222 Broad St, brew pub in old bus barn near the River, bar; pasta, chicken, fish; non-alcohol special drinks are homemade root beer, ginger ale.

Blue Cross Cafeteria, 423-755-6325, 801 Pine St, 10th floor, art in the lobby; bubble elevator to the 10th floor for salads, soups, sandwiches, hot entrees; one of the finest views in town.

Cafe Tazza, 423-265-3032, 1010 Market St, bagels, pastries and coffees; sidewalk musicians after dark; next to Miller Park.

Clearwater Cafe, 423-266-0601, 1301 Chestnut St, lunch is meat and three at a good price with a Monday-Friday daily special; Wednesday and Friday, come at 6 for music.

Durty Nelly's, 423-265-9970, 109 N Market St, an Irish Pub specializing in chilis like Nelly's Wild, broad range of beers at the bar; St Paddy's Day party and Halfway-To in September.

Electric Submarine Rock-n-Roll Cafe 423-266-8999, 347 Broad St, hear 60's sounds of Frankie Valli and the Shangri-Las; the subs come cold or hot; a Guppy Meal for the little ones.

Figgy's Sandwich Shop 423-266-8675, 20 W 8th, downtown lunch spot with soup every day; sandwiches, homemade brownies; interesting mural on two-story wall.

Flatiron Deli, 423-266-2620, 706 Walnut St, just down the street, in 1899, the first Coca-Cola was bottled; brick walls, breakfast and lunch; rotisserie chicken, fresh corn muffins, sandwiches.

Greyfriar's, 423-267-0376, 406 Broad St, three varieties of espresso and 25 teas, sandwiches, bagels and scones fresh baked; Italian sodas, rootbeer, cheesecake.

Le Doux's at Bluff View Inn, *423- 265-5033, 412 E 2nd,* southern dining with a nicely elegant French twist in 1920's house. Three intimate dining rooms, wine served in the parlor.

Lupi's Pizza Pies, *423-266-LUPI, 4th & Broad;* pizzas and calzones in meaty, veggie, or cheezy style; bread loaf with garlic oil for dipping; dine in or takeout.

Market Street Cafe, *423-266-4922, 10 Market St,* sandwiches, including one named The Chattanooga, salads; box lunches in mega or kids size.

Mary's Deli and Bake Shop, *423-266-1356, 724 Market St,* downtown lunch spot with take-out home cooking, specials daily; sandwiches and desserts; a few small tables inside.

Meyer's Deli & Bakery, *423-756-3497, Miller Plaza,* sandwiches, salads, stuffed breads, muffins; open during evening music on the Plaza.

Mom's Italian, *423-266-2204, 1257 Market St,* lasagna, ravioli, manicotti and of course pizza; everything's Mom-made fresh; Mom's family pictures decorate one wall.

Mudpie Coffeehouse and Newsstand, *423-267-9043, 12 Frazier Ave,* old stuffed chairs, a newsstand, tables out back; pizzas, sandwiches, and fancy desserts complement the coffees; beer.

Pickle Barrel Restaurant, *423-266-1103, 1012 Market St,* a spiral staircase to the outdoor deck; food and drink until the wee hours; corned beef and pastrami, the Big Cheese; with a pickle.

Porkers Uptown, *423-267-2726, 1251 Market St,* BBQ plates with baked beans and Texas toast; hamburgers, taters smothered with chili and cheese; coconut pie; old-time malts; beer.

Quixote's, *423-265-4721, 200 Market St;* healthy Mexican food; queso dip, taco salad, tequila lime chicken, or the big burrito; across the street from the Aquarium.

Provident Cafeteria, *423-755-1251, Fountain Square, through the lobby off Walnut;* soups, grill & deli, meat & vegetables, and a giant salad bar; sunny skylit atrium with a view of half the town.

Rembrandt's Coffeehouse, *423-267-2451, 204 High St,* selection of pastries, candies, coffees, inside there's a nice view towards downtown; outside patio.

Sandbar Restaurant, *423-622-4432, 1011 Riverside Dr,* glass-enclosed porch, upper deck, patio, on the river; seafood platter or catfish fillets; key lime pie; section of RiverWalk begins here.

Shapiro's Gift Pantry and *Delicatessen* *423-266-3669, 723 Cherry St,* Cherry Street institution; kosher roast beef, corned beef, pastrami, salami, on rye, pumpernickel, onion roll; salads.

Sneaker's, *423-266-1125, 301 Market St in the Sports Barn,* health spot serves homemade turkey chili; chicken, tuna, and veggie sandwiches; PBJ for the kids; on the Shuttle route.

Soup Kitchen, *423-756-2517, 21 E 7th,* a local treasure, fast-moving lines for soups, salads, sandwiches, and desserts; comfy country look; the sign says "It's a Souper place."

Southside Grill, *423-266-6511, 1400 Cowart St,* classy renovated warehouse, linen-clothed tables and special treatment for old standards with "southern foods reinterpreted," rich desserts.

Thai Food at Chattanooga, *423-267-4433, 340 Market St,* Pud Thai, Panang Beef, and Tod Mun Corn, a fritter with cucumber/onion/vinegar sauce; small buffet restaurant.

The Loft, *423-266-3601, 328 Cherokee Blvd,* a fireplace and highbacked chairs; prime rib, steaks, seafood, Mississippi mud pie; and a comfortable bar; a favorite on the North Shore.

Three Brothers Biscuit & Coffee House, *423-265-9794, 11 W 8th St,* breakfast and lunch; omelets, biscuits and bagels; lunchtime pizzas and sandwiches, Italian sodas and coffees.

Town and Country Restaurant, *423-267-8544, 110 N Market St;* ribeye steaks, broiled red snapper, turkey and dressing; on the North Shore for over 40 years; Bridge Tender Bar.

Two Twelve Market St, *423-265-1212, 212 Market St;* fine international cuisine; an outside deck, extensive wine list, specialty items from every corner of the globe.

Lodgings Lookout Mountain

Alford House Bed & Breakfast, *423-821-7625, 5515 Alford Hill Dr, Lookout Mtn;* Victorian country, three guest rooms, continental breakfast, set among trees on mountain slope. **Chanticleer Inn,** *706-820-2015, 1300 Mockingbird Lane, Lookout Mountain,* stone cottages near entrance to Rock City; some fireplaces; continental breakfast. **McElhattan's Owl Hill Bed and Breakfast** *423-821-2040, 617 Scenic Hwy, Lookout*

Mtn, a wildflower trail and hiking; two pleasant rooms; fresh breads and fruits, breakfast cooked to order.

Restaurants Lookout Mountain

Buck's Pit Barbeque Restaurant, *423-267-1390, 3147 Broad St;.* barbecue, Brunswick stew, lemonade with a log cabin decor.

La Cabriole, *423-821-0350, 1341 Burgess Rd, Open Fri-Sat, dinner at 7:30, one serving only, reservations required,* at the foot of Elder Mountain near the River, farm and classical riding school has a French country restaurant; Reserve in advance for this five-course one-serving-only dinner, Friday and Saturday nights.

Mount Vernon Restaurant, *423-266-6591, 1707A Cummings Hwy;* at the foot of Lookout Mountain; amaretto cream pie, rainbow trout, steaks, veal cutlets with Mount Vernon's own tomato sauce.

Riverside Catfish House, *423-821-9214, Hwy U41, 18039 Cummings Hwy, Central Time Zone, open Thu-Fri dinner, Sat-Sun lunch/dinner,* on south side of Tennessee River, view of the River Gorge. Catfish special is all-you-can eat with cole slaw, hushpuppies, and potato; famous for homemade buttermilk pie.

Soup's On, *423-267-1555, 3103 Broad St,* all-you-can-eat soup bar, with three different kinds every day; three different muffins too, a salad bar, and sandwiches made to order.

Lodgings and Restaurants Around Town

More than 1,000 hotel and motel rooms along I-75 exits 1,5 and 7 east of downtown; almost that many restaurants. Some unusual ones, especially if you are traveling with kids, are **Chuck E Cheese's,** *423-870-3215, 22 Northgate Park;* pizza and salad bar; robotics show, games, rides, and playroom for the kids. **Trip's Seafood Restaurant,** *423-892-6880, 6715 Ringgold Rd,* wooden booths and view of pond with geese and ducks; two buffet tables; all-you-can eat salad and seafood or menu. **Uncle Bud's Catfish** *423-855-0900, 6303 Ringgold Rd,* a giant catfish circles above Uncle Bud's, the table is set with paper towels, white beans, slaw, and hushpuppies; order all-you-can-eat catfish, or a bayou platter with froglegs and gator tail. **Veg-Out,** *423-867-5517, 4801 English Ave,* takeout vegetable plates; meats too: tender chicken, country steak, three a day; and a banana pudding treat.

Index

Newsletter & Mailing List Request

Please add my name to the Phase II: Publications mailing list. I'd like to receive the quarterly newsletter with updates on places to go and things to do in the Southeast, and interesting Travel Tips.

I'd also like to be informed when new books by Phase II: Publications are released.

Keep me posted!

Signed: _____

Print Name: _____

Address: _____

City, State, Zip: _____

Telephone Area Code: _____ Number: _____

Available from Phase II: Publications

- *Chattanooga Great Places*, by Linda L. Burton, ISBN 0-9644760-0-2, $11.95, places to eat, go, shop, stay and use in the Chattanooga area.
- *All Eyes Up Here! A Portrait of Effective Teaching*, by Dr. Tee Carr, ISBN 0-9644760-3-7, $14.95, insights into the art and science of teaching.
- *KickStarts*, by Dalton Roberts, ISBN 0-9644760-2-9, $8.95, a thought a day to get you thinking and get you going.
- *How Come The Wise Men Are In The Dempster Dumpster®?*, by Dr. Tee Carr, ISBN 0-9644760-4-5, $10.95, stories about a school with great teachers and neat kids, available 1997.

Phase II: Publications
5251-C, Hwy 153, #255
Chattanooga, TN 37343
Telephone 423-875-4795 Fax 423-877-4089

Book Order Form

There's nothing like having your own personal copy of *SE Great Trips*. Then you can make notes in it and refer to it whenever the need arises. If you need more copies, for yourself or as a gift for someone else, complete the form below and send with your check or money order.

You'll also want to have the *SE Great Trips* companion, *Chattanooga Great Places,* packed with information about Great Places in the Chattanooga area. With both books in hand, you're set!

On Page 249 read about other books available from Phase II: Publications.

I'd like _____ copies of *SE Great Trips* @ $11.95.

I'd like _____ copies of *Chattanooga Great Places* @ $11.95.

I'd like _____ copies of *All Eyes Up Here* @ $14.95.

I'd like _____ copies of *KickStarts* @ $8.95.

I'd like _____ copies of *How Come the Wise Men Are In The Dempster Dumpster®?* @ $10.95.

Shipping and Handling $3.00 for each book.

My check or money order for $ _____ is enclosed.

Name: _____

Address: _____

City/State/Zip: _____

Telephone Area Code: _____ Number: _____

Allow 4 weeks for delivery.

Phase II: Publications
5251-C Hwy 153, #255
Chattanooga, TN 37343
Telephone 423-875-4795 Fax 423-877-4089